THE GUIDE TO
MYSTERIOUS
STIRLINGSHIRE

THE GUIDE TO
MYSTERIOUS STIRLINGSHIRE

GEOFF HOLDER

Firstly, to all those who, in memory of loved ones, have installed seats and benches on walks and hillsides; my aching feet thank you.

Secondly, to Revd Robert Kirk, a beacon of tolerance in a time of extreme religious prejudice, and a man with an enquiring mind and a generous approach to the outer limits of human experience. 'Love and Life.'

And thirdly, to Ségolène, who said 'yes' on the Fairy Hill of Aberfoyle.

First published 2008

The History Press Ltd
The Mill, Brimscombe Port
Stroud, Gloucestershire, GL5 2QG
www.thehistorypress.co.uk

© Geoff Holder, 2008

The right of Geoff Holder to be identified as the Author
of this work has been asserted in accordance with the
Copyrights, Designs and Patents Act 1988.

British Library Cataloguing in Publication Data.
A catalogue record for this book is available from the British Library.

ISBN 978 0 7524 4768 1

Typesetting and origination by The History Press Ltd.
Printed in Great Britain

CONTENTS

ACKNOWLEDGEMENTS

I would like to thank: J. Malcolm Allan, Hon. Sec. of the Dr Welsh Trust, Bridge of Allan, for his time and knowledge; Howard Allen, monument manager, Dunblane Cathedral, and the other helpful staff at various Historic Scotland properties; the Local Studies staff at A.K. Bell Library, Perth, for their expert diligence and reserves of patience; Alex Phillips of Burgess & Gibson, Dunblane, for saving the day with the loan of a tripod; for sharing information, Louis Stott, Paula Baillie-Hamilton, Leslie MacKenzie of West Highland Animation, and Lawrie and Catriona Oldham of Lochside Cottages; the staff of the Kilmadock Development Trust; Dale Townshend and Beth Andrews of the Gothic Imagination course, Department of English, University of Stirling; Professor Angela Smith; Marguerite Kobs, editor of *The Villagers*; Alaric Hall for his pointers; Rhoda Fothergill of the Perthshire Society of Natural Science for the loan of crucial works; the staff of the Breadalbane Folklore Centre; the Apple company for inventing the iPod; the various people who allowed me to poke around their property; Jenni Wilson for the map; my editor, Cate Ludlow, and her colleagues at The History Press; Dave Walker for driving; and Ségolène Dupuy for wheels, photography and digital manipulation.

Unless otherwise stated, all photographs are by the author.

For more information visit www.geoffholder.co.uk.

The Fairy Hill, Aberfoyle.

INTRODUCTION

This is a guide to all things magical, marvelous, mystical, macabre and mysterious in Stirling District. Witches, demons, ghosts and fairies throng its pages. There is also much on the miracles associated with various saints and their holy relics and wells, as well as folk magic, customs and 'superstition'. Here too are myths both historical and contemporary, and legends and folklore that have become attached to real people from the past. As much of the realm of the uncanny deals with the world of the dead, I give here descriptions of moss-encrusted graveyards and intriguing prehistoric burial sites, as well as places of execution and murder. Ritual locations – from modern shrines to ancient standing stones – also feature, as do gargoyles and bizarre sculptures on historic buildings, and anything else strange, peculiar and wonderful.

The book covers elements from thousands of years ago to the present day, and is organised geographically. You can find everything mysterious and weird about one location in the same place and the places flow logically, with the traveller in mind. Directions are given for many of the places mentioned, particularly hard-to-find sites. Cross-references to other locations are shown in CAPITALS.

THE GEOGRAPHICAL SCOPE OF THE BOOK

Local government boundaries and names can be challenging for the writer of psychogeography – the process of locating behaviours, beliefs and thoughts in a specific place, which is the essence of this book. The book covers the current area under the authority of Stirling Council which, confusingly, includes both the city of Stirling and the vast rural hinterland of Stirling District. It is not the resonant term 'Stirlingshire', as historically that designation included only about the southern half of the current district. Much of the northern area was in Perthshire until local government reorganisations, which also saw exchanges of territory with the councils of East Dunbartonshire, Glasgow, Falkirk and Clackmannanshire. And the recently created Loch Lomond and the Trossachs National Park has only the eastern half of its territory within Stirling District. Faced with this morass of conflicting historical and contemporary boundary issues I have decided the only sensible route is to go with the delineations of the modern Stirling District.

MAGIC AND THE SUPERNATURAL: A FEW KEY CONCEPTS

Ironically, boundaries are essential to one of the key concepts in dealing with magic and the supernatural – *liminality*. Liminality is that which is betwixt and between, a transition, a threshold. A liminal time or place can either make a supernatural event more likely to occur, or it can provide the right conditions to make an act of magic more powerful. Liminal times are typically dusk and midnight, as well as dates such as Halloween, Hogmanay, the solstices and equinoxes, and Beltane (1 May). Liminal events in our lives typically encompass

'And though after my skin worms destroy this body, yet in my flesh shall I see God' – mortuary monument, Old Kincardine burial ground, Blairdrummond.

first menstruation, first sexual experience, starting work, marriage, birth, and the approach of death. Liminal places include caves, bogs, rivers and, very importantly, boundaries.

Other concepts crucial to understanding the realm of magic and the supernatural include:

Apotropaic – That which protects against evil. Making the sign of the cross is a common apotropaic act, as is invoking God or the Trinity, speaking a charm, wearing an amulet, or using a holy object, salt, iron or wood from a rowan tree.

Magical Thinking – This is the thought process that anyone who believes in magic, charms or witchcraft goes through. (Without 'scientific thinking' there would be no evidence-based research which allowed technology to advance; without magical thinking, there can be no magic.) In magical thinking, certain items – a saint's relics, water from a special source, an unusual stone – are regarded as possessing power. The benefits of this power can be transferred to you if you touch the object, or drink or be immersed in the water. To obtain benefit in the afterlife it is best to be buried as close as possible to a saint's grave or an altar, this being the prime reason for the historical emphasis on burial within a church (in, for example, HOLY RUDE KIRK in Stirling). All this is connected to the notion of 'sympathetic magic' – things which have been connected once are connected for ever, so a heart cut out of a bewitched cow, if stuck with nails, can cause a backlash effect on the witch who placed the original curse (see for example THORNHILL). Similarly, items which look like something else can have power – such as St Fillan's Stones in KILLIN, which have organ-specific healing powers because they resemble those parts of the body.

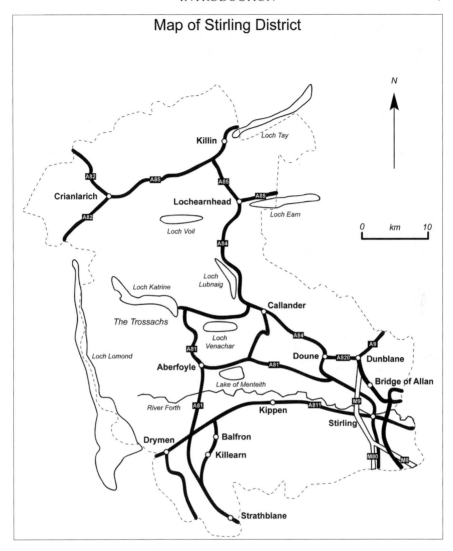

Map of Stirling District

N

Killin
Loch Tay

A82
Crianlarich
A85
A85
Lochearnhead
A85
Loch Eam

Loch Voil
A82

A84

0   km   10

Loch Katrine
Loch Lubnaig

The Trossachs
Callander

Loch Venachar
A84

Loch Lomond
A81
Doune
A820
Dunblane
A9

Aberfoyle
A81
Bridge of Allan

Lake of Menteith

River Forth
A81
Kippen
A811
M9

Stirling

Drymen
Balfron
Killearn
M80
M9

Strathblane

Map of Stirling District showing main routes. (Map by Jenni Wilson)

Simulacra – Natural formations in trees and rocks which we, pattern-seeking apes that we are, interpret as faces, animals and signs from God. Good examples can be seen near STRATHYRE. Some of the 'carved footprints' in the rocks of the north and west (GLEN LOCHAY, GARTMORE and CROFTAMIE) may also be simulacra.

Storytelling – It is in our nature to take a chaotic series of events and turn them into a story. We do it all the time in our daily lives. Paranormal events are often random and confusing, but they quickly become transformed into a 'ghost story'. Historical episodes get retold, usually favouring one individual or group over another. Inconvenient truths and narratively awkward facts get dropped. The 'good story' elements get reworked. Exaggeration, partiality and propaganda have a role too. As witnesses, humans are notoriously unreliable. Moral: don't depend on stories if you're looking for truth. See for example the BATTLE OF BANNOCKBURN.

Doon Hill, Aberfoyle: pendulum offering with the message-draped Fairy Tree in the background.

'Tradition' – Just because there is a longstanding tradition in a certain place, doesn't make it fact. Traditions are subject to the winds of storytelling, and can easily be invented. See for example ABERFOYLE.

'Truth' – Similarly, simply because a respected chronicler from a previous age has written something down, doesn't make it true. And I'm often reporting the words of storytellers (see above), fantasists, liars and journalists. *Caveat lector* (let the reader beware).

THE PHYSICAL SETTING

> Stirling, like a huge brooch, clasps Highlands and Lowlands together.
> (Alexander Smith, *A Summer in Skye* 1856)

Geography is destiny. Never has this statement been truer than when applied to Stirling. In an age of easy travel, of bridges that we cross without paying any attention to them, and of routes made dependable through concrete, steel and tarmac, it is sometimes difficult to grasp how the mighty rivers and mountains of Scotland once severely impeded movement of everyone from traders to armies. The River Forth to the east of Stirling and the treacherous low-lying marshes to the west effectively forged a barrier to north-south communication. The only reliable route was via Stirling, which was not only a solid volcanic rock large enough to build a castle and a town on, away from the wetlands, but also the lowest point on the tidal Forth that could be bridged. As late as 1842 the only road from the south to the north of Scotland went right through the old town on the hill. This geographical bottleneck is the reason why the rock has a major castle, and why so many battles have been fought in the area, from poorly recorded conflicts of the Dark Ages to the great medieval battles of STIRLING BRIDGE, BANNOCKBURN and SAUCHIEBURN, as well as the Hanoverian-Jacobite clash at SHERIFFMUIR.

Stirling is a Lowland city located, along with Bridge of Allan and Dunblane, in the populated south-east corner of its fiefdom, which is part Lowland and part Highland. To the west the flat floodplain of the River Forth now provides fertile agricultural land, a basin hemmed in by hills on two sides and mountains to the north. After the last outposts of the Lowlands to the north and west – Callander, Aberfoyle and Drymen – the Highlands start abruptly. As ever, walking on the moors and mountains requires stout footwear and preparations for changeable weather. The best maps for walking, exploring and finding sites are the Ordnance Survey 1:25000 Explorer series, numbers 364, 365, 366, 377 and 378.

THE SCOTTISH OUTDOOR ACCESS CODE

Everyone has the right to be on most land and inland water providing they act responsibly. Your access rights and responsibilities are explained fully in the Scottish Outdoor Access Code. Find out more by visiting www.outdooraccess-scotland.com or phoning your local Scottish Natural Heritage office.

The key things are to:

   Take responsibility for your own actions
   Respect the interests of other people
   Care for the environment

Access rights can be exercised over most of Scotland, from urban parks and path networks to our hills and forests, and from farmland and field margins to our beaches, lochs and rivers. However, access rights don't apply everywhere, such as in buildings or their immediate surroundings, or in houses or their gardens, or most land in which crops are growing.

Some sites in this book are near houses and other private property; always ask permission – it's simple good manners. Don't disturb animals (wild or domestic). Respect the sites – do not scrape away lichen, leave offerings, or do any damage. I would like to add a personal plea not to drop litter. This is a beautiful part of the world – please do not despoil it. If there is no litter bin, take your litter home.

ARCHAEOLOGY

The area has produced a number of tools used by nomadic hunter-gatherers of the Mesolithic period (very roughly, 8,000–4,000 BC). The Neolithic period (approximately 4,000–2,000 BC) saw the erection of communal burial monuments built from large stones, or megaliths. Often chambers were constructed in the body of the cairn, and some of these chambered cairns, although damaged, can still be seen (such as at EDINCHIP). In the late Neolithic (around 2,500 BC) through the Bronze Age (about 2,000–400 BC) standing stones and stone circles were erected, clearly for ritual and religious purposes. Generally speaking, in contrast to the communal burials of the Neolithic, the typical Bronze-Age burial was individual, either in a small stone-lined grave called a cist (pronounced 'kist') or as a cremation. Some cists are found inserted into the mounds of earlier Neolithic cairns. There is only one confirmed stone circle in the area, at KILLIN, but

Standing stone looming out of the mist on the sports field of the University of Stirling.

Stirling does have three examples of an unusual prehistoric monument, a straight line of three, four or five stones (see GLENHEAD, STRATHBLANE and SHERIFFMUIR). Stirling is also rich in prehistoric rock art, with some standing stones and dozens of rock outcrops and boulders carved with cup marks, enigmatic circular depressions often surrounded by concentric rings (see GLEN LOCHAY, LIX, COWIE and many other sites). The exact purpose of the carvings is unknown – travel directions? Tallies of livestock? Tribal markers? Seasonal star maps? Calendars? Communication with the *deus loci*, the spirits of the place? Illustrations of altered internal states? Symbols of some kind of 'Dreamtime' mythic landscape? No one really knows.

The Iron-Age (*c.* 400-AD 400) monuments that survive are typically hill forts, duns (fortified circular houses) and brochs (twin-walled structures several storeys high with a central space and an internal spiral stairway between the walls). Brochs are mainly found in the far north and west of Scotland; the group in the Forth Valley may be a 'millionaire's row', the dwellings of high-status families who aggrandised their roundhouses into major structures to demonstrate their wealth and power. Many of the brochs were contemporary with the Roman military occupation of the early centuries AD; some appear to have been destroyed by the legions. There are numerous Roman sites, but most survive, if at all, only as crop marks. In the Dark Ages (fifth to tenth century AD) the area was the contested junction of the territories of the Picts, Scots, Angles and Britons.

A good introduction to the area's archaeology is Lorna Main's booklet *First Generations*. Much more detail can be found on the online 'Canmore' database of the Royal Commission on the Ancient and Historical Monuments of Scotland, www.rcahms.gov.uk, and the Stirling Sites and Monuments Record, www.stirling.gov.uk/archaeology. These websites are invaluable, and have formed the background for much of what is written about the archaeological sites in this book. A much more informal view can be obtained from the personal entries on www.themodernantiquarian.com, the community of megalith fans that has mushroomed from Julian Cope's *Modern Antiquarian* books.

A SUMMARY OF KEY HISTORIC EVENTS

1124 – First definite mention of Stirling Castle.
1291 – Edward I of England umpires the contest for the Scottish Crown and effectively annexes Scotland, prompting the Wars of Independence.
1297 – The Battle of Stirling Bridge. Scots commanded by William Wallace and Andrew Moray defeat an English Army.

1314 – Robert the Bruce defeats the Army of Edward II of England at the Battle of Bannockburn.

Fourteenth century – Stirling Castle is variously besieged, destroyed and rebuilt.

1406–1437 – Reign of James I (spent 1406–1423 as a captive in England).

1437–1460 – Reign of James II.

1460–1488 – Reign of James III (killed at the Battle of Sauchieburn by the forces of his son).

1488–1513 – Reign of James IV.

1513–1542 – Reign of James V.

1543–1567 – Reign of Mary I (Mary Queen of Scots).

1560 – The Scottish Reformation. The Roman Catholic Church is forcibly replaced as the state religion by Protestantism. Church properties are privatised, many nobles thus enriching themselves through dubious means. Dunblane Cathedral and Cambuskenneth Abbey suffer.

1567–1625 – Reign of James VI.

1603 – James VI crowned as James I of England – the 'Union of the Crowns'.

1638 onwards – Many Protestants align to the National Covenant in protest at new Church practices imposed by Charles I. Battles between Covenanters and Royalists, with allied violent persecution.

1650 – General Monck besieges the castle on behalf of the Cromwellian Government, which occupies Scotland for eight years.

1688 – James II of England and VII of Scotland deposed for displaying Catholic sympathies. Flees to France – followers are called Jacobites, from *Jacobus*, Latin for James.

1715 – Forces of the new Hanoverian dynasty defeat the Jacobite Army at the Battle of Sheriffmuir.

1734 – Rob Roy MacGregor dies.

1745 – Bonnie Prince Charlie's Jacobite Army avoids Stirling by crossing the marshes to the west.

1746 – The Jacobites, in retreat, occupy Stirling but fail to take the castle.

Eighteenth century – the wetlands drained and converted to agricultural land.

Late eighteenth century – travellers start to write about the Highlands.

1810 – Walter Scott publishes *The Lady of the Lake*. Literary tourism in the Trossachs booms.

1817 – Scott publishes *Rob Roy*. Literary tourism in the Trossachs goes into overdrive.

WILLIAM WALLACE

Despite William Wallace's prominence as a national hero, historically he is a shadowy figure, ill documented, the facts of his life overlaid with a distorting layer of legend and folklore.
(Pete Armstrong and Angus McBride *Stirling Bridge & Falkirk 1297–98: William Wallace's Rebellion*)

The BATTLE OF STIRLING BRIDGE in 1297 was one of the great victories of the Wars of Independence against England. Along with Andrew Moray, who later died of wounds inflicted in this encounter, Wallace was the tactical genius behind the battle. But as Armstrong and McBride point out in their splendid study, what people 'know' about him is derived solely from *The Life of Sir William Wallace*, written by 'Blind Harry' in the 1470s, more than 150 years after Wallace's death. This verse work is filled with errors of fact and chronology, very much a hagiography of a legendary hero, and is to be trusted as much as a miracle-filled medieval 'Life' of a Dark-Age saint. In the early eighteenth century William Hamilton of Gilbertfield revised the almost impenetrable Harry into more comprehensible language, and his heroic epic became the second most popular book in Scotland after the Bible. Wallace therefore became a popular hero; statues were erected to him in Stirling, the WALLACE MONUMENT was built in 1860s, the STIRLING SMITH MUSEUM is full of portraits of Wallace in various heroic interpretations, from medieval warlord through Renaissance Prince to nineteenth-century nationalist, and the epic 1995 *Braveheart* (directed by and starring Mel Gibson) made Wallace a worldwide name. The film is great fun but woeful as history – to give but one example, Wallace is shown having an affair with Isabella, the wife of Edward II of England, even though she would have been an infant at the time. But then Harry got a lot wrong as well. The film's success had a major impact on the Stirling economy, revived the fortunes of the neglected Wallace Monument, and was extensively referenced by Scottish Nationalist politicians.

Demonstrating that much of his current stature is a result of relatively modern myth-making is not to detract from Wallace's achievements. Armstrong and McBride show that his documented early life is shadowy. His success in 1297 suggests he had significant previous military experience, but whether that was in Wales in the Army of Edward I, on the continent or elsewhere, we don't know. He was associated, not with the giant claymore of tradition or fantasy, but with the bow, which he used as a device on his seal. There is also a court document of August 1296 which mentions 'a thief, one William le Waleys' accused of robbing a woman in Perth of goods, chattels and beer. There is no way of telling if this is our man.

As with most legends, popular memory of Wallace is selective. His expert reading of the battlespace at Stirling Bridge is celebrated, and his incredibly brutal execution in London in 1305 is commemorated. The atrocities of Wallace's own Army in Northumberland in October 1297 are conveniently forgotten, as is his defeat at the Battle of Falkirk the following year.

ROBERT THE BRUCE

In 1306 Bruce murdered his rival Comyn in a church, had himself crowned King at Scone in defiance of Edward I, and lost two battles, at Methven near Perth and near Dalrigh in STRATHFILLAN. He then went on the run, and in legend is associated with several caves and refuges (see LOCH VOIL, GLEN DOCHART and LOCH LOMOND). In 1307 he regrouped somewhere off the west coast and launched a new, spectacularly successful, military campaign, which culminated in the triumph of BANNOCKBURN in 1314. Thereafter he founded a number of religious houses in honour of St Fillan, whom he regarded as having delivered success on the battlefield. Both Bruce and Bannockburn are deeply interwoven with myth-making, and both feature extensively in these pages. Again, this does not undermine the abilities and accomplishments of 'Bruce the man', without which modern Scotland would be immensely different, but it serves to remind us that 'Bruce the hero' is a construct, a mix of history and legend onto which successive generations have projected their hopes and fantasies.

FINGAL

The warrior/king/giant Fingal (Fhionn/Fion), along with his war-band the Fingalians (or the Fhianna) was at the centre of an entire Irish mythos of interrelated stories of heroism, love, magic, treachery and supernatural encounters. The tales travelled to Scotland with Gaelic storytellers who adapted them to the local geography, and hence Fingalian place names turn up in many locations.

WALTER SCOTT, ROB ROY AND THE INVENTION OF SCOTLAND

Scott (1771–1832) was one of the most popular writers of his day, with a worldwide readership. He largely invented the historical novel, where fictional characters and plots interwove with, and altered, genuine events from Scotland's turbulent past. So well-known were his works that

William Wallace with
broadsword and ludicrous
Roman toga. The Atheneum,
King Street, Stirling.

Bannockburn visitors' centre;
statue of Robert the Bruce
by Pilkington Jackson.

readers – including many Scots – came to perceive Scotland through the romantic, fanciful lens that he created. In 1810 the verse-romance *The Lady of the Lake* made the Trossachs a locus of mass tourism for the middle classes, a process accelerated greatly with the publication of *Rob Roy* in 1817. Rob Roy MacGregor (*c.* 1671–1734), Jacobite, cattle dealer, cattle thief, extortionist, outlaw and folk hero, was already a legend in his own lifetime, partly through his real exploits and partly through *Highland Rogue*, a fictionalised account of his life written by Daniel Defoe in 1723. Scott's book confirmed him as 'Scotland's Robin Hood', and his story remains popular, as shown by the success of the 1995 film. There are dozens of places in this book associated with Rob. Walter Scott's apogee as the 'Inventor of Scotland' came in 1822 when he organised the visit to the country of King George IV, an event which saw the mass invention of new traditions, from 'traditional' Highland dress to clan tartans.

THE CLANS

Many writers have followed Scott in lauding and romanticising the clans. Today, clan websites and associations flourish, and many people scattered far and wide take pride in their clan name. This sense of belonging, of roots, is a fine thing. But it should not be undertaken whilst wearing rose-hued glasses. The Highlanders' martial prowess, so admired in terms of personal character and its effect on the battlefield, did not spring out of nowhere: to produce warriors, a society must contain violence. Much historical and contemporary writing on the clans seems designed to reassure people with a certain surname that despite a number of their 'colourful' ancestors being murderers, rapists, arsonists, kidnappers, plunderers and cattle thieves, this does not mean they were bad people. It appears that the further back in time an event occurred, the more we are indulgent of appalling violence. A clan ancestry is indeed something of which to be proud; but don't ignore the possibility that many of one's ancestors may stain the escutcheon.

Stirling Castle: the Great Hall from the Nether Bailey.

1

STIRLING CASTLE AND
UPPER STIRLING

Old Strevline…
I love thee more
For the grey relics of thy martial towers,
Thy mouldering palaces and ramparts hoar.
(James Hogg, *The Queen's Wake*)

STIRLING CASTLE

Historic Scotland. Admission fee. 1 April–31 October, Monday–Sunday, 9.30–18.00; 1 October–31 March, Monday–Sunday, 9.30–17.00. NS789940.

Simply one of the must-visit sights of Scotland, the castle requires a minimum of three hours to see properly, although you could easily spend all day here. Aerial views show its shape resembles a great stone battleship. Guidebooks and guided and audio tours are available, so here I will only concentrate on the (allegedly) supernatural and the strange, including the wealth of marvellous and peculiar sculptures that can easily be missed. (For a timeline of monarchs and major events, see introduction.)

The early history of the castle is unrecorded, the first documentary evidence coming only from the early twelfth century when Alexander I founded a chapel. There may well have been occupation on this obvious defensive site in prehistory and the Dark Ages, but the centuries of rebuilding since the Middle Ages have obliterated all traces. This didn't stop early chroniclers (and some later writers) asserting evidence on the site for the Romans, the Vikings, Malcolm Canmore, the Northumbrians, St Modwenna of Ireland (said to have built a chapel here in the ninth century) and even King Arthur, but all this is distinctly dubious.

Some later, well-attested episodes are stranger than fiction, such as the story of Thomas Warde of Trumpington, the Mammet or False King. Depending on which chronicler you read, Thomas was either half-crazed or was a man of skill and talent. He had either been found in service to, or in the dungeon of, the Lord of the Isles on Islay. What made him famous and valuable was that he was the spitting image of Richard II of England. Richard was supposed to have died in 1400 but there was great uncertainly surrounding the claim. Stories were circulating that he had escaped his imprisonment in Pontefract Castle and was in hiding. Under such circumstances a look-alike suited the Scots' strategy, and there are numerous entries in the Scottish Chamberlain's Accounts for the maintenance of 'Richard, King of England'. In the English records there is a denunciation of Thomas for impersonating Richard, and a letter of Henry V which speaks of the conspiracy to bring the Mammet King into England (Mammet comes from *Mahomet*, the medieval term for a figure dressed up for the purposes of deception). After perhaps seventeen years at Stirling Castle Thomas died in 1419 and was buried in a high-status location, on the north side of the great altar of the now-vanished Dominican church. An anonymous manuscript in the Advocates' Library in Edinburgh records the inscription from the tomb:

Stirling Castle from the King's Park.

> Here lieth Richard, who was England's King,
> O'erthrown by treachery of Lancaster,
> Who, strong by treason, gained a wrongful throne.
> Richard died childless, and his later years
> In exile spent, by Scottish bounty fed,
> By Stirling's castled steep his life's sad course
> Ended, when since the year of Jesus birth
> 'Twas fourteen centuries and nineteen years.

Some chroniclers maintained Thomas was indeed the English King. J.E.H. Thomson, on whose 1886 article 'The Mammet King' in the *Transactions of the Stirling Natural History and Archaeological Society* I have drawn heavily, notes: 'This strange story seems to have been an article of faith among Scotch historians.' Hector Boece's notoriously unreliable *History of the Scottish People* of 1527 says Richard II escaped imprisonment disguised as a woman and went into service to a Galloway knight called Macdonald. At last he was recognised and brought to Robert III. Fordun's *Scotichronicon* describes how Richard escaped and was recognised in the kitchen of Donald, Lord of the Isles, by a jester who had been educated at the English courts. Andrew Wyntoun, author of the rhyming chronicle of Scotland, says pretty much the same, but injects a slight note of caution:

> Quhether he had bene King or nane,
> There wes but few that wyst certain.

The royal disputes of the British Isles are full of impostors and pretenders; the story of Thomas Warde the False King is one of the strangest. His story cries out for a cinematic treatment.

Sacred relics played an important role in the Pre-Reformation court. Ordinary people had wells blessed by holy men in the distant past, whereas the monarchy could call upon the very garments that had clothed the flesh of a saint. The Exchequer Rolls testify to the expenses of the Crown for the cost of transporting from Dunfermline to Stirling Castle the chemise of St Margaret, Queen of Scotland 1070–1093. The relic was used to ensure a problem-free birth for Mary of Gueldres, Queen of James II. Both mother and baby were fine, the latter becoming James III. The sacred chemise was again sent for at the birth of James V. (Source: John Ewart Simpkins, *County Folk-lore*)

Another impostor to the English throne, Perkin Warbeck, arrived in Scotland in 1495. James IV welcomed him as the rightful son of Edward IV of England, installed him at Stirling Castle, gave him a pension and a high-status wife, and even made war on England for his guest's sake. The ridiculous charade fizzled out, James and Warbeck quarrelled, and the impostor sailed from Ayr in July 1497. After an abortive invasion of Cornwall, Warbeck was executed at the Tower of London in 1499.

One of my favourite stories from the castle took place in 1507. John Damian, an alchemist and hanger-on known as the French Leech, had been appointed the Abbot of Tungland in Galloway by James IV, but felt he was losing favour at court. To draw attention to his supposed miraculous powers he announced he would fly from the battlements and be in France before the King's ambassadors. A large crowd turned out; he equipped himself with wings made of feathers, leapt into the air – and fell into the dung heap, breaking his leg. Dunbar wrote a satire on the episode, 'The Ballad of the Frenzeit Freir of Tungland'.

In December 1566 an elaborate three-day beano was put on to celebrate the baptism of Prince James (later James VI), the son of Mary Queen of Scots. A masque was arranged by the Frenchman Bastien. Men dressed as satyrs entered the hall as the meat was being served, and wagged their long tails in front of the English guests. A common jibe was that the English had tails, so tempers ran high until Mary addressed the company to calm their feelings. The celebration finished on a happier note, with a pretend siege of an enchanted castle constructed in front of the real one, followed by a firework display.

Five years earlier Mary had been almost overpowered by smoke when her bed curtains caught fire in the castle, thereby coming close to fulfilling an old prophecy that a Queen would be burnt at Stirling. The episode is given as the origin story – or one of them – for one of the castle's noted ghosts, the Green Lady, supposedly the attendant who dreamt that the Queen was in danger, woke up and rescued Mary from the flames just in time. Alternatively the Green Lady was the daughter of the castle governor; she threw herself off the battlements when her lover, an officer in the garrison, was accidentally killed by her father. The Pink Lady, a beautiful woman in a pink silk gown, is supposed to waft between the castle and HOLY RUDE CHURCH. She is identified as:

a) A woman searching for her husband who was killed when the castle was captured by
   Edward I (a date too early for pink silk).
b) The Queen's fire-attentive lady in waiting.
c) Mary Queen of Scots herself.

Attributions such as these probably tell us more about those attributing them than about the identities of the putative ghosts themselves.

THE PALACE

A riot of Renaissance carvings covers three faces of this grand building. Charles McKean's architectural guide *Stirling and the Trossachs* quotes several commentators to show that the statues were not to everyone's taste:

Stirling Castle Palace.

'Obscene groups... the fruits
of an imagination luxuriant
but revolting.' Details of the
sculptures on the Palace.

It is very rich and curiously ornamented with grotesque figures, upon singular pillars or pedestals, each one of which is supported on the back of a figure lying on its breast, which appears a very painful position – especially when encumbered with such a load, and some of the figures seem to wish to be freed of it, if we may judge by the contortion of the muscles of their faces. (Garnett, *Tour Through the Highlands* 1800)

Statues, if such hideous things in imitation of the human form deserve a name. (Alexander Campbell, *Scotland Illustrated: Journey From Edinburgh* 1802)

Obscene groups... the fruits of an imagination luxuriant but revolting. (R.W. Billings, *The Baronial and Ecclesiastical Architecture of Scotland* 1846)

Certainly you can find nudity, monsters, demons and inappropriate inter-species behaviour. Most of the bays have a full-length figure flanked by one or two gargoyles, the statue standing on a pillar resting on the back of a supporter. Some of the statues may well represent Classical gods.

South Face, from left (west) to right (east)

Top row: Bearded man in cloak and hose with mason's set-square; behatted soldier using a windlass to load a crossbow; a man in doublet, hose and codpiece aiming a musket; and a

The Palace: hermaphrodite devil with face on stomach.

The Palace: archer loading crossbow with windlass.

man holding a tube and a foliate shield bearing a face. The figures stand on columns planted on monstrous dog gargoyles, themselves above a string course filled with the heads of angels.

Middle row: First bay: laughing man in a loincloth; flanker – a demon gargoyle; supporter – a man in a toga, with an ugly animalistic face. Second bay: a naked chubby youth with bulbous thighs carrying a shield carved with a face; flankers – two gargoyles, one with a face like a flower, the other a bird with a human or animal head; supporter – a man with elaborate clothes and a monkey's face. Third bay: an incredible, medieval-looking hermaphrodite Devil with horns, ugly bearded face, female breasts, a face on the stomach, penis, knobbed reptilian tail and three-clawed hands and feet; flankers – two gargoyles, one a squatting dragon, the other broken; supporter – a muscular bearded man wearing a cloak and turban(?). Fourth bay: a cheerful fat naked man with coiffed hairstyle, holding a spherical object and a shield carved with a face and attached by a knotted cloth; flankers – a woman whose low-cut ringed dress exposes her breasts and another headless figure in fine clothes, possibly a courtier; supporter – a headless bird.

East face (towards the Outer Close) from left (south) to right (north)
On the corner is a screaming woman with exposed breasts.

Top row: a bearded satyr and three figures bearing scrolls, with short columns resting on the backs of bird gargoyles. Angels' heads on the stringcourse below.

Middle row: first bay: headless figure carrying a small shield with a bearded face; around the feet is an eroded sheep(?) and lyre(?); flanker – a bird-demon encasing a smiling Buddha-like face between its clawed forelegs; supporter – an eroded male figure. Second bay: headless man; flankers – a demon with curled horns and foliate breastplate and a winged sphinx with female head and an animal head on its breastplate; supporter – a man in high status clothes with a diadem of office. Third bay: a man with a scroll; flankers – two chained monkey-demons, one of which is

The Palace: sphinx with animal-headed breastplate. (Courtesy of Ségolène Dupuy)

The Palace: equine demon.

The Palace: demon spitting out a round object. Note human face on its chest. (Courtesy of Ségolène Dupuy)

pawing at its halter; supporter – a woman with a lizard or small mammal on her shoulder. Fourth bay: headless man; flankers: extraordinary foliaceous horse demons; supporter: a leering bearded man with a winged head on his chest. Fifth bay: a naked woman (Venus?) covering her modesty with one hand; flankers – a pair of web-footed bird demons; supporter – a buxom woman in an elaborate dress, with animal faces on her shoulder pads. Final bay, over passageway: two horned, bearded demons each with a human head on its chest. 'I 5' (for James V) above each of the windows. The underside of the bottom string course is carved with faces both human and angelic.

North face (towards the Inner Close) from left (east) to right (west)

Top row: a diminutive figure blowing a musical instrument, the other plinths being empty, and the short columns resting on beast-head gargoyles. String course with angels.

Middle row: Corner: Bearded figure with hat and dirk, James V as the 'Gudeman 'o Ballengeich' (the disguise he allegedly adopted when travelling covertly among his countrymen). Above, a lion holds the crown and a tablet with 'I 5'; flanker – an eroded monster; supporters – two layers of human heads, each with a different expression, a woman pulling her shawl about her, and an eroded lion. First bay: youth holding a jar; flankers – monkey-lion-demons; supporter – a bearded man clutching vegetation(?) to his chest. Second bay: female figure with naked breasts, holding a sphere and a dart and wearing a helmet and curved straps or coverings on the lower legs; flankers – two bird-headed demons; supporter – a woman whose exposed breast is giving suck to a lizard or demon. Third bay: gaunt bearded old man holding a triple-sac bag or purse on a cloth around his neck, his cloak knotted above his shoulder; flankers – a bearded courtier with his hand on the top of his head, and another bearded figure clutching a chain of office(?); supporter – a man handling a snake. Fourth bay: a sensuous female figure dancing with veils and exposing her breasts; flankers – composite monsters with frilled collars, one with a human head; supporter – a bearded man, much eroded. 'I 5' above each of the windows.

If you get down low enough you can see that the underside of the bottom string course is populated by human heads, angels and a Green Man. Inside the Palace, the fireplace pillars of

The Palace: James V as the 'Gudeman o' Ballengeich'.

The Palace: snakehandling courtier.

The Palace: female statue with sphere, dart and shin-guards.

the King's Guard Hall have strange carvings of a four-legged beast split in half with a bequiffed but featureless human head from which springs a pair of wings(?) leaves(?) or gigantic ears(?).

THE GREAT HALL

The west exterior (facing the Inner Close) has a wyvern and mermaid flanking the door and an angel reading from a scroll beneath an empty statue niche. The east face sports two grumpy old men, a monkey-lion, a triplet of faces expressing respectively pleasure, amazement and sadness below an empty niche, a hound bounding towards a rabbit opposite, and several eroded figures: two saints(?) in niches, a walking man, a wyvern and mermaid, and a pair of men with heads hung down. The roof is topped with lions and unicorns sitting in crowns and decorated with gold.

THE CHAPEL ROYAL

When the baptism of James VI's son Prince Henry was celebrated here in 1594, figures appeared representing Ceres, Fecundia, Faith, Concord, Liberalitie and Perseverance. Henry did not become King, dying of disease aged eighteen. The chapel is the temporary home of the reproductions of the medieval tapestry-set 'The Hunt of the Unicorn', the originals of which are in the Metropolitan Museum of Art in New York. When all seven tapestries are completed they will be displayed in the refurbished Palace. The beautiful tapestries are replete with symbolism which has been deconstructed in Lise Gotfredsen's splendid book *The Unicorn*.

Triple head on the Great Hall, Stirling Castle.

The unicorn represents Christ, an identification made as early as the third century AD. The hunters pursue the animal, which is found dipping its horn into a pool to purify the water of poisons, so the other beasts of the forest can drink. The stag represents both Christ and the soul, the powerful lions and panther/leopard are heraldic beasts, and the weasel is a snake-slayer and hence an ally of the unicorn. The hyena is a symbol of Judas. The letters 'A&E' occur five times in each tapestry, but in the third tapestry only ('The Unicorn Leaps the Stream') they are joined by 'F&R'. In the fourth tapestry, 'The Unicorn at Bay', a hunter blowing a horn has on his scabbard the words *Ave Regina C[oelerum]*, 'Hail, Queen of the Heavens'. This identifies him as Gabriel, the Angel of the Annunciation: he is bringing news that Christ will come. The unicorn is then brutally killed and its horn cut off. Around the corpse's neck an oak wreath sprouts thorns, symbolizing the crown of thorns. In the last image, 'The Unicorn in Captivity', the indestructible unicorn has been resurrected and tied to a pomegranate tree, symbol of fertility. This final tapestry, however, is also an allegory for love: the hunter is Love, the unicorn is the lover, and his leash symbolizes the lover's commitment to marriage.

THE KING'S OLD BUILDING

Much of this building was formerly used for military administration and officers' quarters. Most of it is still private apart from the museum. In 1946 footsteps were heard to echo across the ceiling of a room immediately below the roof, on which no one could have walked. The footsteps occurred again in 1956. Their origin story is attributed to a 'sentry beat' along the battlement that then existed over the building. One night in the 1820s a guard was found

'The Unicorn in Captivity', the last tapestry in the 'Hunt for the Unicorn' series, Stirling Castle. (Courtesy of Ségolène Dupuy)

dead at his post with an expression of terror. The Green Lady has popped up here too, causing dinner to be served late in the officers' mess when her appearance made the cook faint.

ARGYLL AND SUTHERLAND HIGHLANDERS REGIMENTAL MUSEUM

The First World War section displays a pocket watch which saved a soldier's life from a bullet, and a tiny New Testament provided by the National Bible Society of Scotland which performed the same task, with the piece of shrapnel still embedded in its pages. These two are typical of the many death-deflecting talismans reported from the annihilatory horrors of the trenches. A press cutting tells the experience of Robert Kincaid who, at a check-up in 2003 following a bump to the head, found he had a bullet in his neck. He had been wounded covering the retreat to Dunkirk in 1940 and had been oblivious to the bullet for sixty-three years.

THE CASTLE EXHIBITION

A stone corbel head from the Great Hall, with his hand on his cheek. A reproduction of one of the wooden Stirling Heads, showing a powerful well-dressed man encircled by winged faces.

THE KING'S KNOT

Adventures are so often told about Arthur that they have become the stuff of fiction: not all lies, not all truth. (Wace, *Le Roman de Brut* 1155)

King Arthur kept the Round Table at Stirling Castle. (William of Worcester, *Itinerarium* 1478)

The King's Knot, where… [with] a sport called 'Knights of the Round Table' the institutions of King Arthur were commemorated. (*New Statistical Account* 1845)

The King's Knot, a geometrical formal-garden structure best viewed from the castle or along the Back Walk by the cemeteries, has a long and confused association with King Arthur. Stuart McHardy in *The Quest for Arthur* locates Arthur as a Dark-Age Christian warrior campaigning against pagan enemies in central and southern Scotland, including Loch Lomondside and the Carse of Stirling. It is only fair to say that the documentary sources for this period are sparse and open to multiple interpretations, and that other writers have used the same sources to make claims for various parts of England and Wales. The search for the 'historical' Arthur continues, with new books, each promoting a conflicting theory, appearing almost every year. The Round Table first makes its appearance in *Le Roman de Brut,* a work of 1155 by the Norman writer Wace. As the quote from Wace demonstrates, by his time Arthur was already acknowledged to be a legendary figure around which many stories were woven. Wace's work was based in large part on Geoffrey of Monmouth's *History of the Kings of Britain* (*c.* 1138), itself a patchwork of legend, myth, pseudo-history and pro-Norman propaganda; in translating Geoffrey's Latin into French, Wace freely added in his own contributions; he probably invented the idea of the Round Table:

> Arthur had the Round Table made, about which the British tell many a tale. There sat the vassals, all equal, all leaders; they were placed equally round the table, and equally served. None of them could boast he sat higher than his peer; all were seated near the place of honour, none far away.

In the slightly later *The Romance of Tristan* by Beroul, a twelfth-century poet, a messenger is sent from Cornwall to find Arthur. His first stop is Caerleon, in South Wales, where he is told that the King and his knights are at the Round Table in Stirling, called by its old name, Snowdoun ('Stirling's tower/Of yore the name of Snowdoun claims' – Walter Scott, *Lady of the Lake*). 'We shall soon be there,' says the messenger, casually dismissing the hundreds of miles to Scotland. It has been argued that what Beroul had in mind was Segontium, the Roman fort near Caernarvon, North Wales, also known as Snowdon. Beroul speaks of a stone slab at Stirling around which Arthur's entire household could sit.

The various Arthurian romances had a huge effect on the chivalric, knightly culture of the Middle Ages. Various 'Round Tables' were set up by English Kings and nobles, including one established by Roger de Mortimer at Kenilworth, where he entertained a hundred knights and their ladies. Participants dressed up as Arthurian characters, banqueted and jousted. The ring in which the jousting and combats took place became called the Round Table – not so much a piece of furniture as a large space, a more or less circular piece of flat ground probably surrounded by a fence or wall. It is possible a similar ring was set up at Stirling, because Barbour's *Bruce,* written in 1375, describes how Edward II, having been unable to take refuge in the castle after the Battle of BANNOCKBURN, went 'Rycht by the Round Table away.' It is also possible this 'Round Table' was set up on or near an older mound which may underlie the Knot, but there is no evidence for this, and this whole subject has to be hedged with caution. There are several references to 'Tilting at The Ring' and jousting competitions being held at Stirling in the fifteenth century, and these chivalric games, often sponsored by the Stuart Kings, almost certainly took place in this area. About 1494 James IV had the Round Table and the surrounding area converted into a formal garden, which is the basis of what we see today. From this time on the place is called the Knot or the King's Knot, although the old name persisted, because in 1539 Sir David Lindsay in his *Farewell of the Papingo* writes, 'Adew fair Snawdoun, with thy towris hie, Thy Chapill Royall, Park, and Tabill Round.'

The King's Knot – a Stuart formal garden, not the Round Table.

Over the years many writers, building on the few written references and captivated by the irresistible glamour of the Arthur connection, have called the Knot the Round Table, perhaps imagining something chivalric and Arthurian taking place on the central octagonal stepped mound. But the Knot, with its geometric terraces, straight lines, hollow squares and its rigid formality, has completely obliterated any earlier structures; this is not the Round Table but the *site* of a ring called a 'Round Table' where a medieval jousting ground once stood. When first created the royal garden was probably covered with flowers, low hedges, paths and water features. These days it is maintained under mown grass, and can be easily visited from Dumbarton Road.

Perhaps the strangest story connected with the Knot is recorded in Charles Rogers' *Social Life in Scotland* (1886). In one of the early days of May:

> Boys of ten and twelve years divest themselves of clothing, and in a state of nudity run round certain natural or artificial circles. Formerly the rounded summit of Dumyat, an eminence in the Ochil range, was a favourite scene of this strange pastime, but for many years it has been performed at the King's Knot in Stirling… The performances are not infrequently repeated at Midsummer and Lammas.

GOWAN HILL

> Fatal mound, that oft hath heard the death-axe sound. (Walter Scott, *The Lady of the Lake*)

This low hill can be seen from the Nether Bailey and is easily visited from the end of the Back Walk or from several paths up from the town – head for the cannons. The Beheading Stone now sits in an iron grille on a plinth. It was used as the chopping block for a variety of aristocratic types – hanging was for commoners – including the Duke of Albany, two of his sons and his father-in-law the Earl of Lennox (all executed by James I in 1425 for not rescuing

The Beheading Stone on Gowan Hill.

him from imprisonment in England, and effectively usurping his kingdom), and Sir Robert Graham, who in 1437 was one of the conspirators who assassinated James I. He was nailed to a tree, dragged through the town and tortured for three days with red-hot irons before being beheaded. Prior to being rescued in 1888 the stone had been used by a butcher at the Old Bridge as a block for chopping off the horns of sheep. The young James V would toboggan down the slope here on a cow's skull, a pursuit called the Hurly-Haaky or Hackit.

ARGYLL'S LODGING

Castle Wynd. Historic Scotland. A ticket to Stirling Castle includes entry to Argyll's Lodging. 1 April–30 September, Monday–Sunday, 9.30–18.00; 1 October–31 March, Monday–Sunday, 9.30–17.00. Interpretation panels.

A superb example of a seventeenth-century nobleman's town house. The extravagant carved panels and window frames around the courtyard include a coat of arms supported by a man in a kilt(?) and a mermaid, the whole thing framed by two human heads; a man's head with a winged helmet, probably representing Mercury; numerous crescent moons; curves ending in foliate birds' heads; crowns; and a woman with a headdress, horizontal ears, and bunches of fruit suspended from her shawl. Winged souls hover over the windows on the exterior walls. Inside, two elaborate fireplaces catch the eye. One has a bearded man and a bare-breasted woman each above a lion's head. The other has two truly strange carvings – human-headed figures whose bodies are covered with intricate vegetation. They have no arms and their feet are those of a three-clawed beast. A crescent moon sits on the central panel. There are vague rumours of ghostly presences, including the sound of a child crying in an empty room, but there is nothing definite.

'I pray all looking on this lodging/with gentle eye to give their judging': the façade of Mar's Wark.

Mar's Wark: detail of mermaid tied to solar face.

MAR'S WARK

Castle Wynd. The ruin of the once-grand town house of John Erskine, 18th Earl of Mar, Regent of Scotland for two years during the time of the young James VI. Built 1571–2 it was capped with turrets and would have been a rival to Argyll's Lodging. The façade is richly decorated with sculptures and carvings, some of which are quite mysterious. Most are heavily eroded. To study them closely you'll need binoculars or a zoom lens, although viewing is not always easy as the traffic thunders past inches from you. Many of the details described here are taken from an article J.S. Fleming wrote for the Society of Antiquaries of Scotland in 1905, at which date the carvings were in better condition. From left to right when looking at the front the carvings are:

South wall

A headless figure with clasped hands wearing an ornamental doublet with a short skirt terminating in foliage. Below, bull's head with a ring in its mouth and a letter 'A' encircled by a coronet, representing Countess Annabella, Mar's wife.

South tower

A rainspout in the shape of a cannon. A headless figure with his hands on his haunches, wearing a doublet with a short scalloped skirt and slashed sleeves with shoulder and elbow bands and cuffs. The arms of the regent, an elaborate construction with a shield and helmet supported by two griffons, with the motto *Je Pense Plus* (I think more) above. On either side are male figures supporting the columns while above two naked female figures each grasp a leafy branch of a flower growing from a pot. The sill of the window below has a pair of mermaids holding a handled mirror between them; each mermaid has a ball (pearl?) in her other hand, while their tails are secured by ropes held on the mouths of two flanking faces, one of which (on the right) may be the sun. Below, a swag and the words I PRAY AL LVIKARIS ON THIS LVGING / VITH GENTIL E TO GIF THAIR JVGING ('I pray all looking on this lodging / with gentle eye to give their judging'). To the right, another cannon rainspout and a male figure holding his chin in one hand. This contemplative figure is wearing a slashed doublet waist cord with tassels. Below, a crown above an 'R' and a swirl around 'I' and '6' (RI6: *Rex Jacobus VI*, King James VI).

Central wall

In the angle with the south tower: a rainspout cannon with a thistle carved on it, and a bearded warrior holding a targe (small shield); he once had a sword. A large heraldic panel carved with the royal arms and crest of Scotland, including two excellent unicorns, and the date 1570. Each of the side pillars has two men dressed in hose with prominent codpieces, standing above two dolphins or sea monsters, and below each of them a male face, the one on the right with a moustache. At the very top are two birds with sunburst human heads, and on the far right is a moustachioed male face with a sunburst hairdo. The angle with the north tower has another rainspout and an eroded soldier whose helmet and armour were once visible. His left hand once held a long pistol called an arquebus; his powder horn is still visible.

North tower

Cannon rainspout, an empty statue support looking like a stylised face, then a headless man with one hand grasping the belt of his doublet; his puffed and pleated sleeves and skirt are still visible. Below, a band around a damaged monogram. A heraldic panel with the arms of the regent impaled with those of his countess, Annabella. At the top is a man spewing vegetation which spirals down the side of the panel. The sill of the blocked-up window underneath has three carvings: the one on the right is a winged bare-breasted female spewing vegetation. The eroded central carving may be an angel or bat, while that on the left has vanished completely. Below, the letter 'A' banded by a coronet, then a gun-port, and another inscription: THE MOIR I STAND ON OPPIN HITHT / MY FAVLTIS MOIR SVBJECT AR TO SITHT ('The more I stand on open height / my faults more subject are to sight'). To the right, a headless man in doublet and skirt strumming a six-stringed lute. At the very bottom right of the door, a mason's mark.

North wall

In the angle with the north tower, another cannon, and a monk with hood drawn back, clutching what may be a bag to his chest. Then the most famous carving – the so-called 'Joan of Arc' figure. This is a woman in what appears to be a nun's surplice, bound by criss-cross ropes which terminate in a knot at the bottom. She stands on a severely eroded plinth with the remnants of two heads and a five-pointed star. The popular story is the Virgin Warrior was placed here because medieval Stirling was full of Frenchmen due to the links with France under the ongoing anti-England 'Auld Alliance'. Her name, Jehanne d'Arc, was unpronounceable for the locals and the statue became known as Jeannie Dark. Fleming, however, writing in 1905, notes the figure was called the 'Bambino', and makes no reference to Joan. The fact that such a repository of local lore as Fleming was unaware of the Jeannie Dark name suggests it might be a twentieth-century invention. A copy of the statue is in the STIRLING SMITH MUSEUM. Below is a man wearing a doublet with chevrons and slashed sleeves. His right hand holds a three-headed flower to his chest. Below the window is a heavily eroded symbol which may be another R16. Next is another cannon and a headless figure holding an open book. For many years the inscription on it was thought to read 'A Revel of Love Grym', but in 1907 W.B. Cook studied a plaster cast of the eroded carving, and concluded it read:

TRA || REVEL
TOVR || IT OVR
TYM || CRYM

'Traitor Time revealed our Crime.' The meaning of this enigmatic phrase is elusive. As Cook noted, 'Whether it contains a clue to the story the architect intended his figures to tell remains, and is likely to remain, a mystery.' After this comes a lion head(?) and a winged angel above the words *Nisi Dominus*, a contraction of a phrase from Psalm 127, 'Unless the Lord is with us our labour is in vain', although perhaps appropriately for a regent, it can also mean 'if not the master, in vain'. Another crowned 'A' follows, then comes a cannon, a headless musician in a pleated skirt beating a side drum, an 'A' surmounting an eroded star (?), a final cannon, and a headless figure in doublet and ornamented belt.

The remaining rooms can be visited from the graveyard. Over the rear archway is a third inscription: ESSPY SPEIK FVRTH AND SPAIR NOTHT / CONSIDDIR VEIL I CAIR NOTHT ('If you speak forth and spare not / consider well I care not'). Many of the carvings on the façade can be more easily studied though the open windows of the first floor.

For antiquarians the inscriptions represented Mar's defiance over the best-known story regarding the building, that he had sacrilegiously plundered the Abbey of CAMBUSKENNETH and/or the Greyfriars church for building stones, and that many of the carvings were taken directly from the abbey. This particular story now seems unlikely, but there was a related scandal which may supply the actual reason. Just before the Reformation Alexander Erskine of Gogar, Mar's brother, sneakily got possession of Stirling's Dominican monastery, along with all its income-generating assets such as lands and the town mills. Mar thus had a quarry close at hand (the monastery has long vanished). The inscriptions may therefore be Mar's way of saying: 'my brother and me, we're rich and successful because we're ruthless and clever; and though it would be nice to be popular as well, actually we don't care what you think.'

CHURCH OF THE HOLY RUDE

This massive medieval church towers over Mar's Wark.

Exterior

On the porch, carvings of a woman with a headdress and a moustachioed, crowned man. The tower has one gargoyle.

Interior

Several consecration crosses on walls of nave and choir. A detached stone corbel with crudely carved staring eyes, next to a triple-arched Gothic monument in the tower. A number of corbels in the choir are carved with bearded male heads, one said to be of James IV; another, opposite, is

Mar's Wark – supposedly 'Jeannie Dark,' Joan of Arc.

poking its tongue out at the King. Burial in church, theoretically banned as a superstitious and sacrilegious practice after the Reformation, continued in Holy Rude for a very good reason: rich people were prepared to pay for it. The bribe – sorry, licence fee – varied depending on the location: the nearer to the altar (regarded as the most sacred part of the church), the higher the price. James Ronald, in *Landmarks of Old Stirling*, notes that burial under the tower cost £30 Scots, £40 for the north aisle, and for the east end £66 13s 4d.

THE TOP OF THE TOWN CEMETERIES

This superb site is divided into the Old Kirkyard, where the most interesting stones are (on the south side, immediately behind Holy Rude kirk), and the Mar and Valley cemeteries to the north, laid out as a sepulchral 'pleasure ground' by the Victorians. The Old Kirkyard is replete with gravestones carved with symbols of mortality (skeletons, skulls, crossed bones, hourglasses – often winged – and the reminder to the living, *memento mori*, 'remember you too will die') and immortality (winged souls, vegetation, the Worm Ourobourus – which eats its own tail in a circular motif of rebirth – and the Angels of Resurrection, recognisable by their trumpets). There are also numerous stones carved with the symbols of various trades: wrights and masons (dividers, square, mallet, wedge), bakers and maltmen (sheaves of wheat, bread loaves, long-handled shovels called peels), hammermen (hammers, often crowned) and weavers (loom shuttle). A reversed '4' indicates a merchant. Several stones are topped with quasi-Green-Men faces spewing vegetation, including one particularly grotesque face with a curled wig, spewing two tendrils which loop around the face of the stone.

Top of the Town Cemeteries: the Sconce Monument, top.

The background to the carved stones was explored in 'Some Early Gravestones in the Holy Rude Kirkyard, Stirling' by John G. Harrison (in *The Forth Naturalist and Historian* Vol. 13 1990), and the best guide is the booklet *Stirling's Talking Stones,* available locally. Gravestones started to be set up in the early seventeenth century after burial within the church became damned as 'desecration' (or, if you were rich and willing, merely expensive). The first stones were the flat or coped stones, known as thrughstones, which imitated the style of burials in church. These were largely set up by the nobility; a few decades later the emergent middle class started to erect upright stones: the licence fee for an upright was about half that for a thrughstone. Unlike the rest of Scotland, where stones were commemorative, the practice in

The Sconce Monument, detail.

the counties of Clackmannan, Stirling, Renfrew and Dunbarton was that stones were put up during the owner's lifetime.

> They should not be seen as memorials but as fashionable artefacts indicating ownership of the site… the owners of these stones could visit them; the symbolism of life and death which they carry is not a message addressed by the dead to the living but an assertion by the owner of his own wealth and orthodoxy. (Harrison).

There are some gravestones which demand especial attention. The Sconce Stone, 1689, an astonishing Renaissance wall-monument, is the largest structure in the Old Kirkyard. At the top a winged long-haired cherub holds a crown and feather; his pudendum and chubby legs rest on a skull and hourglass. Elsewhere there are winged souls and hourglasses, crossed bones, mort-bells, trumpets and grotesque faces. Part of the inscription reads *Ultima Semper Expectanda Dies Homini Dicique Beatus Ante Obitum Nemo Supremaque Funera Debet:* 'We must always await life's last day, and no one should be called happy until he is dead and buried.'

The Service Stone, 1636, just south of the main path between the old and new cemeteries, can be recognised by the circular scene on the west face, and the dents on both sides caused by musket fire during the 1651 siege of the castle. Encompassed within an Ourobourus Worm, symbol of eternity, are three figures, two of whom have cartoon-like speech balloons. The inscriptions and the figures are very worn, so Harrison's article comes to the rescue in interpreting it. The original of the two figures on the left is an illustration from a work by Francis Quarles, *Emblems Divine and Moral,* published in London in 1635. The man on the left covers his face in horror while pointing to a sundial, saying, 'Are not my dayes few! Cease then, and let me alone that I may bewayle me a little' (Job 16:25). The other, a winged haloed angel, is pulling him away – death will not wait. On the ground is an hourglass. A tree separates this pair from a kneeling, praying figure who is saying 'Lord my…' but the rest is illegible. The top part of the stone has been reversed; the angel blowing the trumpet would originally have been above this scene. On the east face a hand

Top of the Town Cemeteries: the stone of Mary Witherspoon, victim of grave robbers.

holds the Thread of Life which is passing through the mouth of a skull. Mason's tools run down the sides.

Close by is Mary Witherspoon's stone, identifiable by the carving of the Grim Reaper, dressed in a corpse shroud and holding a gravedigger's spade, striking a recumbent woman with a staff; the short sword she is wielding cannot ward off the touch of Death. This carving is obviously re-used from an earlier stone, because Mary died in 1822. Three days after her funeral, James McNab, the gravedigger, along with a Daniel Mitchell, dug her up to sell the corpse to John Forrest, a medical student. The two bodysnatchers were caught but due to an administrative error were released. A mob formed and the garrison was called out. Some of the soldiers were drunk, shots were fired, and, after a running riot, order was eventually restored without loss of life. For long afterwards bodies were buried in stone or iron coffins and a watch kept on new graves. Forrest fled to the Continent, became a doctor, joined the Army, and eventually became Inspector-General of Hospitals.

The Victorian cemetery has a few angels and several sentimental or stern statues. That of Ebenezer Erskine has developed an unfortunate stain at the crotch. The most striking monument, however, is the Star Pyramid. Wherever you are your eye is drawn to this staggeringly huge structure. The Pyramid seems to be from some other place; it appears to distort the space around it, a simulacrum of Egyptian mysteries beamed down incongruously into a douce Victorian cemetery. The monument is dedicated to all those who suffered martyrdom in the cause of civil and religious liberty in Scotland. Why a pyramid, though, is unclear. The name 'Star' may refer to the emblem on the south face, a circular wreath surrounding a central sun surrounded by sixteen five-pointed stars. Above this is a staff supporting a triangle of spheres, and then a crown. Each face is decorated with a marble open Bible. Two large stone globes flank the steps;

Top of the Town Cemeteries: the Star Pyramid.

these were once surmounted by bronze eagles, which were stolen in the 1960s or 1970s. In a probably unconscious reflection of the mysteries surrounding the contents and meaning of the internal geography of the Great Pyramid of Giza, when the Star Pyramid was almost complete a Bible and the Confession of Faith were sealed into an inner chamber.

COWANE'S HOSPITAL

Beside Holy Rude church. According to local legend, the statue above the door of the founder, John Cowane (known as Auld Staneybreeks), came down to dance in the courtyard at the last stroke of midnight on New Year's Eve. If he did not do so on any particular Hogmanay this was because the centuries of tolling bells from the kirk had rendered him deaf.

The building is the former Guildhall. Harold Whitbread's book *The Guildry of Stirling* notes a minute of the Guildry records of 19 May 1645. Margaret Niccoll, alewife, had pleaded guilty to illegal sale of wine. The clerk wrote, 'ye said Margrat obleiss hir to abstayne fra doing the lyk in tyme cuming under the pa–', but the sentence is unfinished, the clerk having succumbed to the ravages of the plague. Eight and a half months later the next minute was entered, by a different hand. That plague year, council meetings were held in the King's Park, with members of the council standing in a circle a safe distance from each other. Those with plague in the house had to declare it – usually with a piece of cloth nailed to the front door – on pain of death. Mass graves were dug. One James Davis was given exceptional permission to bury his daughter in his own back yard. Next to the Guildhall is a seat commemorating William Edmonstone, the original planner of the Back Walk. Built into the stones on the left is a small stone, reused from something else. Engraved on it is the word VISITATION, the old, shivery word for the plague. The previous visitation in 1606 had claimed over 600 lives, perhaps more than a third of the burgh; the kirk session did not meet from 14 August until 29 January the following year.

Cowane's Hospital: John Cowane, 'Auld Staneybreeks,' who comes down for a bop on New Year's Eve.

BROAD STREET

Number 10 has a reused sundial and the motto *Nisi Dominus Frustra*, the same as on MAR'S WARK. The window pediments of No. 16, Norie's House, are inscribed in Latin: *Arbor vitae Sapientia* (wisdom is the tree of life), *Bona Conscienta* (a good conscience…) and *Murus Aheneus* (…is a brazen wall), plus initials and the date 1671. The terminal stone of the gable is topped by the stern bewigged head of the owner himself, James Norie, town clerk. The Mercat Cross, once the centre of the market and of public announcements and punishments, was removed in 1791 as a traffic hazard. A century later, when it was proposed to restore the cross, some controversy took place regarding the original design. During the discussion the following rhyming prophecy was published in the *Stirling Sentinel* (2 September 1890):

> When the Cross of Stirling shall go to Redha',
> After that you will see a white craw.

The *Sentinel*'s informant was a man in excess of seventy years of age, who was told the story by Angus McDiarmid, a brewer in Stirling, who died about 1865 at the age of eighty-five, and had a distinct recollection of the prophecy and its fulfilment. When the cross was demolished the steps were taken to East Redhall on the Touch Estate and used to build a farmstead. The following Spring a white crow was seen at Meiklewood, not far from Redhall. The unicorn finial, known as the Puggy, was stored in the Tolbooth and is the only original part. In August 1579 the regent, Douglas, Earl of Morton, hanged William Trumbell and William Scot at the cross for penning a satire on his brutal ways. Despite this lesson, a further ten or twelve 'inventive and despytful letters' circulated, 'tending mickle to the dispraise of the Erle of Mortum and his predecessouris.'

The Tolbooth or Town House, the former centre of justice and administration, was rebuilt in the eighteenth century, and a courthouse and jail were added later. Its predecessor on the same site held all those under trial for witchcraft (see chapter two), as well as for other crimes: in 1547 Marion Ray was hung in a basket on a beam from the tower, as punishment for slandering Agnes Henchman. One of the most notorious executions which took place outside the Tolbooth was that of Andrew Hardie and John Baird, convicted of high treason in 1820 for leading a radical rising during a time of unemployment, high food prices and discontent among the poor. In a scene more medieval than Georgian, both were hanged for thirty minutes to make sure they were dead, placed face down on top of their coffins and beheaded over a chopping block, after which the black-masked executioner held up the heads saying 'this is the head of a traitor'. The executioner's axe and cloak are in the STIRLING SMITH MUSEUM.

In 2000, during the conversion of the building to an arts centre, a skeleton in a pine coffin was discovered beneath the original pend below the courthouse that led from Jail Wynd into the prison courtyard. This was Allan Mair, hanged in Broad Street on 4 October 1843 for the murder of his wife. The events on that day are described in *Stirling: The Royal Burgh* by Craig Mair (no relation). The condemned man, aged eighty-four, was brought to the scaffold seated in a chair. Although he appeared frail he was still full of ire and bitterness, and insisted on haranguing the crowd, claiming he was innocent and going on for so long that people became impatient and shouted for the hangman to get on with it. Mair started cursing everyone connected with his conviction and the crowd itself. Eventually Revd Leitch stepped forward to pray. The hood was placed on Mair, who was still muttering curses. At 8.43 a.m. he was in the middle of saying 'May God be–' when the bolt was pulled and Mair was hung from his chair. For a moment he raised one of his hands, seized the rope, and tried to save himself, but then the grip relaxed and after struggling violently he died. After hanging for the usual time, the body was lowered into a coffin, and taken to a cell, where a death mask was cast.

Before its wholesale renovation the Tolbooth went through a number of roles in the late twentieth century. In an article entitled 'Allan Mair – The Last Person To Be Executed in Stirling' Craig Mair describes how one day he was told by a waitress in the then restaurant that part of the building was haunted by an old man, but only on Wednesdays; she had never heard of Allan Mair, who had been hanged on a Wednesday. The area she indicated as being haunted was the corridor where the skeleton was discovered in 2000. In 1991, when the building was in use by the tourist development department, Craig Mair asked to see the condemned cell. The girl who sat at the desk nearest the corridor told him when she was alone she sometimes felt a man watching her. He only seemed to appear when new staff started, as if to check them

'Puggy', the unicorn on the Mercat Cross, and the allegedly haunted Tolbooth.

out. Neither she nor the other staff knew about Allan Mair. At the time the original courtroom was used as a small theatre in which cameos of Stirling's past were acted out for visitors. Several actors rehearsing in the disused cells above the adjacent restaurant had reported uneasy feelings, chills, or apparitions of an old man walking past.

All of these earlier hints of hauntings went into overdrive with the discovery of Mair's corpse and the opening of the arts centre. Roddy Martine in *Supernatural Scotland* describes the events. Employees saw wine glasses fly off tables and door handles turn in the restaurant. Operations assistant James Wigglesworth heard noises in the old cells upstairs, such as a body being dragged across the floor. A barman in the cellars found the doors of a spirits cabinet shaking violently.

When he opened it bottles fell out and smashed on the floor. In January 2002 a postman saw a man dressed in nineteenth-century clothing pass by and say 'good morning' (this does not sound like Allan Mair, who was more of a snarl than a greeting kind of chap). Karl Kirkland, assistant bar and restaurant manager at the theatre, was reluctant to walk alone in certain parts of the building after he noticed the gas in the cellar kept being turned off when no one was there. Things got so bad that, in May 2002, an exorcist was suggested. A parapsychology team did investigate and 'identified' the spirits of an old man and four others, including a woman. Ironically, as Allan Mair has become established as a regular feature on the Stirling Ghost Tour, the incidents have declined. Perhaps he doesn't care for the publicity.

ST JOHN STREET

The Boys' Club (No. 36), built in 1929, is decorated with several useful instructions: 'Quarrelling is Taboo,' 'Keep Smiling,' and 'Play the Game'. The Old Town Jail, entrance fee, is a popular attraction recreating all the joys and pleasures of Victorian incarceration in the County Jail of 1847. Next door, the Erskine church, now the youth hostel, and fronted by the neo-Classical Erskine Monument, has a small but good selection of little-visited carved gravestones on the grass banks. Look for skulls and crossed bones, hourglasses, Angels of the Resurrection, the elaborated '4' of a merchant, bakers' tools and a wheat sheaf, a complete plough, and the crown, crescent-headed knife and pliers of a shoemaker. The nearby cul-de-sac continues the theme, with the post-war houses decorated with modern versions of old trade symbols, including weavers (shuttle and roll of thread), glovers (shears and glove), fleshers (knife and chopper), shoemakers (crown, curved and straight knives) and tailors (pressing-iron and scissors).

SPITTAL STREET

Stirling Highland Hotel, formerly the Old High School, is populated by an entire menagerie of Victorian gargoyles, including lions, hounds and monsters. The main door is framed with a superb frieze of all the signs of the Zodiac and topped by Art-Nouveau lettering and the *Arbor Scientia* and *Arbor Vitae*, the Trees of Knowledge and Life, while the entrance into the car park is overseen by three small children in Roman togas exploring the wonders of education, exploration and engineering. A figure with astronomical instruments announces the secret of the copper dome: the observatory, a hidden gem with a fully working Newtonian reflecting-telescope in an oak tube, dark wooden panelling, and doors operated by huge cast-iron wheels. Installed in 1889 and restored in the 1970s, this is a time-capsule of Victorian astronomy; it's enough to make you want to put on a frock-coat and grow a patrician beard. The observatory is occasionally open – see www.stirlingastronomicalsociety.org.uk.

CORN EXCHANGE

The façades of the former Clydesdale Bank, now the Varsity Bar, host what may be a veritable portrait gallery of notable Scots: I suspect Robert the Bruce, William Wallace, Mary Queen of Scots and Sir Walter Scot are there, among many others in costumes dating from the Renaissance to the nineteenth century. There are also a number of men, again possibly portraits, associated with the tools of their specialism: art, music, horticulture, architecture and engineering. The upper reaches sprout a lion, unicorn and a helmeted woman, probably Minerva or Athena. The Municipal Buildings is another feast: the main arch flanked by Bruce in full warrior-king mode, and a saint or ecclesiastic, and topped with richly carved arms and Mary Queen of Scots

The Zodiac doorway of the Highland Hotel (formerly the High School).

on the finial. Two heads of warriors wearing helmets decorated with animal and bird crests flank a youth holding a sword and a victory wreath, while the heads of a Queen and abbess similarly chaperone a girl holding a sceptre and a frond; all four heads merge into foliage. Elsewhere there is a portrait of Wallace with a floral helmet and, holding the Seal of Stirling, a pair of angels who look like they've just been goosed. The seal features the crucified Christ surrounded by two trios of archers and spearmen, all on Stirling Bridge; above is a star and a crescent. The library opposite has another version of the seal, and a pair of wyverns above the Stirling wolf. The statue of William Wallace above the porch of the Athenaeum, at the junction with King Street, portrays the hero with medieval broadsword and Roman toga, a rival to the Mel Gibson-alike at the WALLACE MONUMENT for the title of the most ludicrous statue of William Wallace.

BAKER STREET

Nicky Tams Bar markets itself as the most haunted pub in Stirling (www.nickytamsbar.co.uk). The approach is rather obvious – fake cobwebs on the light fittings, etc – but the background is intriguing. Several newspaper reports in a frame refer to disturbances during the pub's renovations. The former owner Andrea Lindsay found a 'secret chamber' that contained a wooden-framed photograph of a man resembling a minister (the photograph is now behind the bar). Voices were heard coming from a cupboard in the gents' toilet, which is still closed up. A plumber called Pete Richardson saw a shadowy figure cross the bar. Two other people witnessed a similar figure drifting from the fireplace, where small balls of light were also seen. The face of a bushy-haired man with sunken eyes appeared in a freshly painted wall. A paranormal investigation group recorded five ghosts – a ten-year-old boy in the cellar, a man from the 1930s outside the gents' toilet, an old man near the doorway and a corner where two chaps from the 1820s sit chatting all day. I learned of other incidents from the staff: a tankard smashed for no reason when two

The Stirling wolf in its lair, flanked by curious symbols, on Wolf's Craig Buildings, Dumbarton Road.

customers were arguing about the music being played; lights in the cellar switched on after being turned off; former supervisor Dave Cuthbertson witnessed the cap of a Talisker bottle fly across the bar; and bangs were heard in the empty pub, which responded to questions being asked.

PORT STREET

A well-worn legend has Stirling occupied in the Dark Ages by Ostric and Ella, two Northumbrian princes. One night when the Vikings came calling a wolf cried out, allowing the Northumbrians to beat off the invaders. The Nationwide Building Society has an elaborate carving of Ostric and Ella emerging out of vegetation. Opposite is the Stirling wolf, which appears in several other places around the city. A horse's head is further along Dumbarton Road. Brass studs in the cobbles mark the site of the main gate into the walled town. Among the shops of the Thistle Centre can be found a well-preserved bastion and bottle dungeon from the town wall. Look for the blazing torches next to WH Smith's.

FRIARS STREET

Number 29–31 is an idiosyncratic red-brick building decorated with mottos – 'Honor Principle' and 'Do Yer Duty' – as well as three peculiar symbols that combine triangles, circles, crosses and straight lines.

STIRLING OLD BRIDGE AND THE BATTLE OF STIRLING BRIDGE

The attractive Old Bridge is pedestrian-only. Being fifteenth century, it is *not* the bridge of the 1297 Battle of Stirling Bridge, which was a wooden structure just upstream to the north. It is,

More curious symbols in Friars Street.

however, a good place from which to get the lie of the land of the battle. William Wallace and Andrew of Moray rebelled against the rule recently imposed by Edward I. On 11 September the English Army was in Stirling, while the Scots were north of the Forth, many of their forces being concealed on the forested slopes of Abbey Craig. The bridge, the only means of crossing the Forth, was narrow, with only room for two soldiers to cross at a time. Once the English vanguard had crossed, the Scots spearmen poured down the Craig and hemmed them in on the marshy ground in the narrow loop of the Forth; the English cavalry could not deploy in the wet, restricted space, and many troops were pushed into the river and drowned. Hugh of Cressingham, the much-hated treasurer, was dragged from his horse, speared to death and his skin cut off in souvenir strips; Wallace had a sword belt made from one portion. Meanwhile the majority of the English Army could only look on from the south bank, unable to cross the bridge. It was a complete victory and established Wallace as a genuine national hero.

2
WITCHCRAFT AND MAGIC
IN STIRLING

Following the Reformation the Reformed Kirk, obsessed with Satan and all his Works, instigated the 1563 Witchcraft Act, which made witchcraft a capital offence. The persecution of 'witches' received a major boost following the North Berwick trials of 1590–1, in which James VI took a personal interest. The King later wrote a book, *On Daemonologie*, which acted as both a philippic against sceptics of witchcraft, and a religious-political justification for hunting down witches.

North Berwick aside, the primary forces behind investigations were the kirk sessions of the local parishes, usually comprising the minister and elders, and the next level up the Church hierarchy, the Presbytery. The sessions dealt with moral discipline, typically non-attendance at church and sexual misconduct, but their remit also included all areas of 'superstition' and magical activity. This varied from practices encouraged by the ousted and now detested Roman Catholic Church, such as pilgrimages to holy wells, through to magically healing people and animals via the use of rituals and incantations, usually called 'charming'. These actions typically attracted the lower level of punishments – payment of a fine, making public repentance in church while wearing sackcloth, and, further up the scale, excommunication, a serious matter with both spiritual and social consequences. All these penalties could be imposed by the session or Presbytery.

Although the boundaries with lesser magical practices such as charming were fluid, the word 'witchcraft' was generally invoked when *malefica* was involved – magic which had allegedly caused serious harm to crops, animals or people. The Church, however, did not have the power to execute – for this, the witch had to be found guilty by a secular court. The usual practice – although this often varied – was that the kirk session induced the witch to confess. Often this involved torture, typically sleep deprivation, which is very effective in inducing confessions of supernatural activity because it produces hallucinations. Sometimes the godly men of the session or their agents employed more direct physical means, such as 'pricking' with a sharp instrument to find the 'Devil's Mark'. Torture was legal in Scotland, and was deemed necessary to ensure the veracity of the confession (when, of course, the result was the opposite – under torture, people will invent anything in the hope that the inquisitors will be satisfied and stop the torment). The typical session included testimony from neighbours who lined up to demonstrate how the 'witch' had done them wrong – often the accused had a local reputation stretching back decades, and community resentments and petty hatreds found their expression in the heightened atmosphere of the session. Once the 'guilt' of the accused had been satisfactorily established by the religious authorities, they could be handed over to the secular arm for a full legal trial. Often the Privy Council in Edinburgh issued a commission for the local landowners and justices to prosecute the witch at a specially constituted local court; sometimes the trial took place in Edinburgh itself; and at other times it was dealt with by a travelling court. If the accused was found guilty they were usually strangled and burnt at the stake. All this describes how things were *supposed* to happen in accordance with the law; in reality there were many abuses, particularly at the local level. Frustratingly, in many cases the records are incomplete: we often do not know exactly what the 'witches' were accused of, or what happened to them – their ultimate fate is often not recorded.

Stirling, having both its own kirk session and the Presbytery which policed other parishes, and being the seat of justice, saw a great many investigations. On 1 September 1562, even before the Witchcraft Act was passed, Jonet Lyndesay from Cambus and her daughter Isabell Keir were found to be witches and banished from the town on pain of death. (In 1604 there is a brief mention of a case against 'Issobell Keir'; this may be the same person.) On 18 and 25 April 1587 the Presbytery found that Margaret Ritchie had slandered Marjorie Robertsone by accusing her of taking the milk from her father's cow by witchcraft. As Margaret could not prove the accusation she had to ask forgiveness from God, the congregation, and from Marjorie face-to-face.

There is often a great deal of fairylore described in witchtrials – in many cases the accused claimed to have received their powers from the Good Folk. One example is the case of Alison Pierson, from Fife, burnt in Edinburgh in May 1588. She suffered from paralysis and fits; during one of her trances she met her cousin, William Sympsoune, a physician and son of the royal blacksmith at Stirling. William had been abducted when young by the Egyptians (usually meaning Gypsies but here referring to the fairies) and had spent twelve years in the fairy hills. He gave Alison an ointment that could cure every disease; with this she healed Archbishop Adamson of St Andrew's (who was excommunicated in 1588). When in trance Alison also met the Queen of Elfland and many fairies whom she saw making their salves from herbs gathered under astrological guidance or on particular days before dawn. The fairies were alternately kind and cruel to her. William seems to have died, because he later came to her as a fairy and told her to cross herself to avoid being carried to Elfland, where she would be part of the annual Teind (tithe) the fairies paid to Hell. On 21 April 1590 twenty-three-year-old Isobell Watsonne confessed to extensive dealing with the fairies. She often met them on a hilltop in Kincardine (Fife). They offered her food which she refused. Her husband became ill and her baby was replaced with a changeling which she threw on the fire. She then promised to serve the fairies if they returned her child. Other people at the meetings included Richie Graham, who was later executed as part of the North Berwick witch panic. The Devil appeared both as an angel and as a man called Thomas Murray. She was asked to renounce her baptism and after the angel marked her on her head and left middle finger she agreed to serve him and the fairies if they protected her. She used rowan wood and a piece of a dead person's finger to cure 'the worm'. While in prison in the Stirling Tolbooth she was visited by a man and asked to identify who had stolen the milk from his cow. Isobell pointed to a man and a woman, both of whom were questioned by the Presbytery. On 10 June she was passed to the civil magistrate with the expectation that she would be executed; but here Isobell vanishes from the records.

Other cases are equally lacking in conclusive details. On 21 July 1590 Marione McNab of Knockhill was accused by Jonet Michell of Lawhed in Knockhill of 'witching' some malt and cursing to cure the sickness of Jonet's husband William. Marione denied the charges but did confess to travelling with Jonet to Kilmahog near Callander to consult with a woman called NcGilers who would somehow repair the malt. Marione was detained in the hands of David Forester, Laird of Logie, for a week, after which Jonet produced twenty-two witnesses to prove Marione was a witch. In her defence Marione called nine of the same witnesses. Clearly this dispute between neighbours was getting out of hand, because even more witnesses appeared on 18 and 25 August, but none of their depositions were ever recorded. On 15 September the Presbytery declared the accusation of witchcraft proven, and ordered Marione to be set free and to attend an assize when called. But there is no further record.

In January and February 1596 Margaret Crawfurd from Denny was investigated for observing the 'Lord's Supper' in a Catholic manner and for some unspecified acts of witchcraft, but she then disappears from the records, as do Elizabet Crawfurd, widow of David Brady, Burgess of Stirling, Jonet Montgomerie, widow of Andro Zung in Stirling, and Jonet NicRomald, widow of Duncan Stewart in Dunblane, all detained for witchcraft in the Tolbooth on 31 August 1597. The following month Jonet Crawfurd and Catherin Kello of Dollar were reported to have made a confession and been imprisoned, but there are no details of any trial, accusations or outcome. And on 26 September James VI wrote a letter from Falkland Palace to the Provost and Baillies of Stirling (I have transposed the original into modern English):

> We command you that you fail not (all excuses set apart) to send to us in Linlithgow, upon Tuesday next, the pricked witch, presently in your ward, that she may be ready there that night at evening attending our coming for her trial in that disposition she has made against Captain Herring and his wife, and for our better resolution of the truth thereof.

On 19 October Patrick Hering was put on trial in Edinburgh for 'certane crymes of Sorcerie and Witchcraft'; it appears the case was abandoned. The identity of the 'pricked witch' requested by James from the Stirling magistrates is unknown.

In July 1612 the Stirling Presbytery noted that, 'charming is varie frequentlie usit in thir bounds' and that each parish should, 'tak inquisition quair any sic thing is committed and as they find to tak ordur yairwith as appertanis and to discharge ye samin publictlie in pulpet.' On 11 October of the following year Issobell Atkine of Jushie was questioned about charming by the Presbytery – they had previously investigated her mother, Helen Nicoll; as Issobell refused to cease using charms the accusation was upgraded to witchcraft and by 16 August 1615 she had been publicly excommunicated.

On 21 February 1614 Grissal Gillaspie was accused of using witchcraft to steal milk from cattle; again there are no details, just as there are none for Issobell McKie, imprisoned in the Tolbooth on 25 August 1617 for 'charming, enchantment and sorcery.' In 1617 and 1621 Jonet Andirsone confessed to charming. On 29 January 1628 Margaret Donaldsoune, wife of James Forsythe, confessed to giving the sark (shirt) of one of her children to Helen Squyar to take to Margaret Cuthbert in Garlickcraig to charm it. Helen denied it was charmed because Cuthbert refused to do it. Margaret and Helen were ordered to sit together upon the seat where the Sabbath breakers sit, and make public repentance upon their knees before the congregation.

The case of Steven Malcome, also known as Stein Maltman, is full of fascinating detail on fairies, protective swords, incantations and the manner in which illness could be transmitted. He appeared before the Presbytery on 6 March, and then 3, 10 and 17 April 1628, where he confessed to curing diseases for nine years, and that he had learned his skill from the fairies, whom he had met in several different places. Based in Wester Leckie near Gargunnock, he was clearly a healer of some renown because he was deliberately engaged by various people in several parishes. In October the previous year Stirling Burgess Adam Neilson sent his sark to be charmed by Stein, who said the words 'God be betwixt this man that aught this sark and all evils in name of the Father, the Sone, and the Holy Ghost, and out on this sark thryse in name of the Father, &c.' Neilson then had to wash his body in south-running water and wipe himself down with a certain napkin and cast it under his bed. Maltman said the water was cast out into a deserted place, while Neilson in evidence said that Maltman had told him the sickness had to be thrown onto a person or an animal; not wanting to harm a human Neilson agreed to pay for a sacrificial beast on which the water would be thrown. Payment for the treatment was a large quantity of meal. On 13 May Neilson was compelled 'to mak his repentence upon the Kirk fluir, in presence of the congregation for his consulting with Stein Maltman ane Witch.'

About six years earlier Maltman treated James Glen, a lunatic at Cambuskenneth Abbey (which was by now a ruin). Between nine and ten o' clock on a winter's night he drew a protective circle around Glen with a sword, then went out into the yard to hold off the fairies. The fee was five merks, only half of which Glen paid. When he met Maltman at the Stirling Fair and refused to pay the balance, Maltman took him by the hand and said 'he should put him in his own place'; that night Glen hanged himself. In St Ninians Maltman was hired by Patrick Wright to cure his son. Stein had Wright take the child that night to a boundary dyke by the water supplying the mill, a highly liminal place. Wright knelt on one side of the dyke with the child in his arms, and handed the boy over the wall to Maltman, who prayed on his knees to God 'and to all unearthly creatures' to heal the child. He then passed the boy back to his father.

In Logie Maltman diagnosed Jonet Chrystie, wife of Andrew Kidston in Nether Craig, as being fairy-struck. He brought in some water from a south-running source and boiled it with an elf-arrow stone. This was a Neolithic arrowhead; such items, being outside the normal run of familiar material culture, and with no obvious provenance, were often thought uncanny; here it was used as a remedy against the invisible and immaterial fairy-shot by which Jonet had been harmed. Jonet drank the potion and immediately Maltman cleared the servants from the room lest Jonet's illness be transferred to them. Later he went out and returned with some cheese, which he distributed to everyone in the house. Agnes Davidson, however, refused to eat it whereupon Maltman said she would 'rew the refusal.' At a session in Logie Agnes later claimed that this had cast Jonet's disease onto her, making her blind and bed-bound. Maltman said he later gave Agnes a remedy, and advised her to 'seek her health from God and all unearthly creatures, for she had gotten a blast of evil wind.' He gave similar advice to John Garrow in Corntoun, and told David Ewing in Westgrange to take his sick son outside between eleven and midnight and shake his sword around the boy's head, as this would banish the fairies. With his own drawn sword he cured John Forrester of Kippen outside at midnight, first ensuring that Forrester's wife shut all the doors and windows and remained silent, no matter what she heard. When Forrester improved and became reluctant to pay, Maltman muttered some threatening words and the man collapsed at his own door and died. Also in Kippen Maltman cured Nicol Campbell by washing him, and healed Walter Millar of Glentirren by rubbing him with an elf-arrow stone while praying to God.

In Gargunnock, his home patch (where he had already appeared before the local session in May 1626 over the healing of a sick cow), Maltman charmed the sarks of several invalids, including James Stewart, and Thomas McLehose's daughter, who was cured of being mute. For the sick son of Johne Dune, he cast two pieces of beef over Binne Craige. He took the son of John Moir of Buchlyvie into the night and did the usual business with the drawn sword, and washed the child with water boiled with his favourite charm, the elf-arrow stone.

On 3 July a commission was granted for the trial of both Maltman and an Agnes Hendersoun of St Ninian. Both were at this point incarcerated in the Tolbooth. We have no details on Agnes other than her name. Maltman's confession included several examples of *malefica*, and so the prognosis would not be good for him, but we have no record of whether a trial went ahead. The exceptional level of detail in this case can be found in two articles by Alaric Hall, 'Getting Shot of Elves' (2005) and 'Folk-healing, fairies and witchcraft: the trial of Stein Maltman, Stirling 1628' (2006), as well as Menzies Fergusson, *Scottish Social Sketches of the 17th Century* (1907).

In January and February 1633 the Presbytery closely questioned Jonet Tailzour of Cambus, also known as 'the Witch of Monza'. Jonet seems to have been one of several difficult, quarrelsome women who had previously been regarded as healers but whom local feeling had turned against. There were examples of successful cures – Jonet unwitched Barbara Dawson by washing her in south-running water, then cutting her hair and nails and baking them in a bannock which was disposed of so that no one would be affected by the disease – but then the witnesses spoke of cursing, cures going wrong, and illness being transferred to other animals and people. Jonet named several other witches, including Jonet and Marion Mathie of Stirling and Helen Keir of Stirling, suspected of being a witch for thirty years. All appeared to have been spectacularly inefficient healers, and had earned the enmity of the community. It is not clear what the outcome was: a note in the kirk session for 11 November 1634 orders Jonet to be drummed out of the town and for no one to shelter her on pain of a £10 fine, but another note in the Presbytery records says she was burned at the stake.

On 30 April 1633 Margaret Chapman, wife of John Bennet of Stirling, was accused by Agnes Bennie, a weaver's wife, of taking her milk from her breast, and laying sickness upon her and her child. Margaret confessed that she had learned from Margaret Dundie in Perth, and Margaret Downie, wife of Thomas Burne, a smith in Stirling, that when a woman lost her milk she should have her infant suck another woman who has milk in her breast; this, when accompanied by nipping of the milk-bearing woman's clothes, would transfer the milk to the woman who wanted it. All this she had done to Agnes.

On 14 and 28 October 1649 John Gibsone and Agnes Hamiltoune confessed to trying to locate the whereabouts of some stolen cloth by consulting 'the dumb man Christie in Stirling', clearly a well-known soothsayer; both had to make public repentance. In 1658 the Presbytery heard the major cases of the murderous and allegedly diabolically inspired Alloa witches, several of whom were executed in Edinburgh (see LOGIE).

Kathrin Black was arrested in Alloa in September 1658 – probably as part of the witch-panic in the town at the time – and after an intervention by the Privy Council complaining about her prison conditions, was released on 28 December suffering from the bloody flux (dysentery). In March 1659 she was in the Stirling Tolbooth along with Elizabeth Black and Isobell (Elspeth) Crockett. They were found guilty of witchcraft and sentenced to be transported but until arrangements could be made were to be kept in the Tolbooth. Incredibly they were still there in August 1661, when they petitioned the Privy Council, who deemed there had been irregularities in the first trial and ordered another one. This took place on 1 January 1662, by which time, through neglect or malice, the three women had been in prison limbo for almost three years. The outcome of the new trial is not recorded.

The year 1659 was a busy year. On 13, 14 and 18 January Helen Ker denounced her neighbour Magdalin Blair as a witch to the Bailie, Minister and Provost. Magdalin confessed to striking and cursing a horse which subsequently died the same day, and to cursing John Steill because 'he had gotten a bairn with her and would give her nothing'; John became ill for a long time and suffered financially. Helen said that after an argument with Magdalin she came home and found a lump of flesh in the shape of a hand between her sheets, after which she became very sick. Magdalin then hinted her neighbour was not entirely innocent, so Helen was examined and confessed she had hired Katharine Greg, who cured her illness with a drink and who had previously charmed the Minister of Dunblane, Thomas Lindsay. Helen Ferguson testified that she had known nothing but bad luck since March 1658 after Magdalin had reproached her for not being kind to Magdalin's husband when he was ill.

Magdalin was brought to trial in March along with two other women. Bessie Stevenson confessed to various healing practices, including placing foxtree (foxglove) leaves under the head and back, reciting words and taking some of the illness into herself. She diagnosed 'heart fires' using a belt and two threads, and cured people who were 'maw turned' (nauseous) by leading them around an oak tree three times while repeating a charm. She could recognise bewitched people 'by the gogling of their eyes and turning hither and tither to ather side.' When she washed the sick person's clothes in ST NINIAN'S WELL she transferred the disease onto anyone she met on the way back from the well. All this she learned from Lady McFarlen's daughter twenty-four years earlier. It is not clear what was the relationship between Bessie and Magdalin, but the other woman at the trial, Issobell Bennet, had been denounced by Magdalin, possibly as a way of getting back at Helen Ferguson. In around 1653 William Luckison, a maltman, fell ill. On a visit to his sister, Katharine, he found her sitting with Magdalin in Andrew Cowan's yard, Andrew being Helen Ferguson's husband. Katharine clearly suspected her brother had been bewitched, and that Magdalin could undo the damage, for she asked Magdalin what was the matter with William. Magdalin questioned William if he had a problem with Issobell Bennet. He said sometimes he threw stones at her chickens when they got into his father's corn. Magdalin said, 'Go to Issobell Bennet, take a firm hold of her coat tail. Drink a pint of ale with her, crave your health from her three times for the Lord's sake, and you will be well.' William did not do this. There was very little other evidence against Magdalin, so she was released.

Issobell and Bessie were not so lucky, and their trial was pursued. Rather cleverly, Magdalin seems to have implicated two people with far more 'form' than herself. Issobell confessed to charming but denied witchcraft. One of her protective charms was to bury a live mole in a box beneath the threshold. For curing maw-turned children she led them around an oak post saying three times, 'Oaken post, stands thou. Bairn's maw, turns thou. God and Saint Birnibane the Bright, turn the bairn's maw right.' (This must be the same as Bessie's practice; presumably they knew each other.) She washed paralysed people with water brought 'from the hollows of the sea' – the hollow ground after an ebb in the sea – then spread meal in the four corners of their bed and made use of a fragment of the shoe of a horse that had been ridden by fairies, a hook and a piece of raw meat, while invoking the Trinity three times. Sometimes she also told the person to pass through a holed stone. Issobell was convicted of charming and witchcraft (although there are no surviving details of any *malefica*) and was whipped through the streets of Stirling the next day. She was then returned to prison until she stumped up £20 as a caution for good behaviour. She was however lucky. Bessie – whose records, once again, contain no harmful magic – was convicted of unspecified witchcraft and executed on 1 April.

January through March 1659 saw one of the more unusual cases in Scottish witchcraft. Wherever Margaret Gourlay went, fires broke out. Flames started up in houses, stables, barns and bedrooms, at any time of day or night, sometimes several simultaneously. Some fires were major and required several people to put them out. On one occasion a fire started where she was standing, but she did nothing about it. The fires were accompanied by strange occurrences giving a sense of proto-Gothic foreboding – a black crow flew back and forth over the house, a clap of thunder was heard at Margaret's window, she was seen speaking to a female stranger wearing a white petticoat and plaid, and there was a banging at her door at bedtime while stones were thrown at her wall.

There is the temptation to suspect Margaret was an attention-seeking pyromaniac with an accomplice, or even that she was the focus of poltergeist activity. Most of the accusations came from Janet Millar, who testified that one Sunday morning Margaret asked her to go and borrow a broom from John Wright. John refused the loan so Margaret took a burning peat-coal and instructed Janet to lay it on top of the wall next to the cows, while she herself went to the far end of her house and went on her knees – which perhaps indicates that she was invoking magical aid in starting the fires. John found the peat before it did any damage. One twilight Janet was waylaid by a black man who laid a heavy hand on her shoulder and questioned her about Margaret. Two nights later she saw him again but committed herself to God, and the man left her alone.

Both Margaret and Janet were put on trial, along with Issobell Keir and Margaret Harvie, James Kirk and Barbara Erskyne. Issobell had been denounced by Janet Millar; she was accused of causing harm to humans and animals. Margaret Gourlay confessed she had advised a woman with a sick child to seek a cure from Margaret Harvie by going to her house, taking three straws from the thatch above the lintel, and asking her for the child's health for God's sake. The woman refused to do this and her daughter died. James was said to have played the whistle at witches' meetings. Barbara confessed to being a servant of the Devil, who had told her to drown herself, but a man rescued her from the water. Margaret Gourlay, Janet Millar, James Kirk and Margaret Harvie were acquitted. Issobell Keir and Barbara Erskyne were found guilty and executed.

Christian Morison was released from the Tolbooth on 5 February 1672, and ordered to appear for trial when summoned, but we have no further details. On 3 December 1677 Janet McNair, Jannet Craig, John Gray, Mary Mitchell and Thomas Mitchell received 'not proven' verdicts in Edinburgh. From April they had been in the Stirling Tolbooth, where in July they had all been pricked and Janet had confessed to a pact with Satan, having got the marks from a grim black man, although the accusation of drowning the two sons of Robert Douglas of Barloch was probably more important. Following the pricking the magistrates of Stirling complained about the cost of keeping the suspects in prison – they had been incarcerated for fifteen weeks – and demanded the Privy Council put up or shut up. The consequent commission deemed the charges were malicious, and released the group. By now charges of witchcraft were getting harder to prove following a groundswell of scepticism, and among the last cases at Stirling were Eupham Wright of Airth (1679) and Elizabeth Naesmith (1683), both of who had their trials deserted without charge.

The last witch-burning in Scotland took place in 1727, and witchcraft ceased to be a capital crime in 1735. A new Witchcraft Act was passed that year in which – in a complete reversal of the belief-system underlying the previous Act – magic was stated to be impossible. Anyone therefore claiming magical or similar powers was therefore, legally, a fraud, and could be prosecuted on that basis. It was under this Act that the medium Helen Duncan, 'Britain's last witch', was sent to jail in 1944 (see CALLANDER).

The cases above are variously taken from: the online Survey of Scottish Witchcraft; Fergusson, *Alexander Hume* and *Scottish Social Sketches of the 17th Century*; Kirk, *Stirling Presbytery Records 1581–1587*; Pearce, 'The Stirling Presbytery, 1604–1612'; Maxwell-Stuart, *An Abundance of Witches*; Larner, *Enemies of God*; Black, *A Calendar of Cases of Witchcraft in Scotland*; Rogers, *Social Life in Scotland*; Davenport Adams, *Witch, Warlock and Magician*; Grant, *The Mysteries of All Nations*; Roger, *A Week At Bridge of Allan;* and Simpkins, *County Folk-lore Vol. VII.*

Nineteen-year-old Alexander Millar, alias Scatters, from Camelon, was hanged in Broad Street on 8 April 1837 for the murder of William Jarvie of Denny. On the scaffold Millar was seen to loosen his shoes and kick them into the street. An old woman in Denny, possibly his aunt, whom he had accused of being a witch, had told him he would die with his shoes on, and he wished to frustrate the prophecy. (Source: William Drysdale, *Old Faces, Old Places and Old Stories of Stirling.*)

FLOWER TREES AND BONFIRES

The Stirling Presbytery set its killjoy face against communal seasonal celebrations that must have been common before the Reformation, such as erecting and dancing around 'flower trees' or poles decorated with vegetation, and the lighting of bonfires and leaping through them. Prohibitions were issued on 9 July 1583, 25 June 1588, 21 October 1589 and 22 May 1593. The key celebrations were Midsummer Eve and 25 October, St Crispin's Day. On 1 August 1607 Thomas Edmane, a piper from Pendreich, along with Nicoll Robertsone, Mathew Huchone, Sandie Carrik, Sandie Gentilman and James Henresone, all from Airthrey, were charged with dancing about flower trees and singing 'superstitious and profane' songs while waving swords. The last case was 14 July 1613 when eight women were summoned for setting up a flower tree in Dunblane on Sunday 27 June and singing 'profane and filthy carols'. After this the practice must have been stamped out. (Source: Fergusson, *Alexander Hume.*)

SUPERSTITIONS

By the nineteenth century the sting had been taken out of tales of witchcraft, magic and 'superstition' and the subject was deemed suitable for antiquarian discourse. In 1901 William Harvey presented a paper entitled 'Some Local Superstitions' to the Stirling Natural History and Archaeological Society:

A person recently visited a house on New Year's Day carrying a Bible, and before the year was out one of the family was dead. On a subsequent 1 January the same person again came in with the Bible and the remark was made, 'who will it be this time?' Before the year had passed another death had taken place in the house. If you borrowed a light from someone on New Year's Day they would be dead within the year.

May Lowrie, suspected as a witch, worked in byre-work by one of the cow-feeders. Many attempts were made to shoot the resident hare of a local tree, and the animal became associated with May. A silver sixpence was quartered and one of the pieces fired at the hare. Next morning May appeared as usual to milk the cows but she had a bandage over one of her eyes.

It was unlucky for newly married couples to meet each other when on their way to be 'kirked' on the Sunday following the nuptials. Three couples were married on the same Friday night. They belonged to three different churches – the Parish, the UP and the Free – but they, being friends, all met on the Sunday when on their way to their respective kirks. Within six weeks one husband had consumption which killed him, the wife of a second couple died of cancer a year or two later, and the third couple never knew much of domestic felicity.

The clock beetle or golach was regarded by many housewives as being lucky and one woman would not rid her house of them, despite her well-known cleanliness. She told Harvey that while they were in the house she had luck, and when they eventually left so did the luck.

Following a death clocks would be stopped and all mirrors turned to the wall or covered with a towel. If the horses drawing the hearse or any of the funeral carriages stumbled or caused a problem, someone closely related to the deceased would die soon; an example of this had taken place in Broad Street.

The Stirling Smith Museum: the Roundel Stone is just to the left of the entrance.

3

STIRLING LOWER TOWN AND ENVIRONS

STIRLING SMITH ART GALLERY AND MUSEUM

Dumbarton Road. Open Tuesday-Saturday 10.30–17.00, Sunday 14.00–17.00. Entrance free.

Like many local museums, the Smith has a number of exhibits of mystical, ritual or Fortean interest. The first item is actually outside, to the left of the door. The Roundel Stone was found on the farm of Townhead, near Greenloaning (NN832068, now Perthshire) in 1822. It has two inscriptions: the upper reads BVAHQATTI IONATI ('Bvahqattis son of Idonatos') and the lower VERGAMEBO NOTVO ('Vergamebos the Notian', presumably a clan or family name). But we can't trust these carvings; the letters were deepened and re-cut by a herdsman after discovery, and others were added by someone else. So it is impossible to tell exactly what was on the stone when it was discovered. The stone is currently neglected: there is no interpretation or sign, and the inscriptions are very difficult to see. Even if it is archaeologically dubious, it needs some care and attention. Some of the interior exhibits are also poorly displayed and interpretation is often minimal.

The museum highlights are:

The axe and cloak used by the headsman in the execution of the two radicals in BROAD STREET in 1820. The Stirling Hangman would not do the job so the task was undertaken by a medical student who had a few days earlier beheaded the weaver James Wilson on Glasgow Green.
A seventeenth-century gravestone from Kippen with superb Masonic imagery – a mason's tools (setsquare, hammer, trowel, mell, level, wedges, dividers), along with a crescent moon, sun and five stars.
Fifteen heads carved about 1540 on wooden decorative panels, originally in a screen in the King's Room of Stirling Castle. The details include several pairs of monsters, winged souls, and dragons, as well as a Green Man.
A bronze bust of Helen Duncan, 'Britain's last witch' (see CALLANDER).
Three charm stones. The red heart-shaped stone was exhibited by David Morris to the Stirling Natural History and Archaeological Society in 1912; it had been found during building work at No. 20 Main Street, St Ninians.
Six links of a chain from ST FILLAN'S POOL near Tyndrum. These may have been used to confine a person being treated for mental illness at the holy pool.
A model by Walter Awlson of 'Jeannie Dark', the statue said to be of Joan of Arc on MAR'S WARK.
A large cup-marked stone, with five huge and one smaller cups, found in 1893 near Mount Alt Farm in Path of Condie.
The 'Figure of Justice' from the TOLBOOTH. This oak figure is suspiciously un-Justice-like, lacking a blindfold, and with the hole for the scales an obvious afterthought. It was probably taken from a religious building, which meant the Protestant justice meted out in the Tolbooth was overseen by a relic of the despised Roman Catholic Church. A modern painted copy stands beside it.

Masonic gravestone, Stirling Smith Museum.

Several whale bones. Fourteen sets of whale remains have been found in the Forth Valley, including Stirling (1859 and 1863), Cornton brickworks (1864) and Causewayhead (1897). Some of the whales may have been caught in a tidal wave which struck the area around 5000 BC. Elsewhere in the museum is a Mesolithic antler with sharpened points found with the Causewayhead whale.

Several items relating to Christian Maclagan (1811–1901), a pioneering archaeologist who studied prehistoric and Roman sites and travelled round the country in difficult conditions making rubbings of sculptured stones. Despite her achievements she was refused full membership of the Society of Antiquaries of Scotland – an insult she never forgave – and so she donated her collection of rubbings to the British Museum. MacLagan developed some eccentric theories – often influenced by her brand of fundamentalist Christianity – my favourite being that all stone circles were simply the decayed remains of brochs. She believed that the original inhabitants of Scotland, although pagan, were all heroic proto-Christians; unlike other antiquarians who were obsessed with Druids, she argued that the noble ancients would have had nothing to do with such idolatry. The museum sells a splendid study, *Christian Maclagan: Stirling's formidable lady antiquary*, by Sheila Elsdon.

Two pieces by the modern Scottish artist George Wyllie. One, whimsical: a portable Stone of Destiny, made of breezeblock in large numbers so many Scots could have their own Stone. The second, grim and powerful: 'Breaking the Habit', a sporting rifle and case sawn up in the shape of a saltire, made following the massacre of children at DUNBLANE.

A caltrop, supposedly found at Bannockburn. Caltrops were a kind of early anti-tank weapon, a multi-spiked iron cluster that disabled horses' feet. There is no record of caltrops being used at Bannockburn, and this and other examples elsewhere are probably fakes. Which leads to the bizarre conclusion that either antiquarians were picking up caltrops and importing them to Bannockburn, or there was a Victorian cottage industry creating fake caltrops.

Sadly for reasons of space most of the ethnological collection is not on display. It includes Japanese netsuke and a shrunken head from New Guinea.

Satyrs' heads, Royal Gardens.

ROYAL GARDENS (OFF ALBERT PLACE)

The houses in this short street sport an excellent selection of carved heads: two horned satyrs, one cat-like, the other with a fierce expression; two bearded men, one protruding his tongue; a foliate lion and dog; and a pair of young men, one with a placid expression, the other scowling.

WELLGREEN

St Ninian's Well was once a major player in Stirling's magical topography; as a holy well its water was often used for charms. These days it is hidden away behind a dull, single-storey locked building in a corner of the car park at the Business Park on Wellgreen. Within are the troughs dating from its use in the nineteenth century as a domestic washplace. In *Stirling Letters*, written in 1894, Isabella Murray Wright describes a coffin being found near the well, in which was 'the skeleton of a knight, which soon crumbled away.' On his breast was a rosette of blue and white ribbon, which decayed after a time, and a silver cross with St Andrew on it, which Wright still had.

KING'S PARK AREA

Murray Wright mentions that her great-grandmother's servant, Menie (Marion) Mackenzie, used to call the road known today as Park Terrace the Witches Road. There are no further details. Somewhere on the hill of King's Park was Patie's or Peter's Well, believed by Menie to promote health, and to which she would carry a delicate child.

ST NINIANS ROAD

A pair of standing stones can be found on the lawn in front of the police headquarters (NS79449244). The 'Canmore' website doubts whether they are prehistoric. By tradition they were set up to commemorate part of the BATTLE OF BANNOCKBURN. Sir Robert de

Clifford and 300 knights attempted a flanking manoeuvre to reach the castle, but were blocked by a company of 500 Scottish spearmen under Sir Thomas Randolph, Earl of Moray. The name Randolphfield, given to this area, seems to date no further back than the end of the eighteenth century, which may possibly suggest the stones were erected by a patriotically inclined Georgian antiquarian.

ST NINIANS

> *It.* Jan. 19 1746 – No sermon, the Highlandmen being here.
> *It.* Jan 26 1746 – No sermon, the Highlandmen being here.
> (Minute book of the parish of St Ninian)

The grand medieval church on Kirk Wynd was used as a powder magazine and blown up – accidentally or otherwise – by Bonnie Prince Charlie's retreating Jacobites on 1 February 1746, an action which killed a number of locals as well as several Highlanders. All that remains is the belfry of 1734, standing proud in the walled graveyard. Apart from a heavily eroded medieval wheel-cross and some mason's tools there are very few carvings. The adjacent St Ninians old parish church, originally built in 1750, has fine carvings of an eagle and the Lamb of God (which appears to be winking) and, around the door, a delightful bird and frog. The small graveyard has several statues of angels, most of them toppled. Minutes of the St Ninians Kirk Session, 1666:

> Jean Anderson went upon a Sabbath day together with Alex Lamb to try, at a certain man who is supposed to be a wizard, if he would show her who had stolen some money she had lost.

THE BANNOCKBURN HERITAGE CENTRE AND THE BATTLE OF BANNOCKBURN

Glasgow Road. National Trust for Scotland. Heritage Centre, 1 March–31 October, daily 10.00–17.30 Entrance free. Grounds: all year, daily. Entrance free.

The Battle of Bannockburn, fought on 23 and 24 June 1314, was the key battle in the Scottish Wars of Independence, with Robert the Bruce (Robert I of Scotland) defeating Edward II of England. The piece of land owned by the NTS is largely symbolic, as the main battle took place elsewhere, on areas now covered by housing and industrial development, but it is still worth visiting for the instructive displays in the visitors centre and the superb statue of Bruce on his warhorse by Pilkington Jackson.

As it has such a pivotal place in Scottish history and patriotic fervour, the battle has attracted more than its fair share of myth. It is often portrayed as a straightforward Scots *v.* English match, ignoring the fact that there were many Scots in Edward's Army, including supporters of the deposed King John Balliol, and the Comyn family (whose chief, John 'the Red', Bruce's main rival for the crown, had been murdered by Bruce in front of the altar of Greyfriars church in Dumfries, a sacrilegious act conveniently forgotten by many fans of Robert the Bruce). So this wasn't so much about patriotism, as the well-known medieval game of shifting alliances called 'Who gets to be King?' The Scots Army carried into battle a reliquary containing the arm-bone of St Fillan, which in his lifetime gave forth a miraculous light to help him read at night. Maurice, the Abbot of Inchaffray, however, fearing the loss of the holy relic if the Scots were defeated, left the bone in a safe place. The night before the battle, the box was heard to click open and shut – and the bone was found to be restored by mystical means. Such is

Frog sculpture, St Ninians old church, Stirling.

the legend. Bruce went on to found several religious establishments dedicated in thanks to St Fillan, including the priory in STRATHFILLAN. The abbot also blessed the Army with holy water, allegedly taken from the Chapel Well at CAMBUSBARRON.

The battle left a negligible archaeological footprint. But if you are going to commemorate a battle, you need to have some kind of focal point. At the centre of the site is a modern cairn which incorporates the fragments of the Borestone. This was said to be the stone in which Robert the Bruce placed his standard, and may be in the general area where Bruce defeated the English knight de Bohun in single combat on 23 June. In 1859 the stone was described as being nearly circular, 3ft (91cm) in diameter and 2ft (60cm) thick, with a 3–4in (8cm) wide hole in the centre. There are several fourteenth-century accounts of the battle, including the anonymous *Vita Edwardi Secundi* (*c.* 1326), *The Lanercrost Chronicle, Scalacronica* by Sir Thomas Grey (*c.* 1355), and Barbour's *The Bruce* (1375), the latter being the main source for the Scottish perspective on the action; none mention the Borestone. In fact, it does not appear on record before 1723. My guess is that an old quernstone was found in an area long associated with the battle, and antiquarian and patriotic enthusiasm put two and two together and got five. The elevation of the Borestone meant that, finally, the site had a ritual focus. Souvenir hunters chipped away at it; it was broken into pieces, which in 1960 were built into a pedestal and protected by a heavy iron grille; the Scottish National Party marched to it on the anniversary of the battle, and pronouncements were made around it about the invidious nature of rule from Westminster; the larger fragments were stolen; and finally the remaining smaller pieces were securely incorporated into the current monument within the circular rotunda, itself garlanded with appropriate quotes. So we have a few fragments of a humble quernstone probably found in the eighteenth century, worshipped as a genuine relic of a pivotal fourteenth-century battle. Such is the power of myth. As the quote from Fiona Watson's 2001 book *Scotland: A History*, displayed in the visitors centre, has it: 'Don't go wandering in the past if you're looking for truth and certainty; it doesn't exist there any more than it exists in the present.'

The Rotunda and Bruce Statue, Bannockburn.

There is a robust thread within Scottish history of political prophecies – pronouncements that allegedly predict the fates of kingdoms or peoples, but which are written *after* the events concerned. Many of these prophecies are attributed to Thomas of Erceldoune, a thirteenth-century seer sometimes identified as the same person as Thomas the Rhymer, sometimes as his son; it is clear later prophecies were attributed to Thomas by default. Such a momentous event as the Battle of Bannockburn could not fail to attract the attention of the popular mythology of prophecy. In *Poems of Political Prophecy* (1996) James M. Dean notes that Thomas 'was regarded as a great oracle who not only could see into the future but could discern the inner structure, the political-spiritual content, of that future.' Dean discusses *Thomas of Erceldoune's Prophecy*, a manuscript from about 1330, sixteen years after the battle, which claims to predict the end of the Scottish wars, and *Ercyldoun's Prophecy*, from about 1340–1350, in which Thomas predicts the end of a dynasty 'when Bannockburn is strewn with men's bones.' A version current in the eighteenth century includes the lines:

The Burn of Bried,	The Burn of Bread,
Sall run fu' reid	Shall run full red
At Banokis borne both water and claye	At Bannockburn both water and earth
Sall be mengyde with mannis blode.	Shall be mixed with men's blood.
The Bretans blode sall vndir falle;	The English shall fall;
The Brysse blode sall wynn the spraye;	The Bruce shall win the fight;
Sex thowsand Ynglysche, grete and smale,	6,000 English, noble and common
Sall there be slane that ilk a daye.	Shall day on that die.

(Note that 'bannock' can mean 'bread'.) This version must be later than the thirteenth-century manuscripts because it includes references to James VI and the colonisation of America. Walter Scott freely modernised the lines in *Minstrelsy of the Scottish Border* (1802), and thus made the supposed prophecy widely known.

Bannockburn continues to throw up strangeness. In the 1990s there was a vogue for claiming the battle was won through the intervention of a cohort of fugitive Knights Templar. The Templars had been brutally suppressed a few years before the battle by Pope Clement and Philip IV of France, allegedly for dabbling in the occult, but in reality Philip had acted for the usual reasons of greed and political convenience. Supposedly a band of these formidable knights had been granted refuge in Scotland, and in return prepared the tactics of the battle and armed and trained the Scots; their appearance at a crucial moment disheartened the English ('It's the Knights Templar! We are doomed!'). The entire story is unlikely in the extreme (again, none of the fourteenth-century accounts mention what would have been a momentous intervention) and the 'Templars Won Bannockburn' theme unnecessarily downgrades the very real military genius of Bruce and the prowess of his commanders and troops. And – the exact site of the battle having been disputed for centuries – on 12 April 2002 *The Sun* reported that Uri Geller was going to locate it by using his psychic powers and a pair of divining rods while flying over the area in a helicopter. He was preparing by watching *Braveheart*...

COWIE

The area around Castleton Farm, south-east of the village, has at least thirteen rocks carved with prehistoric art. The best are given here; all directions are from the farm (ask permission there).

North-west
Three groups of well-preserved markings on top of a ridge (NS85528816); immediately north-west, approximately twenty-three cup-and-rings, with one having nine rings joined by several radial grooves; 50yds(46m) south-east (NS85548811), six cup-and-rings.

North
Five cup-and-rings (NS85878840). Just south, a ring and a natural basin (NS85818831). Further east (NS85988825), over ten cup marks plus rings and connecting channels.

South-east
At least four cup-and-rings, plus three unfinished millstones (NS857878).

South
100yds (91m) south from farm, eight cup-and-rings (NS85718797). Nearby are the fragmentary ruins of Bruce's Castle (NS85708780), nothing to do with Robert the Bruce but owned by the Bruces of Auchenbowie in the early sixteenth century.

PLEAN

Here was once a large moss with a little loch in the middle, occupying a piece of gradually rising ground. After heavy rains the moss slid down the slope overnight. The people had warning and so fled, but in the morning they found sixteen farms covered 6ft (1.8m) deep in liquid moss. (Privy Council Record, 26 December 1629, quoted in Robert Chambers, *Domestic Annals of Scotland*.)

CAMBUSBARRON

Cambusbarron... the place where, if a criminal got under a stair, he was saved from the gallows. In these days, however, this notable privilege no longer exists, there being numerous stairs in the village.
(William Drysdale, *Old Faces, Old Places and Old Stories of Stirling*)

For much of the information in this section, I am indebted to a fine local history publication, *Bygone Days in Cambusbarron* by P.T. Paterson.

The Chapel Well and its accompanying chapel were allegedly visited by Robert the Bruce on 23 June 1314, just before the BATTLE OF BANNOCKBURN; the well also supplied the holy water sprinkled on the field before battle. As a result it became regarded as a place of healing, and was much visited. It is possible some of the people mentioned as being pursued for making a pilgrimage in post-Reformation times to Christ's Well in BLAIRDRUMMOND actually came here, as the Chapel Well was apparently sometimes also called Christ's Well; but the records are ambiguous. In the early nineteenth century a Mr Rennie demolished the now-ruined chapel in search of treasure, a hope unfulfilled. Some of the carved stones made their way into local buildings. The well became a domestic supply, then closed up and used as a midden. In 1979 it was restored and a plaque attached (which has now gone). These days the well is dry, an incredibly dull three sides of very low stones just east of the junction where a set of steps leading down from a path from Birkhill meets the well-made signposted burnside path from the park to The Brae (NS77819251).

A much more interesting visit is St Thomas' Well, off Douglas Terrace across the M9 (NS77889305). This is now a perfectly circular pond, complete with requisite ducks, sitting in the middle of a bijou suburban development. J.S. Fleming, in *Old Nooks of Stirling Delineated and Described* (1898), described steps leading down under the water, and a scattering of carved stones around, including a hog-backed gravestone. Three of the stones bore mason's marks. All this led him to suggest that this was the actual site of the chapel where Robert the Bruce took the sacrament before Bannockburn, and not the Chapel Well. There certainly appears to have been an early church here. Steps and carved stones are all gone but the place still has a pleasant tranquility.

Cambusbarron has several other associations with Bannockburn. There was once a venerable Scots pine atop Gillies Hill (*c*. NS773915) known as the 'Bonnety Tree', allegedly where the camp followers of the Scots Army hung their bonnets before approaching the battlefield as the unarmed but apparently threatening 'Phantom Army' that supposedly caused the English morale to waver. Almost inevitably, as it valorises the role of the 'little people' in the most significant medieval Scottish battle, the story has probably grown in the telling over the years, and everything about it is more popular folktale than history. In 1892, during the digging of foundations of an underground cellar for Cullens the butchers, nine skeletons were found, some of which were over 6ft (1.8m) in height; the immediate local conclusion was that these were the bodies of English nobles buried after the battle.

Paterson quotes an unspecified source of 1852 which claimed the village was a haunt of witches in the time of James VI and 'that at no time since has it lost its demoniacal association,' an assertion somewhat undermined by the only witch named being 'the Widow Dunn', who could shapeshift into an owl. The kirk session records also mention Agnes Law, who in 1703 – very late in the witchcraze – complained that John Douglas and his wife had slandered her by calling her a witch. John had said to his wife, 'Blood her and she will do you no evil,' and the woman had apparently cut Agnes on the face.

One night a man was terrified by a glow coming down the avenue from Polmaise Castle, accompanied by an eerie hooting sound. It turned out to be someone carrying an early electric torch in which the power was generated by a noisy footpump. The building of the castle on Fir Park (NS77769167) in 1865 generated much ill-feeling because it excluded local people from a popular walk and viewpoint; one angry villager pronounced a curse of sterility on the Murray family and predicted the castle would not last a hundred years. The Murrays did succeed in breeding, but the line went though various vicissitudes and eventually died out. The grand Victorian mansion decayed and in 1966 – 101 years after the curse – it was blown up by the Army.

William Drysdale, in *Old Faces, Old Places and Old Stories of Stirling*, tells of James Henderson, weaver, burnt in effigy at the Cross of Cambusbarron in April 1837. He had volunteered to

St Thomas' Well, Cambusbarron. The well has been subsumed in the pond.

go to London to swear that the value of the property of several determined reformers in the village was insufficient to entitle them to vote in the county. A day or two later his wife's effigy was also burnt. In 1901 Revd George Williams, in a paper entitled 'Local Superstitions', wrote, 'Three years ago a greatly respected friend of mine departed this life at Cambusbarron. When he died a woman came, requesting his friends, 'give me something o' his to keep me from dreaming about him.' The dead man had been a clergyman. There was once a Fairy Hill off the Old Drove Road (NS774923).

CAMBUSKENNETH ABBEY

Historic Scotland. 1 April–30 September, Monday–Saturday 9.30–18.00, Sunday 14.00–18.00 (but exterior viewable anytime). Entrance free. NS808939.

Destroyed in 1559 after the Reformation this once-magnificent Augustinian Abbey is still worth visiting for its great bell tower and its numerous carved faces and gargoyles, not to mention the tranquil setting. There is also the grave of James III, killed after the Battle of SAUCHIEBURN, and his Queen, Margaret of Denmark. Their bodies were found in an oak coffin during renovations in 1864, and subsequently re-interred beneath a memorial on the site of the high altar, the cost being borne by Queen Victoria.

The abbey has attracted an extensive skein of stories strange and spooky. Here are the main tales and their sources., which I have paraphrased. Mackenzie Walcott, *Scoti-Monasticon*:

When the spoilers were conveying the great Bell of Cambuskenneth across the ferry of the Forth, without saying an orison in the little wayside Norman chapel, suddenly a dark figure

Carved heads, Cambuskenneth Abbey.

stepped into the boat, which at once sank and left the fatal metal deeply imbedded in the soil below the river.

Norman Adams, *Haunted Scotland*:

A man who lived a few miles away dreamt he was a monk, barefoot or in thin sandals, with an ankle-length robe. He walked up steps worn with age into a tiny austere cell, where the only furniture was a table with a burning candle at either end. When he woke in the morning he found Latin text in his handwriting scribbled on a pink airmail pad on the coffee table. He had never studied the language. The text described a monk who had been accused by a fellow member of the order and burnt at the stake for heresy.

William Drysdale, *Old Faces, Old Places and Old Stories of Stirling*:

A cow belonging to the neighbouring farmer walked up the stairs of the bell tower and had to be removed by pulley as she refused to return the way she came. The wicked laird of Tillicoutry assaulted one of the monks. The laird died shortly after but the morning following the funeral his clenched hand was projecting above the grave. He was reburied every day for more than a week but the hand still thrust out. Hundreds turned up to witness it. The crowd were employed to roll onto the grave the huge stone which now marks the spot in Tillicoutry churchyard, after which the clenched fist no longer appeared. It was one time customary in Scotland when a child lifted his hand to parent to say, 'Weel, weel, my man, your hand'll wag abune the grave for that.'

And finally, and perhaps not too seriously, Menzies Fergusson, *The Ochil Fairy Tales*:

Every Hallowe'en the much-disliked Dean Dalmahoy took the ferry to Stirling to go on a bender, always returning late. One time the ferryman decided not to wait and went to a party, leaving his boat on the abbey side of the river. When Dalmahoy arrived he drunkenly cursed the ferryman and said, 'May the foul fiend drown the sleepy-headed Ferryman and all his bairns!' Straight away the ferry left from the opposite shore. Piloted without oars by Red Cap the fairy, the boat took the monk down the Forth then into a cavern where fairies pricked and beat him, poured vast amounts of whisky down his throat, and threw him into a cauldron of hot water. Struggling up to the surface a third time he promised to repent, and promptly woke up in the boat, which had drifted down the river as far as the Manor Pow, where it had come aground, and where he was found asleep by the monks the next day. Thereafter he stopped drinking and was nice to children.

4

BRIDGE OF ALLAN AND AREA

THE WALLACE MONUMENT

A magnificent neo-medieval monument to the great man, built 1861–9 on Abbey Craig (NS80949565) from whence the Scottish troops descended to win the Battle of Stirling Bridge. The construction largely obliterated a Dark-Ages fort on the site. Within is a worthwhile exhibition, the highlight of which is Wallace's (alleged) two-handed sword, but the best experience is simply to walk up the hill and marvel at the towering edifice. The worst part of the experience is the Mel Gibson-alike statue of Wallace at the car park, a new nadir in kitsch.

THE UNIVERSITY OF STIRLING

The attractive campus contains two standing stones, one on the west side of the road running from the Pathfoot building to behind the halls of residence (NS80609687), the other a massive block of stone, incongruous in its current setting of the new sports facilities to the east of the loch (NS81409650). Both are easy to access. The former is not in its original position; it was broken and lost for years, and when re-erected in the 1960s it was moved a short distance up the slope for safety. This was the centre of the vanished original clachan at Pathfoot. Hector Boece, in his sixteenth-century *History of Scotland*, claims both stones were erected to commemorate the victory of Kenneth MacAlpin over the Picts in AD 843, the battle that established the political and military status of the Scots and which eventually led to this country being called Scotland. The battle certainly took place, and may have happened somewhere in this general area, but the standing stones were here at least two and a half millennia earlier. Roughly 100yds (91m) north of the stone in the sports field, in the general direction of the golf clubhouse, is another curiosity, three slabs of stone cemented together in a triangle (NS81419661). 'P' is visible on the northern one, a damaged 'C' on the eastern one and the southern one is completely eroded, but it once read 'S', this being the boundary marker of the point where the counties of Perthshire, Clackmannanshire and Stirlingshire once met.

There are a number of sculptures in the courtyards of the Pathfoot building and around the loch, the best of which is one entitled 'The Search for Knowledge', a blue man dressed in working clothes, sitting on a pillar and contemplating a gem. The English department runs a postgraduate course called 'The Gothic Imagination'. As well as covering eighteenth- and nineteenth-century Gothic literature, from *The Castle of Otranto* to *Dracula*, the course is a broad church of contemporary and global expressions of the Gothic aesthetic, drawing on vampire sub-cultures, Spiritualism, occultism, opera, painting, architecture, videogames and horror films. Modules include: 'Transmutations of the Vampire in Contemporary Fiction and Film', 'Monstrosity in the Work of Stephen King' and 'Gothic and Serial-Killing'. For more information visit www.gothic.stir.ac.uk.

Above: The Wallace Monument.

Left: The repaired standing stone at Pathfoot, University of Stirling.

'The Search for Knowledge'
sculpture in front of the Pathfoot
Building.

A post on the website of the University's fortieth anniversary (www.anniversary.stir.ac.uk) by Colin Rogerson recalled that during the very hard winter of 1983/4, somebody drove an Austin Mini out on to the ice on Airthrey Loch, where it remained in view until the ice gave way. It might still be there.

From Back o' Dykes, the old track immediately north of the campus, there are several routes up into the pleasant Hermitage Woods, named after a Romantic grotto built about 1785 (NS80779700). The now-ruined retreat was based on that inhabited by the eponymous hero of Oliver Goldsmith's poem 'The Hermit' from his novel *The Vicar of Wakefield* (1766). Edwin, a virtuous but poor youth, is ignored by his true love Angelina, the daughter of a lord, and so becomes a hermit. One day, Angelina turns up at his cell in men's clothes and, not recognizing him, relates her sad story. Edwin then reveals his identity, and the lovers are reunited. The poem must have had a considerable effect on the landowner, James Alexander Haldane, for not only did he build the grotto, he painted verses from the poem on the adjacent rock, including the following lines:

> Then, pilgrim, turn, thy cares forego
> All earth-born cares are wrong:
> Man wants but little here below,
> Nor wants that little long.

Haldane finally advertised for a live-in hermit. Several interviews took place but no suitable candidate was found.

LOGIE

The ruined Old Kirk (NS81529697) has dozens of superb carved seventeenth- and eighteenth-century stones crammed into its miniscule graveyard. You'll lose count of the number of skulls, crossed bones, winged souls and other symbols of mortality. Many of the stones were erected by their owners well in advance of shuffling off the mortal coil. On 26 December 1610 the Presbytery of Stirling sacked Malcolm Toir or Toward, the reader at Logie Kirk, for consulting with the Egyptians (gypsies) and for 'being bewitched by them and giving them gear [money or goods] for remedies'. Ella MacLean in *Bridge of Allan: The Rise of a Village* (1970) says there was an anti-bodysnatching iron coffin and grating in the graveyard, but both may have been snatched since then. There was a church on the site by at least 1178 and the graveyard holds two heavily eroded eleventh-century hogback gravestones (east and south-east of the church, by the stream). The early church was supposedly dedicated to St Serf, although this suggestion is based solely on the connection with the 'Airthrey Miracle'. The source is Andrew of Wyntoun (1355–1422), the prior of St Serf's Priory, Loch Leven. His *Chronicle* contains a great deal on the miracles of St Serf, an historically indeterminate saint, possibly active in the sixth century, who supposedly battled a dragon at Dunning, drove a spirit from a demented man in Tullibody, and in Tillicoutry raised a woman from the dead.

This haly man had a ram	This holy man had a ram
That he had fed up off a lame…	That he had fed since a lamb…
A theffe this schepe in Athren stall	A thief this sheep in Airthrey stole
And ete hym up in pesis small…	And ate him up in pieces small…
Bot sone he worthyd rede for schame	But soon he became red with shame
The schepe thare beltyd in his wame	Because the sheep bleated in his belly

The consumed creature vocalised when the man denied the theft on oath while touching the Saint's staff, a holy object which was thought to distinguish between truth and lies.

At the right time of day (or night) this can be an eerie place. Rennie McOwan, in *The Green Hills* (1989) notes that a friend who jogged along the Sheriffmuir Road always sped up when passing the ruin, and a visiting teacher from Japan, new to the area, walked past the graveyard and said to her friends 'Bad spirits here!' The area certainly has a reputation for witchcraft, both folkloric and historical. On 1 December 1613 Helene, Annas and Issobell Erskine, daughters of John Erskine, and Johnne and George Kirk, sons of Johnne Kirk, all of Logie, were accused in Edinburgh of witchcraft, poisoning and murdering Johnne and Alexander Erskine, sons of the laird. There are no more details. John Monteath's *Dunblane Traditions* (1835) records witchcraft stories set in the unlikely late date of 1718 or 1720 – the historical records are from 1658, so it is probable Monteath is recording traditions which had been elaborated on top of the actual events. The Witches O'Logie met atop Carlie Craig, the cliff above Old Logie Kirk, where the Devil would appear as a large black dog with big teeth and red eyes, or as a human bearing a flaming brand, 'his blue torch being socketed *a posteriori*', that is, in his bottom. In the Glen of Jerah, up on Sheriffmuir (NS838991), he took on the shape of Auld Donald, a Highlander, who pretended to be in distress so as to lure shepherds to their doom in the ravines. Whatever form he took he could be recognised by his cloven hooves, which he could not metamorphose. One evening an Elder of the Kirk was returning from a shooting expedition, carrying a musket which he had some years before picked up on SHERIFFMUIR, some days after the battle of 1715. He thought he saw the Devil-as-Dog on Carlie Craig, so he slipped a small silver coin into his gun, uttered a short prayer, and shot the Foul Fiend, who tumbled to the bottom of the cliff. The marksman rushed to see the minister, exclaiming, 'The De'il's dead noo, Sir.' At dawn the two men investigated the kill-site, to discover not a hound, infernal or otherwise, but the corpse of a pet goat, the prize property of a poor woman.

Above: Logie Old Kirk: gravestone.

Right: Graveyard of Logie Old Kirk, with the witch-haunted Carlie Craig behind.

According to Monteath, maleficent magic caused 'Auld Lizzy Monteath o' Park' to have a 'bairn like a ghaist', while the 'Auld wife o' Jerah' blamed her illness on the witchcraft of 'Auld Meg o' Ashintrool' and 'Black Kate o' Parson-lees' (her husband threatened them with a gun loaded with a silver button, and they removed the spell). Meg and Kate may well be respectively Margaret Taylor and Katharine Rainy, named in the confession of Margaret Duchill of Alloa (or Dollar, it is not clear) on 23 June 1658. Margaret Duchill's incredible narrative includes child murder, assault, shape-shifting into a cat or a large black dog, the killing of cattle and other animals, and sexual intercourse with Satan. In his highly recommended book *An Abundance of Witches* (2005), P.G. Maxwell-Stuart suggests that these extraordinary claims were so far removed from most Scottish witchcraft confessions up to this point that they were probably derived from a learned work recently read by the interrogators and inserted into the questioning. The most likely candidate was *Disquisitiones Magicae* by the Jesuit Martín Del Rio, which describes a dramatic (and, to us, stereotyped) view of Sabbats, including flying, demonic sex, dancing, music etc. It is not clear why Margaret Duchill confessed to the terrible crimes and implicated the others, but it may have been out of deathbed spite – by 3 June, when the other women were questioned, she was dead, presumably from illness. On 3 August Margaret Taylor and Katharine Rainy, along with Bessie Paton and Janet Black, were convicted in Alloa, and burned in Edinburgh a week later. This, then, is the real-life horror behind Monteath's folklore.

Ashentrool is now a group of sheep pens on Sheriffmuir Road (NS819998) while Parsonleys, thought to be in the area of Pendreich Farm, has disappeared. In *The Green Hills* McOwan muses on the link between landscape and legend: all the local witch sites are 'linked to, or close to, terrain that is canyon-like, deep-cut gorges, steep glens, ravine-like, oppressive, overhung, dank and dark grottos.' Robert Louis Stevenson noted that some coastlines 'cried out' for stories of shipwrecks; the dangerous moors hereabouts may have a similar effect on the imagination.

BLAIRLOGIE

Blairlogie Castle, also known as The Blair (NS82759696, private) is a mostly sixteenth-century structure. Charles Roger in *A Week at Bridge of Allan* (1853) notes it had a small oak cabinet, once fixed to the wall of one of the upper apartments, where a hidden spring opened the cabinet which led into a secret staircase leading to a turret. This escape device was said to have been built by a Cambuskenneth monk for reasons unknown.

THE OCHIL HILLS

The Iron-Age fort on Dumyat (NS83249736), a popular walk, has become a destination for Christian celebrations at dawn on Easter Day. What may be a standing stone lies beside an old trackway at Lipney (NS84369803). In his 1922 book on cat behaviour and lore, *The Tiger in the House*, Carl Van Vechten relates the tale of a poverty-stricken ploughman who was dying of hunger in his home at the foot of the Ochils. His cat Mysie brought him a freshly killed rabbit every night for a month until he regained sufficient strength to return to work, after which Mysie's gifts immediately ceased. Sometime between 1979 and 1982 a Mrs C. of Glenrothes saw a big black cat while out driving along a road in the Ochil Hills:

> It came out of a wood and was about to cross the road. It was huge, like a big black cat with enormous green eyes, when it saw our van it turned and went back through a hedge and towards the wood. There were six people in the van and we were all in no doubt of what we had seen that night. (Source: www.bigcats.org.)

BRIDGE OF ALLAN

Robert Louis Stevenson and his mother were frequent health-tourists to Bridge of Allan. It has long been rumoured that Louis Stevenson based the central character of *The Strange Case of Dr Jekyll and Mr Hyde* on Gilbert Farie, proprietor of Farie's the Chemist, guidebook publisher, house-letting agent and all-round finger-in-many-pies Victorian entrepreneur, a man who made the most of the spa boomtown. The youthful Robert disliked and feared Farie, writing that he was 'a… terror to me by day and haunted my dreams by night.' Pretty much anywhere Louis Stevenson paused for thirty minutes tends to be claimed as the 'inspiration' for one of his later classics, but my scepticism was banished when local historian J. Malcolm Allan confirmed to me that Farie did indeed have a double life; he was a voyeur. Farie would sneak out from the back door of his garden and secrete himself in Lower Westerton Wood, from where his trusty spyglass gave a fine view of the ladies in the rooming houses on Henderson Street. Already disliked for his ruthlessness in business, when his pastime was discovered he was held head first over the bridge and told to mend his ways. There is a good chance Louis Stevenson knew about this scandal. Farie's business is to this day trading as Strathallan Pharmacy, No. 65 Henderson Street; it still has all the original ingredients' drawers, labelled in Latin, and the original Victorian floor tiling.

Two archaeological finds can be viewed and handled in the library on Fountain Road: a broken rock fragment with a single large cup mark, and a metal mould for a circular or spherical object and some kind of short bar; they were found whilst ploughing near HIGHLANDMAN'S WELL. They belong to the Dr Welsh Trust and are kept in Cupboard 4 of the Reading Room, along with a number of plant fossils. Sir James Edward Alexander, Laird of Westerton, was the man who eventually retrieved Cleopatra's Needle from the shore in Egypt and brought it to Britain. The story is that he wanted to install the great obelisk on the triangular patch of grass at the junction of Keir Street and Westerton Drive, but this plan was vetoed and the prize remained in London. The footpath parallel to Henderson Street, up the steps from the bridge

The prehistoric cup-marked stone kept at Bridge of Allan library.

The Fairy Knowe on the golf course, Bridge of Allan.

passes a former tollbar stone and, a few metres before joining Well Road, a coffin stone (now broken) lying next to a former icehouse (NS79099761).

The Fairy Knowe (NS79619818), on the northern edge of the golf course, has been reduced by digging but is still an impressive Bronze-Age round cairn some 60ft (18m) in diameter and 7ft 6in (2.2m) in height. The 1868 excavation found a central cist with cremated bone and charcoal, and beaker inserted higher up the cairn, and several arrowheads. There are many fairy stories associated with the knowe, some of which were collected by Revd Menzies Fergusson in *The Ochil Fairy Tales* (1911). The beautiful wife of a Menstrie miller was seduced by the King of the Fairies who lived in the knowe, and just vanished. The miller consulted an old woman said to be a witch. She told him to return to the mill and when he was riddling the corn to give the riddle a certain magic turn. He went back to work and heard his wife's voice singing:

O! Alva woods are bonnie
Tillicoultry hills are fair
But when I think on the braes o' Menstrie
It makes my heart aye sair

For days he heard the same song but he could never make the right magic movement. Eventually he managed it and she dropped down at his feet. Sandy Stewart and Willie Clason from the Middle-town of Airthrey paused to admire the view from the Knowe at noon on New Year's Day. The side of the mound opened and they saw wee dancers in green, grey, red and blue. Willie went in for a bop and the door closed on him. Sandy had to wait until next New Year's Day at noon to rescue him. A piper from Rannoch Moor called Sandy Sinclair met the fairies at the Highlandman's Well (see page 77) and was taken by them into the Fairy Knowe, abandoning the cattle on his drove; piping was thereafter often heard from the Knowe.

Janet Coklay was the vain and flirtatious wife of Davie Rae, a Tullibody farmer. One day when Davie was ploughing he met a small man dressed in green, and told him of his marital woes. Red Cap (who appears in many of the local tales) gave Davie an elfin stone, which would make Janet more obedient. Instead of putting it on her plate, however, where she would not have seen it, Davie placed the stone in the broth pot, so Janet found it and threw it out.

At Hallowe'en Davie went to a gathering at Pendreich. Passing the Fairy Knowe at midnight he met Red Cap, who told him he and his fellows had been lurking unseen at Pendreich, 'in the garden when the lads and lasses came out to pull the stocks, and running round the stacks when they thought nobody was near them.' He warned that if Janet did not curb her flirting before next Hallowe'en the fairies would carry her off. Janet did not, and her scandalous behaviour came to the attention of the Church. At the next Hallowe'en Davie, fearful of Red Cap's promise, persuaded Janet to stay at home. In the morning she was gone and the servant girl had not seen her. The door was still barred. The following day some children saw Janet, 'wearing the same peculiar mutch [nightcap] which she had worn when she lived in Tullibody' on the back of a funny cloud sailing over the top of Dumyat in the direction of the Fairy Knowe. Janet was a real person – she is recorded in the kirk session records – and when Fergusson was writing the tradition of her abduction was still current. The best way to get to the site is up the Coppermine Path through Mine Wood, passing the closed-off adit of the eponymous mine and following the edge of the wood alongside the golf course as far as you can, then striking north to Green 13/4. Note that golfers have priority and watch out for low-flying white spheroids.

Lecropt parish church (NS78059794), which sits above the motorway to the west of the village, is an 1827 Gothic-Revival structure with carved human heads on all four faces of the tower and on the west gable. A Green Lion glowers from the lowest part of the south face of the tower, its face formed from vegetation. The garden of the lodge next door is home to Snow White and the Seven Dwarves and other gnomish delights. The first church at Lecropt, built in the thirteenth century, was further to the west and dedicated to the Celtic missionary St Moroc, who, traditional states, was buried here around AD 800. His shrine, a focus of pilgrimage, was visited by James IV six times between 1497 and 1507, but was destroyed at the Reformation. In 1826 Lecropt Village, including the medieval church, school, manse and cottages, was demolished by the Laird of Keir and the ground enclosed within the policies of Keir Estate. Typically – many local writers being in thrall to the great landowners in one way or another – this act of vandalism and naked greed passed without much adverse comment. The nearby holy well was destroyed when the M9 was built in 1972. All that remains of the community is the old walled and gated graveyard (NS77879811), which has a superb collection of eighteenth-century gravestones carved with symbols of mortality. Moss-covered, dark and tree-shrouded, with only the endless roar of the adjacent motorway to disturb the atmosphere, it appears to have changed little since Thomas Wallace reported to the Society of Antiquaries of Scotland in 1912 that: 'it is the gloomiest and most desolate and neglected place I have ever visited.' A cross marks the position of the old church. Access to the graveyard is ad hoc – seek permission at the former gatehouses on the southern edge of the estate, then head straight up the hill through the trees until you reach a well-made track. Follow this to the right to the graveyard.

On 13 July 1608 James Wright of Inverallan on the west side of Bridge of Allan was accused of performing a magical charm. The records – given verbatim in Fergusson's *Alexander Hume* – are very confusingly written, but it appears his cattle had sturdie, also known as turnsick, a brain disease which caused livestock to run round and round. He cut the head off an infected stirk (a year-old heifer or bullock) and buried it in the passage so the cattle had to pass over it. But the dogs dug it up. He then brought to the village Jonet McCome from Greenoak, a farm on the Teith. She told him to take a new calf to the threshold and bore its ear with a nail, and to consult another woman called Murrochie 'for charming of his goods that they may mend'. This may be Jonet Murriache (see DUNBLANE). Murrochie twice brought James some water and told him to cast it on the cows in the name of the Father, the Son and Holy Ghost. For this she was paid a shilling. On 20 July James' wife Jonet Brok confessed that she had performed the actions as advised. None of this seemed to have worked because after the charms were cast two of the calves died. The couple were ordered to make public repentance in the parish church of Lecropt. On a lighter note, Katherine Steuart's *By Allan Water* (1901), a kind of pseudo-fictional historical reminiscence, describes the adventures of the Black Laird, a travelling tailor from Dunblane who had met many 'ghosts, bogles, wraiths

Green Lion, Lecropt parish
church, Bridge of Allan.

Lecropt old graveyard.

and water kelpies' on his travels, saw a vast number of little fairy women gathering windle-straes (grass used for making ropes) in a stubble field as he walked between Alloa and Dunblane, and encountered Satan at Mill Seive Bank as he was returning home late from Stirling. The Black Laird had been using herbs against the spells of a Logie witch called Piece-morning, and the Devil turned up to tell him to lay off.

SHERIFFMUIR

No preaching, therefore no collection. Everyone away watching the battle.
(Church records, Alva, 13 November 1715)

The 1715 Battle of Sheriffmuir was fought between the Jacobites, commanded by the Earl of Mar in the name of James Edward Stuart, son of the deposed James VII, and the Hanoverian forces commanded by the Duke of Argyll. The terrain meant that neither commander had clear sightlines over their respective forces or indeed the battlefield itself, and there was much confusion and miscommunication on both sides. The battle was indecisive, the left wings of both armies being defeated by their opposite numbers, with the Jacobites being driven as far as the Allan Water and Argyll's left wing routed almost to Stirling. However, the Jacobite plan had been to proceed south to link up with other friendly forces, and as this was prevented – Mar, a strikingly poor commander, did not press his numerical advantage on the day, and after the battle withdrew to Perth – it was essentially a victory for the Government. Since then historians have argued about where exactly the fighting took place. I have found the best guide to what probably happened where and when to be Bill Inglis' *The Battle of Sheriffmuir Based on Eye Witness Accounts* (2005).

War is of course the crucible of folklore. Wherever there is the prospect of sudden violent death, and wherever post-battle stories told by relieved survivors mix with propaganda, biased written accounts and wishful thinking, so shall there be tales that may be versions of the truth. The folklore starts the night before the battle, when the Jacobite Army camped at Kinbuck to the north of Sheriffmuir (NN7905) and witnessed a major display of the Aurora Borealis, thought to be a bad omen. And then there was the Clach-na-bratach, a rock crystal supposedly found attached to the standard of Clan Donnachaidh when it was lifted from the ground just before the victory at the BATTLE OF BANNOCKBURN. Thereafter whenever the clan was about to go into combat the chief consulted the rock to foresee the outcome. On the eve of Sheriffmuir a large internal flaw was observed for the first time, an omen of the impending defeat. The stone, with its flaw, is now kept in the *ad hoc* Clan Donnachaidh collection in Bruar, Perthshire. There is a persistent tradition that on the morning of the battle some Highlanders, in pursuit of a supposed Celtic need for first blood before a battle, killed an unarmed man suspected of Hanoverian sympathies and spread his blood on the White Stone, on the very northern edge of Sheriffmuir (NN80630420). None of the sources written soon after the battle mention this incident, which may be apocryphal. The White Stone, also known as the Whittieston Stone, is a 10ft (3m) high prehistoric standing stone with eight cup marks. Like many stones in the area it is supposed to have been set up by William Wallace. It can be seen from the A9.

The main focus for the folklore of the battle itself is the Gathering Stone (NN81090218). For years this was assumed to be where the clans gathered on the day, and this supposition shaped perceptions of the stone – not least in terms of a symbol of Scottish resistance against the English. The Highlanders were said to have sharpened their dirks and claymores on it – in 1848 the weapon marks were still suspiciously clear. In the late nineteenth century it had a plaque stating: 'The Gathering Stone of the Highland Army on the day of the memorable battle of Sheriffmuir, fought in November 1715.' And on the centenary of the battle, 600 people assembled around the stone and enjoyed whisky, bagpipes, speeches, songs and dancing around a bonfire. As recorded in George Charles' 1817 book *History Of The Transactions In The Years 1715–16, and 1745–46*, an extraordinarily convenient and strangely productive archaeological dig also took place:

> Two graves, or rather trenches, were opened, when, to the astonishment of all present, the bones appeared nearly entire. [One man] took away a skull with seven teeth in the lower jaw…The compiler of this work measured several thigh-bones, and has in his possession one 18 inches long, in a wonderful state of preservation.

Even if the bones were genuine discoveries there is no guarantee they were of Sheriffmuir soldiers. In 1913 John Shearer tried to dispel some of the growing myths in his *The Battlefields Around Stirling*:

> A few years ago the writer of a popular hand-book thought it was no sin to help this story by adding to it, that along with the bones 'claymores, swords and bayonets were discovered.' It is marvellous how many people accepted this silly addition to the story.

There is no record of any genuine archaeological find relating to the battle. Sadly for Jacobite romantics the stone's reputation is post-battle mythology. It was not the clans but their enemy, Argyll, the Hanoverian commander, who used the Gathering Stone as a vantage point (see, for example, the detailed study of the site in David Clark's 1996 book *Battlefield Walks: Scotland*). And the 'weapon marks' date from a day in 1845, when a number of navvies working on the construction of the railway, having suffered an onslaught of anti-English feeling in a local pub, marched to the Gathering Stone and blew it up in retaliation. (The date may be significant – a hundred years after the start of the 1745 rebellion, which may be what had kicked things off in the pub.) The various parts of the stone were then covered with iron railings to prevent any further damage. Bernard Byrom, in *Old Dunblane*, is one of several writers who have this version of events. But there is even more to the stone than this. It was probably a prehistoric standing stone. A 1766 plan of Sheriffmuir calls it the Karling or Carline Stone, as does William Marshall (*Historic Scenes in Perthshire,* 1879) and Alexander Barty (*The History of Dunblane*, 1944). *Carline* is an old Scots word for witch. An article in *The Scottish Journal of Topography, Antiquities, Traditions* (1848) calls it the Belted Stane, from a grayish sort of belt encompassing it, and quotes a local tradition that when:

> The twa ends o' the belt embrace,
> A bluidy battle will tak' place.

It seems possible that earlier traditions associated with the stone have been eclipsed by its purported role in the battle. The Gathering Stone can be easily visited from the tall memorial cairn erected on the roadside by the Clan McRae Society on 13 November 1915, exactly 200 years after the battle (NN817019), and the smaller adjacent monument put up by the 1745 Association, which pointedly mentions James VIII (not James Stuart) and uses the word 'Rising', not 'Rebellion'. As if unable to take the mythological weight attached to it, the Gathering Stone, encased and broken, seems rather sad and dull.

The battle continued to find its way into various channels of folklore. Walter Scott in *Letters On Demonology and Witchcraft* noted a variant of the 'Sleeping Warriors' theme: a horse-trader received his money from a mysterious man in the Eildon Hills who turned out to be the immortal Thomas the Rhymer. In a cavern the trader saw a cavalcade of warhorses and armed men, all fast asleep – 'All these men,' said the wizard in a whisper, 'will awaken at the Battle of Sheriffmoor.' Sleeping heroes ready to return at the hour of need – Arthur, the Fingalians, even Robert the Bruce – are a well-known motif, and this tale, with the name of the pertinent battle

The Sheriffmuir prehistoric stone alignment. Stone 'E' with stone 'D', the Wallace Stone, in the background.

suitably altered, dates back to at least the sixteenth century. In contrast to all this grandiose mythology, Fergusson, in *Logie: A Parish History*, notes that at the time the tenant of the farm of Ashintrool hid his money in a magpie's nest atop a tall tree, and so kept it safe from the Highlanders.

The Highlandman's Well, also known as the Holy Well or the Fairy Well, was a former healing well on the east side of the road where it makes a right angle at the feed to the Cocksburn Reservoir (NS81359804). For more on the witch and fairy lore of Sheriffmuir see LOGIE.

The most interesting site on the moor is the alignment of five substantial prehistoric stones, focused on the only one still standing, the Wallace Stone (NN83240226). This is a very strange place: the stones are in a perfect straight line, almost south-west – north-east, and about 75yds (67m) apart each, but on what were they aligned? I'm surprised more attention hasn't been paid to this unusual monument. Take the field gate diagonally opposite the Sheriffmuir Inn car park and head towards the Wallace Stone (Stone D) on the horizon; Stones A, B and C will reveal themselves on your right if you look hard enough – find any two stones and use the alignment in the heather. The stones are large, and originally would have been an impressive sight. Stone A, the most south-westerly, has twenty obvious cup marks. Stone B is split in two. There may have once been more stones – early twentieth-century accounts mention six, and John Monteath, in 'Statistics of the Parish of Dunblane' (1831) describes them as the Seven Stones (but only one was upright even then). The only tradition I can find attached to the stones is that they were, somewhat inevitably, erected by William Wallace, this time to mark his victory over 10,000 troops under the English general, Woodstock. A post dated 7 December 2001 by 'winterjc' on the 'Modern Antiquarian' website notes that a 2000 visit found animal bones and a skull around the stones. This shows a continuity of some kind of ritual activity – in February 2008 I found sheep bones on all but one of the five stones.

The final battle scene of *Monty Python and the Holy Grail* (see Doune Castle) was filmed on Sheriffmuir, many of the medieval-clad types being played by students from the university, including a young Iain Banks, noted novelist of this parish.

The most surprising monument on the moor is Hitler's Atlantic Wall, mock-ups of the German anti-invasion beach defences constructed during 1943 as part of the intensive rehearsals

Mock-up of Hitler's Atlantic Wall defences on Sheriffmuir, used in preparation for D-Day.

Mock-up of a German 'Tobruk Shelter', Sheriffmuir.

for the D-Day landings. Standing in the middle of moorland, the ruins of shell-blasted concrete and twisted metal are incredibly potent. The wall at NN83790367 is obvious from the road. Nearby are a low-lying Tobruk shelter, a blockhouse, two concrete bunkers and a network of trenches and ditches. A fallen standing stone atop a hill north-west of Pendreich (NS81379967) is reputed to have been knocked down by a tank during manoeuvres, although this may just be a good story.

5

DUNBLANE AND DOUNE

DUNBLANE CATHEDRAL

Historic Scotland. Entrance free. 1 April-30 September, Monday– Saturday 9.30–17.30; Sunday 14.00–17.30. 1 October-31 March, Monday–Saturday 9.30–17.30 (closed for lunch 12.30–13.30); Sunday 14.00–16.30.

Christianity was probably established on the site by St Blane, a late fifth-/early sixth-century missionary whose later biographies (for example the *Breviary of Aberdeen,* compiled in 1508) are full of typical miracles. His mother, Ertha, had crossed from Ireland to Bute with her brother St Catan. Ertha refused to disclose the name of the child's father (it may have been King Aidan, although Ertha seems to have inclined towards a spirit living in a local fountain), so Catan sternly set both mother and baby adrift on the sea. Despite having no oars they floated back safely to the north of Ireland. Lacking illumination one night during his youthful training, Blane produced fire from his fingertips. Returning from an unlikely pilgrimage to Rome with sacred soil from the Holy City for the consecration of his main church on Bute, he travelled on foot through England where he restored a dead youth to life. Blane's Dark-Ages Celtic foundation was succeeded by a twelfth-century Roman Catholic diocese. After the Reformation the choir became a simple parish church, while the nave was abandoned, its roof collapsing through neglect around 1589. In 1649 a large sculptured cross in the churchyard was destroyed by order of the Synod of Perth, who deemed it idolatrous. The nave remained a ruin until a wholesale restoration in the 1890s, with a further upgrade of the choir in 1914.

From the outside the cathedral presents an austere, almost dour, impression, but once within it proves itself full of wonders and marvels, although many of the carvings are perhaps initially hard to spot.

The Nave

The most amazing sight here is the Chisholm stalls, a set of elaborate medieval canopied stalls carved with an entire menagerie of monsters and the arms of Bishop Chisholm (consecrated 1487, the stalls generally being dated 1520). The misericords are carved with, from left to right (south to north): a shield with the Chisholm boar's head, and a bishop's mitre, all supported by two angels; a shield with foliage; a wonderful wyvern (a two-legged winged dragon); IHS, the sacred monogram of Jesus, with foliage; the words GRACIA DEI (the Grace of God) in ornate lettering; and a shield, with mitre and foliage. The canopies, from left to right: stall 1 – a centaur carrying a thick club with a dog above. Note the centaur seems to have a second creature's face on its posterior. In the central 'triangle', a tiny difficult-to-see face spewing foliage with a strange holed hat. Stall 2 – a centaur and (damaged) dog as before, plus a wyvern fighting an amphisbeana (a dragon with a second head at the end of its tail – the word means 'able to go either way'). The central 'triangle' houses a mermaid with naked breasts, holding her bipartite fishy tail. Stalls 3, 4 and 5 each repeat the combative monsters, centaur and dog, and have a spewing head in the triangle (in Stall 5 this head is bearded, with Asian features), while

The monster-populated medieval stalls, Dunblane Cathedral. (Courtesy of Ségolène Dupuy)

Stall 4 also has two human-headed monsters at the very top. In Stall 6 the dragons remain as before, but the centaur is replaced with an incredible composite human-headed monster with bat ears, sharp teeth, long neck, reptilian wings and clawed limbs, one paw lying over the back of a chained, muzzled dog. The central triangle houses another spewing face, but the hat is so eroded it looks like a frog mask. What the symbolism means is open to conjecture – some kind of medieval morality tale, perhaps? Sadly we'll never know, especially as there were once twelve canopies, not just the current six.

The carvings on the nave pews were designed by Sir Robert Lorimer, noted for his idiosyncratic and delightfully playful approach to ornamentation. The plants on the ends are delicately carved, with no two alike. The bookboards of the front pews have armrests in the form of a bloodhound, lion, ram and boar. A search among the pews reveals several gravestones from the time when the nave was roofless and used as burial ground. Each of the arches has a central carved stone head, most heavily eroded.

The Nave, North Aisle

A Pictish stone with, on one side, a Celtic cross whose moulding ends in two serpents' heads with protruding tongues, and on the other a panoply of enigmatic sculpture: two animals on their haunches with entwined legs and a spiral; below, a key-pattern and a rectangle enclosing five circles (a die?); a small, ringed Celtic cross; a horseman with spear and dog; a disc enclosing a Greek (equal-armed) cross; a group of small spirals and abstract designs; and a man holding a staff lying down with his feet against a spiral. The stone probably dates from the ninth century and was found beneath the chapter house during the restoration; it may possibly have been cast down when the Vikings raided the Celtic monastery in

Dunblane Cathedral misericords – wyvern. (Courtesy of Ségolène Dupuy)

AD 912. Next to it is a much smaller stone with interlace and other decoration on one edge. The Strathallan Tomb has a coat of arms bearing two club-wielding wild men with hirsute arms and legs, and underpants made of foliage. Close by are effigies of Malise, 5th Earl of Strathearn, and his Countess. The pews against the wall of the aisle have armrests carved with a hen, cock, camel, beaver, hare and a nut-munching squirrel. The pulpit has two female angels on the stair entrance, one solemn, the other with a half smile. Three masons' marks can be seen on the first column west of the pulpit; there are sixty-two such marks around the cathedral, of forty-six different types.

The Nave, South Aisle

The Clement Chapel, up the short flight of stairs, was restored in 1964. Originally it may have been used to hold various treasures. After the nave roof fell in a poor, possibly mentally ill, woman took up residence, the room thus gaining the name Katie Ogie's Hole. During 1828–32 Dunblane suffered the depredations of bodysnatchers. Men patrolled the nave (which had been used for burials) and churchyard with gun and lantern, but more often were to be found sheltering from the weather in Katie Ogie's Hole. The session minutes of 8 June 1828 record a spat with the procurator-fiscal who had apparently failed to take action on a recent theft of a corpse; after an exchange of name-calling between the church and the judiciary no more is written on the subject, so we have no conclusion.

The pair of baptism pews by the small font are carved with a tiny rabbit, rat, squirrel and bird. The tall stone inscribed with quotations commemorates the sixteen children and their teacher who were murdered at Dunblane Primary School on 13 March 1996 in a killing frenzy by local man Thomas Hamilton. Hamilton committed suicide at the scene. The appalling crime left a deep scar on the national psyche, with memorial gardens, trees and cairns being set up throughout the land. For examples of how people responded, see the STIRLING SMITH MUSEUM and the Fairy Hill at ABERFOYLE.

The Choir

The wooden screen between choir and nave was erected during the 1890s restoration. As well as figures of Moses, David, Isaiah, Jeremiah, John the Baptist and St Paul, its columns have multiple dancing figures, some showing their bottoms. Elsewhere are winged souls, lions and female angels whose lower bodies transform into foliage.

Choir stalls, Dunblane Cathedral. One of several hundred such carvings. (Courtesy of Ségolène Dupuy)

The stalls, organ and the screen behind the altar in the choir were designed by Lorimer, and present an astonishing number of creatures from both the natural and the mythical worlds. By my count there are twenty-eight dragons and wyverns, eighteen griffons, nine sea monsters, twenty-one other composite monsters, ten angels (four playing bagpipes) and one phoenix, as well as forty-six lions and panthers, forty-one monkeys, thirty-six dogs of various breeds, thirty-three sheep and rams, twenty-three boars, twenty-three birds, sixteen rats and mice, sixteen stags and deer, eleven wolves, eleven squirrels, ten foxes, nine goats, eight rabbits, seven eagles, seven pigs, six owls, five hares, bears, crocodiles and swans, three each of elephants, beavers and cats, a pair each of antelopes, wildcats, pelicans, kingfishers, cocks, peacocks, lizards and frogs, and one ape, one bull and one badger. Dozens of the creatures are spewing foliage or foliaceously transforming. Be warned, once you start noticing the menagerie, you won't want to stop until you've seen them all.

Also in the choir are more sets of medieval stalls, lacking canopies but garlanded with splendid misericords. There is a pard, a fierce spotted beast; the pard is described in early bestiaries from the seventh century on as being fierce, swift and with a spotted coat. It is clearly a leopard, but the bestiaries insist the latter beast is the degenerate offspring of a pard and a lion. Other carvings include a crowned Green Man spewing an extensive selection of foliage and fruits, and a bat with spread wings. In 1807 Robert Forsyth, in *The Beauties of Scotland*, wrote that there were thirty-two stalls in the cathedral. By 1874, when Revd Mackenzie Walcott wrote his monumental description of old churches in Scotland, *Scoti-Monasticon*, there were only eighteen stalls remaining, twelve with canopies. Today the total number of medieval stalls stands at only sixteen, six of which have canopies. Remnants of some are in the cathedral museum, but many have clearly been lost, including those

Dunblane Cathedral misericords – pard. (Courtesy of Ségolène Dupuy)

Dunblane Cathedral misericords – bat. (Courtesy of Ségolène Dupuy)

with misericords carved with, as described by Walcott, a sleeping fox; a monkey on an ass; and a vampire. That is his description: a vampire. Initially I thought he must have meant the bat, but if the erudite Dr Walcott meant to write 'vampire bat', surely he would have done so. And he would also surely not have leaped to the conclusion that the bat on the misericord was a vampire; only one Latin American species drinks blood, and non-vampire bats would have been familiar to him. I then thought Dr Walcott might have been influenced by *Dracula*, but Bram Stoker's novel – which was the first publication to make the link between (in)human bloodsuckers and vampire bats – was not published until 1897. There were however numerous pre-Dracula vampires sloshing about the plays and novels of Victorian Britain; Walcott would certainly have known what a vampire was and did. I can therefore only conclude that maybe there was once in Dunblane Cathedral a misericord carved with some kind of fanged human-type creature.

In 1746 a portion of the cross on the east gable was shot off by one of the Duke of Cumberland's soldiers, who was instantly killed by the fragment. The cross has since been repaired. One night the cathedral bell began to toll for no reason. A black face and hoofed feet were seen – it must be the Devil! The minister bravely set forth armed with a Bible, only to find someone had tied the bell rope to a black-faced ram. The graveyard has a small number of carved eighteenth-century stones with the usual symbols of mortality. Over the years building work in the area has revealed three stone-lined cists which may be anything from Bronze Age to medieval; one contained the skeletons of a woman and two children. The north-west part of the graveyard, opposite The Haining, is said to be the plague pit for the 1646 'visitation'; no graves were dug here thereafter.

DUNBLANE TOWN

The museum opposite the cathedral is in the former dean's house, dating to 1624. The highlights are some of the original carvings from the cathedral stalls, including a magnificent lion and a 'Green Devil' with vegetation issuing from its mouth. Open 10.30–16.30 Monday–Saturday, May to first week of October (closed for renovations until 2009). Entrance free. Across the road is the Leighton Library, containing hundreds of books donated by Robert Leighton (Bishop 1661–1670) and added to since. The oldest purpose-built library in Scotland, its treasures include a 1554 map of Europe in *Cosmographicus* by Sebastian Munster, who has chosen to put Italy at the top and Britain and Scandinavia at the bottom. The library is open from 11.00–3.00 Monday–Friday, May–September. Entrance free.

An old curling stone can be seen built into the wall of the Chimes, the pub on Kirk Street. Numbers 22–24 High Street has a carved Masonic panel dated 1726. Over the years Barbush Quarry (NN78750255), not far from the cemetery, has yielded a silver coin hoard, a corn drier, prehistoric cremation burials, pottery, a jet armlet, flints, a possible Iron-Age grave, a possible stretch of Roman road, and three circular stone-lined Bronze-Age cists (one with a skeleton of a child between nine and twelve years old and another a cannel coal necklace now in the museum). The so-called 'Faery' pedestrian bridge over the Allan Water was originally built before the First World War (it was replaced by a new bridge). The name has no fairy connection, being instead a corruption of the then new material, ferro-concrete. Laighhills Park (NN778019), north-west of the town, once had a small loch called the Egg (it was filled in when the railway came, 1845). The loch's central island was reputed to be haunted. Children would run round it singing, 'Hosie, hosie, peep, peep! Whaur's the man wi' the cloven feet?' At one time it was inhabited by two ill-favoured old women. As proof of their supposed witchhood, the following tale was told: a Cromlix farmer called McFarlane shot a hare there one evening; the hare gave an unearthly but human-like cry, McFarlane got his dog to trace the hare, it swam over to the island, the farmer followed, and found that one of the women was injured in the thigh.

MAGIC AND WITCHCRAFT

Such folkloric witchery aside, Dunblane's ministers and elders were dealing with cases of charming and witchcraft. There are no confirmed records of executions, but there were certainly abuses. The records begin on 11 June 1610 when Moreis Scobie of Balhadie admitted working charms for Jacobe Zair in Dunblane, Colin Campbell (a son of the laird of Lundy) and James Nevein. The trial clerk recorded Scobie's doggerel charm, which he claimed to have learned from 'Sir Andro Hudsone, ane preist in Glendevon.' The parts in square brackets are missing.

> The Lord is blessed that heirin is baith mirrie in hairt and hand
> The Lord is blessed that heirin is he salbe thy warrand
> God of his gudeness that he can call and he sendis hestallie
> The fusone of middilyird God send it hame to the […]

The Lord he can, the Lord he zid, he zid syne hestallie

Quha hes bein heir, this nyght he sayes, quha hes bein heir this day?

The Elriche King hes bein heir this nyght, and rest fra me away

The pouar of woman and mankind, and bayth sone grant thow me

The fusone of mirrie middilyird he hes tane fra me away

Grant me the gift sone againe that I granted to the […]

Or ellis thow sall have hell to thy dwelling and damisday at zo'dur

The father the sone and holy gaist and him

I laive with thee.

Scobie was ordered to return several times but didn't, his clients denied they had consulted him, and the case just vanishes from the record.

On 19 April 1615 in Logie parish Johnne Gentilman had to answer for telling his servant Elizabet Chrystie to, on his behalf, seek his wife's health on her knees from Walter Bryce (alias Watty Bryis), a Dunblane man alleged to be 'ane witch, the instrument of Sathan'. 'Seeking health' while kneeling was a powerful request, often made before individuals thought to have bewitched someone. Johnne denied he had told Elizabet to do any such thing, but he did confess that he had asked Bryce to come without the town so that he might ask him if he had done his wife, Margaret Duncansone, any wrong. The brethren considered Johnne had been acting on his servant's superstitious advice, and on 3 May fined both Johnne and Elizabet and ordered them to make public repentance in the parish kirk in linen clothes. Johnne refused to obey.

Then things started to get ugly for Bryce. On 13 May Adam Ballenden, Bishop of Dunblane, applied to the Privy Council for a commission to try this 'pestilent fellow'. By 17 May Bryce and Jonet Murriache were in the Tolbooth of Dunblane, where they had apparently confessed to witchcraft, sorcery and enchantment. At this point we enter a mix of the Presbytery records and the highly excitable account in John Monteath's *Dunblane Traditions* of 1835. The secular commissioners – the lairds of Keir and Kippenross and Sir George Muschet of Burnbanke – were, it appears, dismissive of ideas of witchcraft. The Bailies of Dunblane, William Blackwoode and John Morrisone, cited James VI and John Knox as authorities for the reality of witchcraft. Kippenross noted that the ministers of the Reformed Kirk were so illiterate and ignorant they even preached that the natural phenomena of solar eclipses were 'nothing else than miracles performed by the direct interposition of heaven, that poor benighted Scotland might profit thereby.' Blackwoode countered that such teaching on eclipses was true, at which point the lairds, clearly fed up with this credulous malarky, and against the express wishes of the Bailies, ordered Bryce to appear so he could confront his accusers. At which point Bryce complained that the Bailies had kept him awake for three days and nights, and while he was bound had 'stabbit wi' swords, dirks, and daggers'. The lairds noted that even the Bailies themselves would confess to witchcraft if treated in such a manner, and proposed to attempt the experiment. At this point the Bailies retired in shame and confusion. Only one witness appeared against Bryce, an old woman called Elspat Whirrit, whose sole testimony was that Bryce had, thirty years earlier, appeared in a dream and told her to leave her husband for another, after which her life had taken a downward spiral. This evidence not being exactly convincing, Bryce was released. One of the intriguing aspects about this case is that the Church must have thought they had a good case – Bryce was already noted as a notorious witch – yet no credible witnesses appeared against him, the judges were on his side, and he was acquitted. We'll never know what went wrong. Monteath claims that the Laird of Cromlix later had Blackwoode and Morrisone hanged on the Gallows Hill, where Keir Street now stands. This seems unlikely, and may be a 'poetic justice' addition to the tale. The records are, sadly, silent on the fate of Jonet Murriache.

Later that year, on 1 November, the Presbytery noted that neither Johnne Gentilman, nor Marione Henresone, wife of Thomas Bowsey in Aithrey, had fulfilled their punishment for consulting Bryce and Murriache. Two leaves of the register are here torn out. On 31 January 1616 Johnne was ordered to obey on pain of excommunication. He still denied the charge and appealed to the Bishop of Dunblane. This wasn't allowed and he was excommunicated. Sometime during the period covered by the missing pages, Watty Bryce had died. We have no more details.

The next few years give up only a few scraps. For two cases we have merely the names – Bessie Finlaysoune on 16 July 1618 and John Hog and his wife Margaret Nicolsone on 12 November 1629. In 1648 it was recorded that in this district witchcraft, turning the riddle, fortune telling and superstitious cures were common. On 23 June 1658 Sybilla Drummond of Dunblane was mentioned by Bessie Paton at her trial (see STIRLING) but other than that Sybilla was consulted about childbirth, and had allegedly been burned, there are no more details. The following year on 25 September Janet Finlayson of Dunblane was accused of casting sickness on Katharine White's son. John Buchanan, giving supporting evidence, told the session that when Janet had took him by the hand, 'such a grip, he never saw the like.' He accused her both of making him ill in the first place, and then of taking the illness off. Again, the case fizzles out. On 24 February of the same year Katharine McGregor or McGrigore was summoned because 'she lives and charmes by carrying water out of ye superstitious well at Cullens.' This was probably the spring at Cullens which supplied Cromlix House (see KINBUCK). On 3 March she confessed to taking the water several times into Stirling and giving it to a woman, and meeting her again at Elsie Scobbie's house in Bridge of Allan. Katharine complained that Isobell Ker in Bridge of Allan, the sister of the woman in Stirling, paid her only 12s Scots for her travel – very little money for a lot of work – and she then lost half of it. She denied washing the woman or sprinkling the water on her but admitted casting the 'fairie wispe' that stopped the bottle into the fire. The reason for burning the stubble stopper may be related to the role fire plays in the charm she repeated during the action:

Sanct Jone lay in ye mouth of a lyon
And he forgot himself to faine
And something came to him with a dreime.
Will yat it burn him be stake and stane
Will it brunt him to ye bane
For all the ills yat ever may be
Let it never byde with thee
But in ye aire and into ye flame
And let it never come again to thee.
Ryse up Mother Marie for deir John's sake
And charme this man with yor ten fingeres
With your great gold rings
For blood and melt for shotes and grippe
For all the ills yat ever may be
Let it never come again to thee
But into ye aire and into ye flame
And let it never come again to thee.

Collecting and distributing the charmed water seems to have been Katharine's stock in trade: she confessed to taking the water Jone Robisone in Row for his hens, but denied she had carried water to the Minister of Dunblane. Walter Reid, a tenant at Cullens, gave evidence that Katharine had said to him 'I am summoned and sall thank you before it be longe,' implying she blamed him for the summons. Consequently one of his stirks did not return from watering, the implication being that Katharine had killed it in revenge. But there, once again, the records dry up. On 2 August 1660 Helen Bryce (possibly a relative of Watty?) accused Alexander Jack of slandering her by seeking his health from her on his knees – the implication of this being that she had bewitched him. The kirk session ordered Jack to confess his slander publicly while sitting on the Stool of Repentance.

The saddest and strangest case is the last of the witchcraft records in Dunblane. On 24 July 1664 Thomas Lyndsay, minister at Dunblane, reported 'several pregnant presumptions of witchcraft upon Barbara Drummond.' Barbara, wife of William Robison at Tenantry of Kilbryde, was imprisoned by the Laird of Kilbryde until the Presbytery could question her again on 17 August, when she was again incarcerated, this time until 14 September, when finally some evidence was presented. Geills Finnie of Kilbryde accused Barbara of bewitching her, and then healing her with bits of cloth dipped in water, the feeling of healing being like pins going through her whole body. The episode was said to be related to Geills wetnursing the child of the Laird of Kilbryde, although the connection is not clear from the evidence. Barbara denied the charges, sniped at Geills and was insolent towards the Presbytery, who recommended she be imprisoned for further trial. At this point Harie Blackwoode, the Bailie of Dunblane (and probably a relative of William Blackwoode, Bailie during the 1615 Watty Bryce case) declined to keep Barbara in the Tolbooth. She had already been imprisoned for forty days, there was no commission granted by the civil authorities for an actual trial, and her attendance was 'troublesome to the towne [at] the tyme of harvest, which gave the towne occasione to grumble at him.' The Laird of Kippenross also tired of the matter and withdrew. The Laird of Kilbryde, however, was keen to proceed – there is a hint that there was an animus between him and Barbara, possibly connected to the wetnursing of his child by Geills, and Barbara's alleged bewitchment of Geills. The Dunblane worthies were having none of it, so the Laird somehow managed to get Barbara transferred to Edinburgh for trial. The Privy Council, however, was just as uncooperative. A commission for trial was granted to James Seatoun of Touch and others on 18 December 1664, but two days later the trial was abandoned and the council ordered it should take place in Barbara's home Presbytery.

By 22 December she was in the Tolbooth of Stirling. And there she lay for months, not brought to trial. On 15 June 1665 – eleven months since her first incarceration – she, or more likely a relative, petitioned the Privy Council to end the wrongful imprisonment, naming the Laird of Kilbryde as her persecutor, and noting her lamentable condition in the Tolbooth, 'where she now lies in great misery, and no person appears to insist against her.' The council ordered those responsible to meet within fifteen days under pain of being denounced and their property forfeited. A week later more commissioners were added, and were ordered to try Barbara before 20 October. On 31 January 1667 Barbara again appealed to the council saying that her accusers had refused to attend the trial. The commissioners were ordered to appear before the council to explain why no trial had been held. Clearly they did not do so, and on 7 May 1667, having been imprisoned for almost three years, Barbara was finally released without charge.

Quite what was going on is difficult to judge. Sorcery and charming were listed on the accusation, but no details of what Barbara was claimed to have done were recorded, and we are left with the possibility that the Laird of Kilbryde was carrying through some kind of obsessive vendetta against Barbara, but that he and his fellow commissioners realized that the evidence was too weak to gain a conviction, and so stalled the Privy Council for years. (Much of the material on Barbara Drummond comes from the Survey of Scottish Witchcraft database (www.shc.ed.ac.uk/Research/witches) and Fergusson's *Scottish Social Sketches of the 17th Century*.)

KINBUCK

The spring of Cullens was thought to have healing powers and featured in various cases of folk magic (see also DUNBLANE). The following episode is pieced together from elements in Alexander Barty's *The History of Dunblane* and a 1953 article in the *Bulletin of the Society of Friends of Dunblane Cathedral* by James Webster Barty. On 24 April 1650 Robert Cusing from Kincardine-on-Forth (now in Fife) was charged with having consulted a man in Kinbuck to seek the health of the wife of John Aitken in Torryburn, near Culross. Aitken's wife was said to be bewitched. Cusing denied the charge but the Kirk Session of Culross reproved him sharply.

The case then went into the Kirk Session of Torryburn and 27 April they charged John Aitken with consulting witches. It turned out Cusing had previously assisted in the healing of a man called James Young. The man from Kinbuck, named Drummond, had told Young to go to a certain south-running water, put in his neck and wash himself three times all over and go thrice about in an anti-sunwise direction (widdershins) while saying, 'all the evil that is on me be on the gowan'. The gowan, or lucken gowan or globe flower, was held in great repute as a charm. Aitken, on hearing this, persuaded Cusing to go to Kinbuck on behalf of his wife, taking with him the woman's night-cap. When Cusing returned he informed Aitken that his wife had 'gotten wrong by those he had suspected; that she would be dead before he went home, that her picture was burnt; that he brought with him three pieces of rantries [mountain ash]'. Aitken was to lay them under his threshold and keep one of them upon himself with seven pickles of wheat, because 'seven was set for his life'. Cusing also brought with him an orange coloured salve which he kept because Aitken's wife was dead before he could use it on her. Cusing confessed it all to the Presbytery on 14 May 1650, and had to make public repentance in sackcloth.

KILBRYDE

...O the brae is stey and weary tae Kilbryde Kirkyard,
An' the brig is auld and eerie near Kilbryde Kirkyard;
'Twas the howff where witches met,
Ere they forced the iron yet,
Tae keep their midnicht cantrips in Kilbryde Kirkyard.
('Kilbryde Kirkyard', by Revd William Blair, quoted in Alexander Barty's, *The History of Dunblane*)

Kilbryde Kirkyard, a short distance north of Kilbryde crossroads (NN75550277), has a fine collection of eighteenth-century stones carved with skulls and crossed bones. The medieval church has long gone, replaced on the site by the crowstep-gabled Gothic of the Mausoleum of the Campbells of Aberuchill, built 1864. South of the crossroads and west of the road, the pair of enormous Grey Stones (NS755025) are probably glacial erratics, but had the reputation of coming from across the ocean. Way up on the moors, beyond Dalbrack, sits the Judge's Cairn (NN73940561), supposedly named from the unlikely tradition that the sheriff used to hold his court here.

Kilbryde Castle (NN75580367, private) is entirely Victorian, replacing a late medieval castle on the same spot. The old fortalice had its fair share of stories weird and gruesome, many of them recorded in Barty's *The History of Dunblane*. It was said to have been built by Sir John Graham of Kilbryde, known as 'Sir John of the Bright Sword', in 1460, but this is at least a century before the actual foundation. Whenever a senior Graham warrior was due to die, his bloody shade would be seen in the adjacent dramatic Kilbryde Glen, while the corridors of the castle echoed with grim wails and moans. A great treasure, much searched for through the centuries, was hidden in the Glen. An underground passage supposedly led from the dungeon to a pool on the burn called the Wife's Lynn, a place of execution for women. A circle of trees on a hill on Gallow Hill marked the more conventional spot. A gamekeeper called MacGregor once heard someone knocking at a window of the castle and saw a strange face. He instituted a search with the gardeners, but found nothing. An old blacksmith often saw the White Lady of Kilbryde but whenever he spoke to her she melted away. Blood was seen on a stone in the rear passage, where the lady had been murdered. There are two versions of the event – 1. A daughter of Kilbryde Castle used to cross the burn at the stepping stones in Kilbryde Glen to surreptitiously meet a son of the Cromlix family; she was eventually murdered. 2. Almost identical, but she was a Cromlix and he was from Kilbryde. The latter version is better recorded, being in Marshall's *Historic Scenes of Perthshire* and Monteath's *Traditions of Dunblane*: Lady Anne Chisholm of Cromlix fell in love with Sir Malise Graham, 'The Black Knight of Kilbryde', another fictional owner of the castle. Either he seduced and then murdered her, or she rejected him until he mended his violent ways and he killed her in response. Malise buried the body at the dead of night and went through a pantomime of grief at her loss. The ghost of a lady in a bloodstained white gown was then frequently seen in the glen, wringing her hands and beckoning as if for help. When Malise died – typically, in a dispute of his own making – his nephew inherited the castle. This Graham, a bold warrior, confronted the spirit, which pointed to a certain spot. The knight had the body dug up and buried in a Christian grave, after which the White Lady walked no more.

In a report for the Stirling Natural History and Archaeological Society in 1897/8, J.G. Christie wrote of 'The Fairy Knowe of Kilbride, of old famous for the pranks of the fairies.' Barty has many of these pixie pranks: at Kilbryde fairies were more dreaded than devil and witches, because they were supposedly allowed to kidnap 10 per cent of all unchristened children from their mothers' side. One resident recalled coming home at night and seeing a room lit up by the fairies; when she clapped her hands the light went out and they left. A farmer's horse would not pass a large company of bagpipes-playing fairies on the Stirling road near Keir. They disappeared when he clapped his hands. Green-coated fairies often played at the Fairies' Knowe, above the Kilbryde Burn, not far from the meal mill.

The daughter of the last miller used to tell how she had heard them dancing and singing at the knowe. A solitary pedlar called Scobie who lived at Brighill earned his living from dealing with the Good Folk. One night he had been at a farmhouse when he appeared 'fay-like'. The farmer walked with him part of the way home, and when taking leave of him invited him to return, as they both heard strange noises in the dark. Scobie insisted on continuing and the following morning was missing. 'Dr Ure, the warlock [see FINTRY], was consulted. Dressed in leather breeches, green-sleeved coat and red nightcap, with his witch book and black art stick.' Shaking with terror he said, 'He's awa' wi' the fairies. Ye'll find his corpse in a little glen within sight of the Chapel of Kilbryde.' Some months later the body was eventually found, in the spot indicated. Barty finishes the tale with an enigmatic sentence: 'It is not recorded what was the fate of the poor pedlar's pack, but it was not the fairies who got it.' Which suggests Scobie's fate was not fairy abduction, but simple greed-based human murder.

Monteath's *Traditions of Dunblane* has more dastardly deeds, possibly more folkloric than fact-based, though he claims this tale was told to him by an old woman who had been told it seventy years previously by her grandmother, who had personally witnessed the events. Three siblings, Willie, Robin, and their sister Mal, lived at Blenboard (present-day Blenboard cottage is on the Dalbrack Road at NN748033). They were all incredibly ugly, and obsessed with the fear that they would as a consequence be arrested as witches. Despite living in squalor, they were also immensely wealthy. The Laird of Argaty coveted these riches, so he feigned sickness and accused the trio of bewitching him. In short order they were apprehended, convicted and burned, and the Laird got the dosh. I can find no record of this witchtrial.

DOUNE CASTLE

Historic Scotland. Open Easter–30 September, Monday–Sunday 9.30–17.30. 1 October–Easter, Monday–Wednesday and Saturday–Sunday 9.30–16.30.

> On the opposite bank of the river, and partly surrounded by a winding of the stream, stood a large and massive castle, the half ruined turrets of which were already glittering in the first rays of the sun.
> (Walter Scott, *Waverley*)
> Your mother was a hamster and your father smelt of elderberries!
> (Taunting Frenchman to the Knights of the Round Table, *Monty Python and the Holy Grail*)

Above: Doune Castle from the battlements. Giant wooden Trojan Rabbit and taunting French knights not shown.

Left: Victorian gargoyle, Doune Castle.

Two steps to heaven: buy the Pythons' Holy Ale, drink it from the Holy Grail.

Doune (NN72840107) is a magnificent fourteenth-century castle, some of it restored in 1883. It is worth visiting for its own sake, but also because it was the premier location in the film *Monty Python and the Holy Grail,* and hence has developed as a cult locus for fans of what, for many, is one of the funniest films ever made. The film's plot (such as it is), revolves around King Arthur recruiting his Knights of the Round Table, who then have to complete various quests which they face while using coconut shells to simulate the sound of their imaginary horses. Along the way Arthur and the knights have a personal visitation from God, and encounter the three-headed knight, the knights who say Ni!, Tim the Enchanter (who can make things explode with a gesture, and has a flamethrower in his wizard's staff), a soothsayer, a castle-full of lustful virgin damsels, a witch whose guilt is proved because she weighs the same as a duck, the mystical Bridgekeeper of the Bridge of Death, a dead sheep and a Trojan rabbit fired from catapults, flagellant monks who hit themselves on the head with wooden boards while chanting a phrase from the Latin Requiem Mass, a black knight who keeps on fighting despite having lost all his limbs, the Killer Rabbit of Caerbannog (which is disposed of using the Holy Hand Grenade of Antioch), the last words of Joseph of Arimethea, and the Legendary Black Beast of Aaaaarrrrrggghhh. Not to mention some outrageously grotesque French knights who taunt them from the battlements of the castle (see opposite).

The castle has a guidebook for sale and so here I will concentrate on the elements of direct interest to the remit of this book, including any Python references (marked *HG*). To get the best from your visit, it's probably a good idea to view the *Holy Grail* DVD before you come (the special edition includes the invaluable documentary 'The Quest for the Holy Grail Locations', hosted by Pythons Michael Palin and Terry Jones). At least that way you'll understand why, during your visit, there may be people spouting ridiculous epithets in a silly French accent from the battlements. The Historic Scotland shop will loan you coconut shells if you wish, and also sell two kinds of Holy Grail goblets as well as bottles of Holy Grail Ale, 'tempered over burning witches.'

The open-air courtyard

In *HG* the psychotic Sir Lancelot (played by John Cleese) rushes through the gate-passage and into the courtyard, where, under the mistaken impression that he is saving a damsel in distress, he proceeds to slaughter all the guests at a wedding. The north wall of the courtyard has five ferocious gargoyle heads inserted during the Victorian restoration.

The Lord's Hall

This is on the first floor of the gate-tower, and owes its present décor to the 1883 restoration. After closing up, one of the custodians saw a dark figure in this hall, which she assumed was her colleague – but her co-worker had been elsewhere. A wooden stool tells us that 'The furniture of the Barons Hall is made from the Old Gallows Tree which grew in front of Doune Castle blown down in 1878'. One of the chairs has a carving of a hind holding a flag with three stars, and a pelican bleeding her breast to feed her young. A hinged lid in the sill of the northern window looks down into the machicolation above the castle gate, providing a means of delivering blunt force or hot liquid trauma to unwelcome guests. The first-floor chamber leading off the hall has a chair carved with '*Drede God Ano Dom 1615*', the pelican motif, and a group of armed warrior nobles and a bishop standing round a crown. Below them is a quote from the Roman poet Horace, *Murus Aeneus Consientia Sana*, 'A Sound Conscience is a Wall of Brass'. This chamber, the one above it, and the conjoining spiral staircase, have a considerable number of masons' marks. The wall walk, accessible from here, is the favourite spot for *HG* re-enactors to spout the tauntings of the silly French knights, although much of the filming for this used a small section of wall built at ground level. Even if you have no desire to taunt, the view is excellent, and includes Old Newton Castle to the east (see below).

The Upper Hall

Six of the corbels have human faces, some elongated, all austere. The central window alcove was used as an oratory or chapel and has a pointed credence for holding the consecrated vessels and an octagonal piscina for washing them. In *HG* the hall doubled as both the bedroom of dopey Prince Herbert of Swamp Castle, and the setting for Lancelot's second slaughter of the wedding guests.

The Great Hall

The wooden bench at the east end is elaborately carved: two pairs of coiled dragons, one breathing fire and the other flicking pointed tongues, a quartet of winged four-legged dragons with pointed tongues and curled pointed tails, two coiled serpents with pointed tongues, eight sea monsters with foliate tails, two bewigged men composed of abstract shapes, coats of arms, birds, fruit and vegetation, the date 1654 and the mottos PLENTYE AND GRASE BEE INN THIS PLACE and THE LORD BEE PRAISED. This wonderful piece is actually something of a mystery: like the other examples of carved seventeenth-century furniture in the other rooms, it appears to have turned up some time after the restoration and has no clear provenance. The 'Camelot/Spamalot' song-and-dance routine in *Holy Grail* was filmed in this hall.

The Kitchen Tower

The servery and kitchen. If there is any ghostly activity in the castle, this area seems to be the focus, but the stories do seem to be very vague. There are more masons' marks, and an eroded stone in the floor which used to read 'Remains of oven used by the MacGregors while holding the castle for Prince Charlie in 1745'. In *HG* the tempting of Sir Galahad the Chaste by the eight score young blondes and brunettes of Castle Anthrax takes place in this room.

Every Scottish castle seems to have a legend of a secret passage; it's probably required in an old charter or tradition or something. For years there was a belief that a tunnel ran from Doune Castle to Old Newton Castle, an L-plan sixteenth-century fortalice on the other side of the

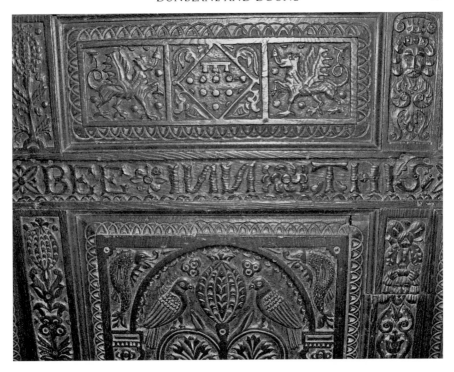

Detail of the carving on a wooden bench in the Great Hall, Doune Castle. PLENTYE AND GRASE
BEE INN THIS PLACE.

Not a secret tunnel leading from Doune Castle under the river to Old Newton: simply the entrance to
an ice-house.

No. 11 George Street, Doune,
designed by Thomas MacLaren.
Primitive carved face and
inverted horseshoe.

Ardoch Burn (NN73140122, private). During mid-twentieth century alterations at Newton a
large chamber was found hidden behind one of the fireplaces; this was thought to connect to
the underground route. And outside Doune Castle, just to the east, there is indeed a low brick
passage running into the slope (NN72910109). It was revealed when Castle Farm was moved
from here at the time of the 1883 restoration. Sadly for the legend, this is only the entrance to
an eighteenth-century ice-house, now sealed. And anyway, what medieval engineer is going to
build a secret tunnel under a deep, wide fast-flowing river?

DOUNE VILLAGE

Much of the information in this section comes from Moray MacKay's *Doune: Historical Notes*. This
wonderful compendium of local lore and history was first compiled in 1950 and is now available in
a modern edition from the Information and Heritage Centre of the Kilmadock Development Trust
at No. 52 Main Street. Mackay was a son of the minister of the United Free Church in Doune.

The 1824 east church opposite the Information Centre has on its tower the arms of the Earl
of Moray, as well as four male figures whose awkward posture has led them to being called the
'Puddocks on the Auld Kirk', a puddock being a frog. The foundation stone was laid 8 April 1820,
when Revd Dr Patrick Murray 'poured corn, wine and oil on the stone', a Masonic echo of a
pagan prayer for fertility. There was once a small cross inlaid in the rough paving a few paces west of
Hall Lane which marked where 'the plague', sweeping from one end of the village, had stopped and
left the rest untouched. The last outbreak of actual plague was between 1645 and 1650, so this was
almost certainly the 1848–9 cholera epidemic. No one could be found to bury the dead, so a big
Irishman named Ned Chambers was induced to do it by a promise of whisky. The 'dead cart' 'went

Male figure on the East church, Doune, displaying the awkward posture that has earned the name 'puddock' (frog).

The Devil's Head standing stone, with surrounding Victorian-era bank.

round the village collecting bodies, and many were the whispers that "some o' the folk werene' deid but only in a trance" when Ned enthusiastically committed them to the grave.' (Mackay).

The wonderful sandstone and whitewash confection of Nos 1–11 George Street, designed by local architect Thomas MacLaren in 1894, is described by Charles McKean in his architectural guide to *Stirling and the Trossachs*: 'Crow-stepped gables, corbels, inset doors, turrets, craft panels and similar idiosyncrasies produce a Scotland that should have been but never was.' On the door of No. 11 is a motif incorporating an upside-down horseshoe, and above that an incredibly primitive and crude representation of a face, presumably reused from the previous building on the site. A small road leads off Balkerach Street to the signposted Doune Ponds nature walk. In the corner of the car park here is a standing stone known as the Top of the Devil's Head (NN72560182). According to Moray's grandmother the children of the village used to join hands in a ring around it and sing:

> Olie, Olie, peep, peep, peep;
> Here's the man wi' the cloven feet.
> Here's his head but where's his feet?
> Olie, Olie, peep, peep, peep.

Note the similarity to the chant about Egg Island in DUNBLANE. In the eighteenth century cattle deals were struck at the stone during the annual Doune Fair. A low mossy bank can be seen around the stone; this may be a Victorian 'Druidic' addition. The Trootie Well, opposite Glenardoch, on Castle Farm Road, apparently always had a little trout in it, which led to suspicions it might have been restocked surreptitiously.

MAGIC AND WITCHCRAFT

On 20 March 1650 Murdoch Ferguson accused Margaret Spittell, of Earne in Kilmadock parish, of witchcraft. He said he and his wife Jonet Buchanan were coming out of Earne, she being ill and on horseback. Margaret came to Jonet and gripped her and said, 'God send you the relief that is nearest you.' After which Jonet was paralysed from the waist down for two years. Murdoch went to Margaret and sought from her his wife's health but she ignored his request. Murdoch told the session he 'never had health thereafter.' Other witnesses then testified. One day Margaret visited a neighbour for a drink. When the neighbour returned she found Margaret with the newborn calf in her arms, after which the cow would not take the calf and the milk was turned to blood. The woman came to Margaret later and requested the return of the milk, which she got. Johne Bachop, now in Stirling but formerly Margaret's neighbour, found something strange like raw flesh on his midden; the description is not clear but presumably this was thought to be a charm or curse. Margaret threatened James Haldin of Sachane after an argument between him and her husband, and said she would bring 'ane evil end upon him and his guids.' Margaret then appeared at the Presbytery on 3 April, where she contradicted herself in many things and denied what she had already confessed to the minister, William Edmistone. She was ordered to be incarcerated by Harie Blackadder, Bailie of Dunblane. And then she disappears from the records. The details are in Fergusson's *Scottish Social Sketches of the 17th Century*. In *An Abundance of Witches* Maxwell-Stuart mentions Margaret Henderson from Kilmadock, who in January 1659 sought a cure from a woman called NicOstrich, who was travelling in the area. On 7 February the Session was told she did nothing to Margaret except 'take her by the wrist and looked at the hollows thereof, and said that she could do her no good, for she had got a blast' (illness brought on by witchcraft, or also paralysis). The case dragged on until October, at which time NicOstrich denied she had divined by 'turning the riddle' (sieve) but she had seen it done a long time ago. The session passed her on to the civil magistrate for further trial, and again the case disappears. The only recent 'witch' that Mackay could find was Jenny Merton, d. 1825. 'Her witchery does not seem to have been specially potent and little is known about her.'

AROUND DOUNE

St Fillan's Chapel (NN73440037) was one of six reputedly erected to the saint by Robert the Bruce to commemorate the victory at Bannockburn. In the nineteenth century it was converted into a mausoleum. The three standing stones at Glenhead (NN75480045) run in a line approximately north-east to south-west for 30ft (9m); there is a fourth block which

St Aedh's church, Old Kilmadock burial ground: incised grid above lintel.

appears to have split off the northern stone. The central stone has at least twenty obvious cup marks. The alignment can be seen from the road but access into the field is easy. Aerial photography has identified a possible 105yd (96m) long rectangular ditched site some 300yds (275m) m to the north-west, possibly a Neolithic mortuary enclosure or long barrow. A single standing stone 7ft (2.1m) high is built into the wall of the forestry plantation on the east side of Glenhead farmhouse (NN75520100). The single cup mark on its top was clearly not meant to be seen. A cairn at the farm was opened in the 1880s; several cists were revealed, one of which contained a perforated stone macehead and a food vessel, both of which are in the National Museum of Scotland. In 1951 quarrying operations near Auchinteck (NN75660170) unearthed a cist containing a crouched skeleton and, nearby, a circle of six shallow pits each lined with small flat stones. All were destroyed. On the road a little south-west of the Glenhead stones is a statue to Colonel Sir David Stirling of Keir House, founder of the SAS (NN755004).

Old Kilmadock burial ground (NN70660247, marked on the map as St Aedh's church), an easy walk along the Teith from Doune, sits on a beautiful spot above the river. If you like your graveyards in classic horror-film format with be-mossed and lichened gravestones leaning at crazy angles, this is the place for you. Carvings on the stones include scissors, spade, dagger (?), hammers, winged souls, skulls and crossed bones, sexton's tools, hourglass, a heraldic animal, coats of arms, and the sock and coulter of a plough. One of the stones on the sole remaining gable of the ruined church, which was abandoned in 1746, is incised with a grid of three horizontal and two vertical lines, while three more blocks have masons' marks. The small room with the sloping roof was, at the time of my visit, a sheep graveyard, with the remains of at least five ovine skeletons within.

Mackay records an entry in the kirk session records of 12 January 1823: the church officer was made to promise under oath 'that he would not be concerned in the raising of dead bodies in the churchyard of Doune, of Kilmadock, or any other churchyard or be accessory to such nefarious practices in any shape whatever.' The graveyard watch recorded no incidents but there were many stories of graves having been opened. A stranger called Rab Stevenson stayed in the village in 1827, leaving for a period, then returning. He had no obvious employment. Some time after Rab left for good, Peter Ferguson, a Doune lad, moved to Edinburgh, and married a servant to one of the well-known doctors in Surgeon Square. She told him that late-night callers often came asking for the key to the cellar. One night Peter answered the knock, to find the caller was Rab. He had been employed to 'do' Doune as a resurrectionist. A year later the scandal over the murdering and bodysnatching activities of Burke and Hare erupted. Another entry in the session records reads: '15 June 1863. It was agreed to supply the gravedigger with Bags or Slips in order to contain any portion of the remains of the deceased unavoidably turned up in the digging of graves.'

A 'Judge's Seat' once existed near Severie Cottage. Mackay notes that: 'It has been suggested that the judgement given here may have been more vengeance than justice, and that the stones formed a sort of sacrificial altar more than a seat.' The site of the 'chair' is probably the damaged cist on a knoll to the south of the cottage (NN70460792), which has two compartments separated by a slumped slab.

The A84 south from Doune crosses over the Brig o' Teith, which bears a pair of scissors and the inscription: 'In the Year of God 1535 founded was this bridge by Robert Spittal, tailor to the most noble Princess Margaret, spouse to James IV.' Tullock Knowe, a little way along the B8032 (NN71780119) is a large cairn with a reputation as a fairy hill. Gartincaber Tower, a ruined Gothic folly erected in 1799, stands on a hill to the west (NN69760080). It was supposed to mark the centre of Scotland.

BLAIRDRUMMOND

Old Kincardine burial ground (NS72129874), across the busy A84 from the attractive Gothic parish church of 1814–16, has another splendid crop of eighteenth-century carvings, often covered with moss. As well as the usual symbols of mortality and coats of arms, there are some truly extraordinary monuments. The Muschet burial enclosure, built in 1686, has above the door a skeleton, one of whose hands is holding a book inscribed with a quote from Job 19:26, 'And though after my skin worms destroy this body, yet in my flesh shall I see God'.

One of the table tombs has a support carved with a man who appears to be rubbing his stomach with one hand while holding some sort of covering over his head with the other. Next to this is an upright slab with carvings of George Bachup, dressed in a tightly buttoned frock coat and his wife Jennet Forgeson, wearing a gown. Between them is an open book; the inscription, in mixed characters, now almost illegible, reads 'For he remembers we are dvst and he our frame wel knovs • frail man his days are like the gras • as flowr in field he grows for over it the', at which point it cuts off, perhaps because the carver ran out of room, or the quote was presumed to be continued on the hidden next page. It is a version of part of Psalm 103: 'For he knoweth our frame; he remembereth that we are dust. As for man, his days are as grass: as a flower of the field, so he flourisheth. For the wind passeth over it, and it is gone; and the place therof shall know it no more.' Below are carved the couple's ten children, the first of whom wears a frock like his father's while the remaining nine are nude and anatomically male. Two are almost holding hands: were these twins? There is no information on the stone about the brood. There is also a Gothic triple-arched monument, whose inscription tells us it contains stones brought from Dunblane Cathedral after its restoration in 1893. Outside the graveyard wall is what looks like a modern reconstruction of a well or font.

The woodlands of Blair Drummond estate, to the east, hide two sites of particular interest. An obelisk with the date '1780' stands on a rise at the western end of the woods (NS72489867). it is reached by crossing a small rustic bridge and ascending an inward-turning spiral up a knoll, all clearly another part of the designed landscape. On one side is an intriguing inscription: 'For his Neighbours as well as for Himself was this Obelisk erected by Henry Home. Graft Benevolence on Self Love the Fruit will be Delicious.' Henry Home was Lord Kames (1696–1792), an energetic proprietor who not only landscaped his estate but drained the 6–12ft (2–3.6m) deep moss to reveal the fertile land beneath, employing poor people from Balquhidder to wash away the moss using

The ten children of George Bachup and Jennet Forgeson, Old Kincardine burial ground, Blairdrummond.

a huge water wheel. William Drysdale, in *Old Faces, Old Places and Old Stories of Stirling,* tells a characteristic story of Kames: on his deathbed he told Dr Cukken that he earnestly wished to be away, as he was exceedingly curious to learn the nature and manners of another world. 'Doctor, as I never could be idle in this world, I shall willingly perform any task that may be imposed upon me.'

The clearing of the moss revealed a number of archaeological items, including: an Iron-Age bronze cauldron (now in the National Museum of Scotland); a second cauldron, now lost, a whale's skeleton with a piece of perforated antler, probably Mesolithic; various bronze axes, spearheads and swords; several polished stone axes and perforated maceheads; and a section of timber track.

The main focus of interest, however, is Christ's Well (NS72919890). For at least sixty years after 1581, the Reformed Kirk waged a campaign against the large number of people who persistently visited this well to be healed. This dedication was not altogether surprising – the pre-Reformation church had encouraged pilgrimages to holy wells, and there is always a demand for healthcare. The kirk session records of several parishes, from Fintry and Kippen to the Hillfoots, Culross and Kinross-shire mention the pilgrimages, an indication of the distance people were prepared to travel – only a few examples are given here. On 20 August 1581 the Presbytery of Stirling ordained every parish minister to compel any of their parishioners who had attended the well to explain their behaviour in front of the kirk session. But 1583 was the big push. On 7 May the Presbytery again investigated the great abuse caused by 'the rascall sort of pepill' who practiced 'idolatrie or superstitoun' at Christ's Well, and the ministers at Dunblane, Kilmadock and Kilbryde were ordered to enact fines and other forms of punishment. Men and women confessed to praying on their knees, washing their afflicted parts and leaving a piece of clothing or silver behind. The well seemed to be efficacious for migraine, 'sickness of the heart,' sore limbs, skin disorders, lameness, blindness and a multitude of other ailments. A woman claimed washing her child in the water saved its life. Several people testified that they went to the well because their parents had done so before them.

On 14 May the brethren of Dunblane were commissioned to go to the well the following Saturday to report the names of those who attended. On 22 May Malcolme Alexander in

Overgrown and forgotten: Christ's Well, Blairdrummond.

Menstrie, James Baird at Mockart Miln and Jonet Mairschell his wife were charged. On 28 May 'ane gret number of pepill' had been reported attending the well. 4 June saw Margaret Wryght and Johnne Kidstoun of Cambus and Thomas Patersone of Black Grange summoned to the session for the second time, on fear of excommunication. A week later Jonet Talizor, spouse to Robert Cowane in Touch, Marione Watsone, Marjorie Fargusson and Margaret Downy in Polmais and Jonet Mayne in Mossyd were all also summoned for failing to appear at the session when ordered. On 9 July Johnne Adame of Kippen confessed to saying that if he could get his health at the well he would go there no matter who tried to stop him. At various dates in July Jonet Mayne and Jonet Gray did public repentance in their parish church of St Ninian, and on the 23rd Robert Andirsone of Tullibody was threatened with excommunication for failing to obey several summons about the well. There are dozens of other examples.

Perhaps this campaign delivered a short sharp shock to the populace, because the records are quiet for a decade. Then in 1593 it all started up again. On 29 May James Baird was ordered to make repentance in sackcloth in Dollar Kirk for going to the well two hours before sundown on 12 May and washing his wife's legs and arms. Also at the well were Ewffam Wilsone from Blairhill and Alaster Leany of Culross. Crystie Cadzear in Alva and his wife had been cured by the well. On 14 May 1595 Helen Jameson in Fossoway confessed that during a previous visit she washed the trousers of her blind and mute child in the well, and the child was cured. This year she returned to the well to give thanks, leaving the child's sark behind. Clearly May was the favoured month for visiting the well, although there appears to have been no particular day.

On 23 April 1600 yet again the ministers were ordered to preach against visiting the well in May. Jonet Rob in Pendreich was charged on 29 July 1601. On 1 July 1607 nine people from Airth and Bothkennar parishes confessed they went to the well, took the water and left something behind. In 1610 three more people were admonished. A Stirling woman took a pint of water from the well on the first Sunday of May 1617 for the benefit of a sick female relative, and left part of the woman's headscarf behind on a tree near the well. Usually the punishments involved the payment of a fine and making public repentance in church, but in 1624 the bar was raised when the Privy Council appointed commissioners to wait near the well and to imprison in Doune Castle anyone who attended. In 1628 the Session at Falkirk ordered:

> If any person or persons be found superstitiously and idolatrously after this to have passed in pilgrimage to Christ's Well, on the Sundays of May, to seek their health, they shall repent *in sacco* and linen three several Sabbaths, and pay twenty pounds for ilk fault; and if they cannot pay it, the Baillie shall be recommended to put them in ward, there to be fed on bread and water for eight days.

By now the numbers attending were clearly falling. On 1 June 1630 a cutler, weaver, cook and their various wives and relatives were ordered to make public repentance the next Sunday, but there are no more occurrences until 1643, when, in the last recorded punishment, several women were summoned, including Marion Ewing who was admonished for taking water to sprinkle on her cattle. The various records can be found in Rogers, *Social Life in Scotland*, Fergusson, *Alexander Hume*, Pearce, 'The Stirling Presbytery, 1604–1612', Kirk, *Stirling Presbytery Records 1581–1587* and Roger, *A Week At Bridge of Allan*.

After 1643 Christ's Well disappears from the records. Indeed, so successful was the Church's campaign that the very location of the well was forgotten. At some point, presumably during the eighteenth-century landscaping of Lord Kames, the well was rediscovered and rebuilt in a Romantic rustic grotto. It is currently enclosed in a rectangular barrel-roofed structure with a low doorway, the whole thing surmounted by a mossed-over and beferned rockery and surrounded by a pool, with a modern standing stone on the bank behind it. Above the lintel is a stone inscribed GD ER 1690. So overgrown and secluded is this damp bower that it is exceptionally difficult to find. Locate the south fence at the bottom of the slope of the woods, east of the obelisk, and keeping the safari park to your right, follow the fence (on the woodland side – do not cross into the safari park) until you are opposite a large Cedar of Lebanon – recognizable by its spread of horizontal branches – in the park's field; the well is among the rhododendrons about here. In summer the density of the vegetation may well defeat you. Note that the woodlands are used to rear pheasants and so are not always accessible – ask permission at the site office of the Blair Drummond Caravan Park on Cuthil Brae (NS726992). The caravan park itself is home to a large tumulus next to the play area (NS72539906), 82ft (25m) in maximum diameter and 11ft (3.3m) high. Two cists and a cremation burial were found in the 1920s. Note the woodlands are *not* connected to, or accessible from, Blairdrummond Safari Park.

West along the A873 stands Margaret Drummond's Grave, also known as the Plague Grave, hidden away behind iron railings in the garden of a house on the south side of the road (NS70959875). The original is a flat tombstone, now illegible, with the nineteenth century upright copy beside it, itself subject to obscuration through lichen and vegetation. The inscription reads:

> Here lyes the Corpes of Margaret Drummond, Frid Daughter to the Laird of Invermay, and Spouse to Sir George Muschet of Burnbanke, Her Age 26, Departit this Lyfe in the Wisitation with her Frie Children at Burnbanke, the 10th of August 1647.

Margaret was the wife of Sir George Muschet; the grave is sited in what was once the orchard of Burnbank. Ask permission at the house. The B8031 leads south-west from here, passing the site of Coldoch Broch (NS69639812). Although greatly damaged, the entrance is visible as are three chambers and a stairway within the thickness of the wall. As a boy Moray Mackay remembered one chamber being roofed and part of the stairway still standing. In the eighteenth century one of the wall chambers was visible and was exhibited as a 'Roman well'. Lewis Spence, in *The Magic Arts in Celtic Britain* describes Coldoch as a centre of initiation into the fairy cult, the passage being the metaphorical route into the Otherworld. Cuptree, a farm on the A873 at NS690993, marks the site of a tree which had been cut into a certain shape, and so was known as the Egg Cup Tree.

6

CALLANDER AND THE TROSSACHS

CALLANDER

> Callander, a village that embraces Highland and Lowland at a single crossroads. Its long main street
> is a spear aimed at the heart of the mountain.
> (Jim Crumley, *The Mountain of Light*)

Callander dawdled along in its quiet way until Walter Scott's *The Lady of the Lake* (1810) and *Rob Roy* (1817) transformed it into, in the felicitous words of Charles McKean, 'a hitherto unknown Eldorado of the noble savage.' In the eighteenth century both visitors and residents left detailed accounts of the still-extant 'superstitions' of the local people, in particular the festivals of Beltane (May Day) and Hallowe'en. Thomas Pennant, who was here in 1769, noted that on the first of May the herdsmen gathered together, cooked up a kind of custard, poured some of the mixture on the ground 'as a libation', and then stood facing the fire while throwing behind them an oatmeal cake and chanting to the supernatural powers: 'This I give to thee, preserve thou my horses; this to thee, preserve thou my sheep.' This was followed by gifts to natural predators: 'This I give to thee, O fox! spare thou my lambs; this to thee, O hooded crow! this to thee, O eagle!' The custard was then eaten. A similar, but differently structured, piece of propitiatory magic was described in the 1794 *Old Statistical Account*. Here, after the custard was eaten, the oatmeal cakes were placed into a bonnet from which everyone present drew a sample. The person who picked the one cake blackened with charcoal had to leap three times through the fire, as a substitute sacrifice to the dark powers.

These two descriptions, only a few years apart, have much in common: both ceremonies are designed to propitiate the forces of destruction, whether totemic spirits of predatory creatures or even greater powers; both involve a symbolic sacrifice; there is a celebration involving good food; and the oatmeal cake is the medium through which communication is opened with the Otherworld. But there are also differences – the first account suggests it is a ritual of adults, the second that of youths, and it is possible to discern the relative seriousness with which the respective actions are undertaken. The boys are having a bit of a laugh; but the men are making sure their livelihoods are protected.

On 7 March 1791 Revd James Robertson, Minister of Callander, wrote a letter on 'the Superstitions of the Highlands' to the Right Honourable James Drummond of Perth. In 1829 it found its way to the *Transactions of the Society of Antiquaries of Scotland*. The letter is so full of detail on the rituals of a late eighteenth-century Highland Hallowe'en that it is worth quoting at length. When the bonfire was spent,

> Every person in the company got a small stone, such as they could conveniently carry in one hand,
> and distinguishable by some particular mark, that each stone might be easily known from every
> other stone. The oldest person laid down the first stone upon the very verge or circumference
> of the ashes of their fire, saying to the rest that this stone was his. All the rest were prepared to do
> the same, and took precedence according to their seniority, until the whole stones formed a circle

round the spot on which the fire had burnt. And if any person was absent, the rest put in a stone for their absent friend. This was generally done by the nearest relation of the absentee.

The following morning the stones were examined, and if anyone's stone was turned out of its place, they would die within a year.

No person went near that haunted place all night but by the break of day it was approached with awe, and every circumstance supposed to be of importance relative to the stones and ashes examined with care. *All this I have seen myself.*

Robertson then went on to describe marriage divination rituals which took place after the bonfire:

The person went to a barn, which must have two opposite doors. Both doors were opened. A riddle [sieve] was taken into which a piece of money was thrown; no matter whether a coin, or brooch, or piece of plate. The person began immediately to riddle the silver, in the name of the Evil Spirit, or of the Worst Man, as he is commonly called in Gaelic. During this transaction the figure of a person came in, and took the riddle from the person who was employed; and this vision was understood to have the exact figure, and stature, and appearance of the future spouse.

Robertson then, with a sense of awe, related a tale told to him by a man who witnessed the events while staying at his grand-uncle's house many years previously.

His grand-uncle's servant went to the barn, to riddle the silver... There came in the figure of a woman, who took a faint hold of the riddle, but not so as to take it out of his hand. He continued still to riddle, and there came another female apparition, and passed in the same manner. Immediately thereafter there came in four people, carrying a coffin on a bier, in the ordinary way used at funerals, and passed through the barn. He was so terrified that he started back till this procession passed away. But before he could make his escape, the figure of a third woman came in and took the riddle from him. He left the barn instantly, and came to the dwelling-house in great terror and agitation. The person who told me was at that moment in the house. The master of the family examined his servant strictly, in the presence of all, where he had been—what he had been about—and if he had seen any thing. The servant told every circumstance as above narrated. The old man replied, 'You shall be three times married, and you have already seen the funeral of your two first wives.' The man was actually married three times—buried two of his wives—and died himself before the last wife.

The minister had also heard similar tales where women riddling saw apparitions of bloody or wet men, and their husbands ended up dying in battle or drowned, but these were 'friend-of-a-friend' tales and he could not find a reliable witness.

Robertson concluded his letter with a miscellany of other divinatory practices on Hallowe'en, including a stone with an overlapping series of liminal properties – 'taken from a rivulet making a boundary between two estates, and from a ford where living and dead do pass – gall cut with the teeth by a person blind-fold and dumb', and a cake baked from the first egg of a young hen, 'with one shellful of soot, another of meal, and a third of salt', cooked on 'a fire made of straw taken from the cradle of a woman's first son'. For a divination with added *diablerie*, the recommended procedure was to take some wool from a black sheep, immediately spin it while remaining silent, then in the name of Satan throw it into the pot of the drying kiln, wind it back up, and when the yarn snagged, ask: 'Who holds my clew [thread of life]?' From below, a demonic voice would answer with the name of the seeker's future spouse. Presumably the heat of the kiln was an analogue of the fires of Hell. It all makes 'Trick or Treat?' look rather weedy.

Tom Na Chisaig, possible site of St Kessog's church, Callander.

In 1944 the medium Helen Duncan was jailed under the Witchcraft Act of 1735, an unusual prosecution and result – 'fraudulent' mediums were usually skewered with just a fine. But Helen was different. Despite a career that encompassed many clear acts of fraud, some of her séances produced sensitive wartime information. The authorities did not really care whether she was genuinely communicating with the dead or obtaining the information through other means – with the D-Day landings impending she was a security risk and had to be silenced. Once the invasion of Europe was a success, Helen was quietly released. She was born Helen MacFarlane at No. 96 Main Street, Callander in 1897, and manifested the second sight early, seeing visions of a long-dead soldier and a man alive in a snowdrift, and predicting futures – typically involving marriage or violent death – for her schoolmates. When asked questions by teachers on subjects for which she had avoided studying, the answer would simply appear in her head. A much-told story is that the numbers 1066 (or 1314) appeared on her forehead, apparently predicting the death of a teacher who died while teaching a lesson on the Battle of Hastings (or Bannockburn). Helen left Callander in her teens and never returned. Marriage, multiple children and a grinding working-class existence in Edinburgh and Dundee followed, during which she embraced Spiritualism. After many extraordinary psychic episodes she eventually embarked on a long career as a professional medium. She was one of the last people prosecuted under the 1735 Act. Her full, fascinating story is told in Malcolm Gaskell's excellent *Hellish Nell: Last of Britain's Witches*.

Tom Na Chisaig (NN62660789), easily accessible between the Meadows car park and Bridge Street, is a strikingly conical flat-topped mound which is probably a medieval motte. Traditionally this eye-catching structure was the site of a church dedicated to St Kessog, also known as Kessock, Kessaig, Cassog, Cassoc, Mac Kessog and Mackessock. Like that of many Dark-Age saints, Kessog's biography is typically vague and garlanded with legends. He is supposed to have been born in the sixth century in Cashel, Ireland. As a boy he resurrected a coterie of drowned princes. A similar tradition in Scotland has Kessog restoring to life a boatful of people who were drowned crossing a river. Next to the mound is St Kessock's graveyard, with an anti-bodysnatching watchtower and mostly Victorian gravestones, lichened and bemossed in the approved atmospheric style. The local speciality was clearly the carving of a three cheery cherubs. Somewhere in the burial ground may be the re-interred remains of a young woman who was found in a shallow grave by peat-diggers on Greenock Farm. The report in the *Stirling Journal* (13 June 1822) noted that the body was wrapped in a sheet and although it could not be identified, it was probably that of a young red-headed girl who got pregnant and mysteriously disappeared some fifty years previously.

Paul McGinlay's *Tales from the Trossachs* relates a series of hauntings reported from the Dreadnought Hotel. Guests have reported feelings of intense cold, someone apparently sitting at the bottom of the bed, sounds of a child crying, and a vision of an infant on a bedroom wall. The source events are taken to be the supposed drowning of a child in a well in the basement, and/or the actions of the hotel's founder, Francis, Chieftain of the Clan McNab, who is alleged to have both thrown his pregnant mistress out of one of the windows and bricked up his wife in one of the rooms and left her to die. When his portrait in the bar is moved, Francis himself is said to patrol the hotel corridors in full clan regalia.

There are carvings of human heads on School Lane (a pair of bearded heads) and the Old Bank on Main Street (a man with long hair and a fulsome curled beard, crowned by an unusual triple boat) and a full set of mason's tools above the doorway of Ivy Cottage in Bridge Street. The Italianate Callander Kirk on South Church Street is decorated with vermiculated quoins, rectangular blocks each carved with an unusual individual pattern of 'worm treads'. The Roman Camp Hotel is so-named from the account of a 1724 traveller, Thomas Graham, who misidentified several natural glacial mounds as the vestiges of a Roman structure (the genuine Roman fort is to the west of the town). The delightful gardens are open to the public and include sundials, statues, a marble wellhead, and stone crocodiles on gate-piers. The glasshouse has a Latin inscription from Horace, *Ille Terrarum mihi praeter omnes Angulus ridet*, 'this place above all others smiles to me'. There are vague suggestions the hotel has a ghost.

A circular walk up Bracklinn Road has several items of interest. As you cross over the old railway bridge a small issue of water on the right marks Bogle Well. The name is suggestive – 'bogle' being a Scottish spirit or uncanny entity – but Archibald McLaren in *Callander in the 1890s* says it was named after Revd Bogle, the Free Church minister (the well is in the garden wall of the priory, which was formerly St Bride's Manse). Carrying on up the steep road brings you to the signposted Red Well, a recently restored chalybeate spring with vivid orange and foul-tasting water. In March 2008 I spotted a pair of trainers thrown over the telephone wire on this road. This is an example of an act which is so widespread it has had folklorists around the world comparing notes. Theories include: markers for drug dealers and gangs (admittedly an unlikely reason here); indicators of leaving school for the last time; trophies taken by bullies from smaller kids; displaying your worn-out but very cool trainers to the world forever (or at least until they rot); drunken dares and/or feats of prowess; signifiers of losing one's virginity; and because it's fun. Ultimately, only the trainer-throwers themselves will know the purpose (if there is one).

Returning down the road a signposted path leads east from the car park to the Bracklinn Falls, which thunder through a gorge strewn with truly Cyclopean rocks. Retracing your steps to the seats on the brow of the hill, and then turning south-east through forestry you join a well-made track which loops west to the caravan park, at which point you are passing right across the Scottish Neolithic equivalent of the Great Pyramid of Giza, Auchenlaich Chambered Cairn (NN64980715). Auchenlaich is an astonishing 352yds (322m) long, the longest prehistoric burial mound in Scotland. Unfortunately it has been so mutilated and robbed that for much of its length it just looks like a field wall, and was not actually identified until 1991. The burial chamber itself is in the large mound at the south-east end, and can be inspected from the caravan park. You can trace a concave forecourt and the chamber. About one third of the cairn's length along from here can be seen the remains of a side chamber, which was cleared out in

Vermiculated quoins on Callander
Kirk, South Church Street.

Trainers on a telephone wire, near
the Red Well, Callander.

the 1950s, but no finds were recorded. The big question remains, of course: why did the people who build the monument feel the need to construct something on this scale?

The high ground to the north and east is home to a significant concentration of prehistoric burial sites, most of which require good hillwalking skills to find and to reach safely, and most of which turn out to be quite dull when you get there. The lower summit of Uamh Bheag (NN69611175), at 2,172ft (662m) a challenging trek from Glen Artney, hosts a circular cairn with a collapsed chamber. As prehistoric burial sites go, it is mountainously spectacular. And on 23 April 1994 *The Sun* found the reason: it was apparently a UFO base. Claiming that 'UFO experts' were to mount a '24-hour a day vigil', the report noted 'ex-cop Robert Lie called in Scottish Earth Mystery Research after claiming he saw dozens of alien ships land… Norwegian born Robert, seventy-two, of Kinbuck, said "I've no idea what they are doing there".' Fans of lexilinking – the apparent process whereby personal names seem to intertwine with destiny – will note that 'Lie' is an unfortunate surname for both a police officer and a UFO witness.

Paul McGinlay in *Tales from the Trossachs* has a cautionary ghost story from the early eighteenth century. The Laird of Cambusmore was a strict and godly man but his gamekeeper James MacFarlane was not a frequenter of the church, preferring to spend time with a number of young women. One day the laird lectured James on his morals, saying he would give him a fright that would change him forever. That night James, returning along a woodland path from an assignation in Doune, tripped over his employer's body. He reached down and his hand passed right through the apparition. Taking to his heels James arrived at the laird's house, to be told the master had died earlier that evening. As is inevitable in moral tales of this kind, James mended his ways and became a pious man full of prayer.

South of the A84, on the west bank of the Keltie Water, is the site of St Mary's Well (NN65090559), now impossible to access because of quarry workings and dangerous quicksand. The small stone-lined well was dedicated to the Virgin Mary, and had a reputation for healing, although we have no specific details. In the mid-seventeenth century the Presbytery rebuked the Elders at Callander church for allowing 'scandalous persons' to visit a certain well in the parish 'in a superstitious way.' Presumably this was the well concerned. Robertson's letter on 'the Superstitions of the Highlands', quoted above, had something to say on the practice of dealing with sacred waters:

> To this day, when the Highlanders go round any thing with a degree of religious veneration, they go round in the same direction as the sun goes round the world…i.e. from east to west, by the south side. This is the direction in which a bride is placed by her bridegroom, when they stand up to be married; the direction in which the bridegroom turns round the bride to give the first kiss after the nuptial ceremony; the direction in which they go at least half round a grave before the coffin is deposited; the direction in which they go round any consecrated fountain, whose waters are supposed to have some medicinal virtues, which they expect to receive by immersion or drinking. I have heard it said that, in certain places of the Highlands, the people sometimes took off their bonnets to the sun when he appeared first in the morning.

'The Auld Knowe' (NN65260480) is a prominent mound easily accessible from the road. It may well be a dun (possibly Dark Ages) inserted into a hillfort (probably Iron Age), with near the base, a single standing stone which appears to be all that remains of a small Bronze Age five-stone circle apparently destroyed in 1980. That's a stone circle. Destroyed, not in previous centuries, but in 1980. The gods weep. Neither accessible nor visible from the road – or from anywhere else, access not being encouraged – is the truly odd MacGregor Monument (NN68390293), hidden away in the trees of the Lanrick Estate. First comes 30ft (9m) of masonry in the form of a tree trunk with the 'scars' of branch stumps. Then there's a crown from which rise three 15ft (4.5m) pillars supporting a circular platform, and a central column rising just short of the platform. On the platform three flame-like ornaments surround another central column which used to end in an acorn-shaped finial (now fallen off and lying at the base). This unique, puzzling monument, replete with obscure, personal imagery, was once thought to be a joint monument to the fallen of the MacGregor clan and a celebration of the lifting of the prohibition of the MacGregor name, but it was in fact built by Sir John MacGregor Murray in memory of his brother, Colonel Peter Murray, who was killed in action against the French off the coast of Ireland in 1803. For all this and more on the Scottish Baronial Lanrick Castle (which was controversially demolished in 2002) see Paul McGinlay's informative booklet *History of Lanrick Castle*, available locally.

The area to the west of Callander is also full of interest. Little Leny, the ancestral burial ground of Clan Buchanan (NN62180765), is south of the cycle track and footpath on the dismantled railway. The approach is often waterlogged, this being the flood plain at the confluence of two rivers. In a parallel development to Tom Na Chisaig, there is a substantial mound right next to the burial ground. It was here that the chapel, now long gone, once stood, and is currently occupied by the more recent gravestones. One lichened pillar, about 5ft (1.5m) high, has very much the look of a standing stone. It is unmarked and may be a modern memorial. A finial above the enclosure reads 'The Buchanan Chapel – 1214', although it is unclear when this was put up. There are slabs carved with skulls, crossbones, a heart, spade and winged soul, and three eroded human figures, one within an arch, another encircled by vegetation, and a third holding something (musical instrument? weapon?) Diagonally left as you enter the enclosure are two upright stones with intriguing dates. One, in memory of John Buchanan, claims he died in 1882 aged seventy while his wife passed away at the age of seventy-two in 1811, seventy-one years earlier. Near to it is the stone in memory of Isabella Buchanan. It has been claimed this reads 'Died 24th July 1848 Aged 128 Years' but on my visit the inscription was illegible. 128 is very old, but it is not outside the bounds of recorded longevity.

The cycle track now passes next to the walls of the first-century Bochastle Roman Fort (NN61420790) and provides good views of the ramparts of the Iron-Age fort of Dunmore (NN60140759), also known as An Dun and Dun bo chaistel. If you wish to do the short but stiff climb to Dunmore, turn west along the A821 when the cycle track crosses it and at the layby at the junction with the minor road take the gate and rough track uphill. After a sharp bend in the track on your right you will see Samson's Putting Stone, a huge glacial erratic boulder which, from some angles, has the simulacrum of a human face. The fort itself is to the west, across a burn. Turning right on the A821 brings you instead to Kilmahog Burial Ground (NN60910826). The site can also be reached by road, west from Callander. Access is via a kissing gate into the field. Experts disagree on the dedication of the vanished church (and the provenance of the Kilmahog name itself), candidates including saints Chug, Luag, Kessog, Mahog and Cuaca, some of whom may be the same person. There is a small collection of symbols of mortality – skulls, crossed bones, etc – but the clear local favourite is the pelican, which, as an allegory of Jesus, was supposed to pierce its own breast to shed blood to feed its young.

BEN LEDI

> In August 1508 light candles shone before the sun on the tops of the mountains, and two armies
> battled in the sky 'to the grate astonishment of maney thousands that did behold the same'.
> (Sir James Balfour, *Annales of Scotland*)

Virtually everywhere in Callander the horizons are dominated by this majestic mountain, the first of the Highlands. The conventional wisdom is that the name is derived from Beinn le Dia, the hill of God. The strangely flat and smooth summit was accounted for by nineteenth century writers who spoke of the vast crowds attending a Druidic festival lasting three days and nights at the summer solstice. In Jim Crumley's mystical novel *The Mountain of Light* (another possible meaning of the name) the mysterious Wanderer and his lover Bella transform into swans on the top of Ben Ledi. About 1,500yds (1.4km) north of the summit is the tiny Lochan nan Corp, Lochan of the Bodies. Archibald McLaren relates the mournful origins of the name. A funeral party of Kessanachs, possibly also known as McKessaigs, were taking Black Colin from Glean nan Meann over the shoulder of Ben Ledi and down the side of the Stank Burn, to St Bride's burial ground, far below on Loch Lubnaig-side. To save a long circuit they crossed the winter ice of the lochan, which shattered, taking almost 200 of them into the freezing waters. A little to the south is Bealach nam Corp, 'Pass of the Bodies'.

LOCH VENACHAR

In 1812, C. Randall, in his *The History of Stirling*, recorded 'a rude image, graven in stone, resembling the head, neck, and shoulders of a human being' kept on the wall of an enclosure at the western boundary of the farm of Cuilinteogle (now Coilantogle, NN594068). 'The stone is different from any other species found in the country: it rings a little when struck upon the chin with another stone or metal.' Sixty-seven years later, in a 1879 report to the Stirling Natural History and Archaeological Society, C.B. Macdiarmid called this the 'Tombea God'; it was on the farm of Annie, had once been at Coilantogle, and was now sunk into the ground; it might prove to be 'of colossal dimensions'. Randall also reported another stone, 'somewhat similar,' in the corner of a garden at Tarndoun, 'about a mile nearer Callander.' Annie and Tarndoun are now gone; and the Tombea God, whatever it once was, is sadly lost. The forestry plantations around Invertrossachs House, on the south side of the loch, were planted by the owner in imitation of the disposition of the Allied armies at the Battle of Waterloo. The loch has a water-horse whose favourite food is human babies.

BRIG O' TURK

Taking the narrow road to Glen Finglas – past the tea room, which is something of an institution – leads you to the Iron Eating Tree or Bicycle Tree, which has swallowed not just a bicycle but an anchor and various other bits of scrap metal since it was showered with junk as a small sapling in the late 1930s, when the adjacent blacksmith's closed down. A few hundred paces further on is the small graveyard (NN53420682), famous for the 1888 table-top tomb of Donald Campbell complete with cast-iron shepherd's crook.

GLEN FINGLAS

This is the setting for Walter Scott's first serious attempt at poetry, *Glenfinlas, Or, Lord Ronald's Coronach*, in which two lairds, staying in a hunting bothy, express a wish for female company and are swiftly joined by their sweethearts, each dressed in green. Lord Ronald goes off with his gal but the other, Moy, recognises his companion as an evil spirit and fends her off with prayers and sacred music from his jaw harp. The succubus-witch changes shape into something the height of the roof and flies off, and in the next moment Ronald's blood, sword-arm and finally his severed head, drop from the sky. The poem can be found in *The Minstrelsy of the Scottish Border*. Scott's notes make it clear the idea was based on an extant Highland legend, and that Glen Finglas was known as the Glen of the Green Women.

LOCH ACHRAY

Such has been its popularity over the decades, the exaggerated candle snuffer turrets and grand frontage of Tigh Mor, 'the Big House', probably define Scottish Baronial architecture for many. Formerly the Trossachs Hotel, begun in 1849 and aggrandised variously throughout the nineteenth century, it has dominated the tourist trade – and the scenery – at the heart of the Trossachs. Before he became one of the founder members of the pioneering New-Age community at Findhorn, Peter Caddy had a career in hotel management. In 1957 he was managing the Trossachs Hotel, then in something of a decline. As related in his autobiographical *In Perfect Timing*, he noted that both the hotel and the staff quarters to the rear, called Woodlands, were extensively haunted. There was a bad atmosphere, the previously coherent team fell apart, and there was talk of an 'inbuilt evil'. The chief suspects were two people supposedly killed on the hotel staircase during a fire in 1864 – the ghosts had been disturbed by the relocation of the staircase. There is no documentary evidence for this alleged fire, although two female staff members did die during a fire on 28 July 1941. Further tales can be found in a locally available booklet, *A History of Tigh Mor Trossachs* by Paul McGinley.

After going through several owners the hotel was rebuilt as an upscale resort and leisure centre owned by the Holiday Property Bond (HPB). Reconstruction work in 1992 saw the loss of several rowan trees, the traditional protector of Highland homes against evil spirits. Inevitably, the building work became dogged by problems and it rained every day; when new rowans were planted the weather instantly improved and remained benevolent for the remainder of the job. Security guards felt uneasy at night, claiming to have seen figures walking corridors of floors that had yet to be built. Guard dogs would not go into the building. The architect's dog, a ferocious Rhodesian Ridgeback, bolted from an old part of the building and, terror-stricken, refused to go back in. Geoffrey Baber, managing director of HPB, noted the hotel was the most haunted building in the company's portfolio, and had a priest conduct Holy Communion and bless the place before it was reopened.

McGinley relates a small number of incidents from recent years. A young married man, alone in his apartment, twice heard his name called. A woman, feeling someone behind her, turned to see a figure dressed in grey disappear through the door, accompanied by church music. A guest in the new Corrie A'an building was awoken by her name being called, and saw three men with long red hair and unkempt beards, trying to rise out of the ground. They looked like they had been burned. There were frequent sounds – shouting, singing, men talking, children laughing – the atmosphere was 'red', and as she moved between sleep and wakefulness for the rest of the night, the woman experienced a sense of great sadness. The clues to this latter incident, at least, are that the woman was woken by the experience, and then moved between sleep and consciousness – all classic symptoms of a hypnagogic state, in which the recently awakened brain is struggling to match the new sensory input of the 'real' world with the vivid imagery of the still-operating dream world. McGinlay himself had an odd experience while driving home from work at Tigh Mor at about 11.15 p.m. on a clear moonlit July night. Passing the lodge house at Glenbruach, two houses down from the hotel, he saw an agitated figure dressed in light grey whose clothes were blown about as if in a wind – although it was a still night. Not wanting to cause an accident on the bend he drove off; nothing more was reported. The nearby Loch Achray Hotel is also supposedly haunted by a Green Lady dressed in antique garb, who accompanies single men walking from the loch towards the hotel, but disappears at the bridge.

A few years ago, about 1870, a most respectable gentleman belonging to Edinburgh, devoid of superstitious fear, told the writer: 'I gained the friendship of a venerable clergyman, whose charity and piety were known far and near. While I had my residence in the Trossachs Hotel, the clergyman, I was told, one day was dangerously ill. Next morning, before starting with a few friends up Loch

Katrine, I sent to inquire after the invalid's health. The answer returned conveyed the impression that he was fast sinking. We proceeded up the lake, and came back by the last boat for the day. We took outside seats on the coach, and while turning a corner of the road, about half-way between the lake and the hotel, I and several other passengers (including the captain of the Loch Katrine steamer and the driver) observed a gentleman passing us, whom we all declared was the clergyman... The sight struck all, who recognised in the traveller the invalid minister with amazement, and some with fear. On the coach arriving at the hotel, a messenger was despatched to inquire after the reverend gentleman's health. The answer received disclosed the startling intelligence that the clergyman had expired shortly before the time we saw his figure walking with slow step and sad countenance towards Loch Katrine. (James Grant, *The Mysteries of All Nations*, 1880)

LOCH KATRINE

Travellers who wish to see all they can of this singular piece of water generally sail west, on the south side of the lake, to the Rock and Den of the Ghost; whose dark recesses, from their gloomy appearance, the imagination of superstition conceived to be the habitation of supernatural beings. (Robert Forsyth, *The Beauties of Scotland*, 1807)

Forsyth's 'Den of the Ghost' is Coire na Uruisgean, a natural amphitheatre on the lochside of Ben Venue (NN483078). It was the general assembly building of all the urisks of Scotland, who were granted this space when the Earl of Menteith relieved them of their task of building a bridge of sand (see LAKE OF MENTEITH, where, however, the supernatural beings are referred to as fairies). Urisks are variously described, although generally they are hairy human-sized anthropoids, sometimes with goat-like legs. They were variously called satyrs, goblins, spirits and lubber fiends. They lived in the wild places of the Highlands and Islands, and in many tales are mischievous towards or even dangerous to travellers. They could talk, and were immensely strong. In some stories they were more domesticated, doing farmwork in exchange for a bowl of cream and some clothes, although here they may have been confused with brownies. Like brownies, they were quick to take offence, and the urisk of Glasahoile further along the shore (NN465088) disappeared at dawn with a horrible shriek because he had been dissatisfied with his cream. Coire na Uruisgean became celebrated in the nineteenth century because it already had a supernatural association through its name, and writers saw its awe-inspiring scenery as a suitable stage for the uncanny. First was Patrick Graham, in his *Sketches of Perthshire* (1806): 'huge and rough masses of moss-covered rocks, piled on each other in wild confusion; upon the spongy bogs, and blood-congealing damps which exhale from the darksome recesses of the cove... a place suited only to the residence of the lubber fiends.' Walter Scott drew on Graham's work in *The Lady of the Lake*:

> Grey Superstition's whisper dread,
> Debarred the spot to vulgar tread;
> For there, she said, did fays resort,
> And satyrs hold their sylvan court,
> By moon-light tread their mystic maze,
> And blast the rash beholder's gaze.

When Scott's work became a best-seller, the fame of Coire na Uruisgean was assured.

In one legend Katrine was a beautiful lass who lived in the fertile farming glen that once existed here. Her job was to guard the well on the slopes of Ben Venue. One day the local urisk appeared to her in the guise of a handsome man, and offered her a drink from his bowl. She accepted and fell into a deep sleep, whereupon the urisk opened all the sluices and caused the well to flood the valley, drowning everyone. When Katrine awoke she was so overcome with remorse she drowned herself in the newly created loch. This motif – guarded well floods valley creating loch – is widespread, being responsible for Lochs Ness and Tay among others.

W. Wilson's 1908 book *The Trossachs in Literature and Tradition* contains 'A Legend of Glengyle... contributed by Miss Alison Sheriff Macgregor of Glengyle, from traditional hearsay'. In the valley of Glen Gyle, beyond the western end of Loch Katrine, where the Glengyle Water divided, there was once a place called Kil-mi-challaig, Kil-mi-chailleach or Kilmacallach. There was a graveyard, in which were buried the notable dead of the area, and the village was ruled by a number of women who acted as local judges (all of which suggests this might have been a community of nuns, the site possibly dedicated to Abbot Cellach of Iona, 802–815). The women were revered, but then one day pronounced an obviously guilty man innocent of horse theft, the steed being found culpable for running off with him. The horse was duly hanged, which led to ridicule and eventually the downfall of the community. There are indeed the ruins of several structures in the area on the stream of Lag A' Chuirn (NN35871478). Some further ruins about 750yds (685m) further west, where a small tributary from the slopes of Beinn Ducteach meets Lag A' Chuirn, are said to include one called Tigh na Cuirte, this being the 'court-house'. Sadly none of these structures can be identified as specific buildings now and there is no trace of a graveyard. Suggestively, though, the pass to Balquhidder is named Bealach nan Corp, Pass of the Bodies (NN365157) perhaps indicating a former coffin-road. To the north-west of the pass can be found Lon an t-Sidhein, the Meadow of the Fairies' Knoll (NN363163), and Sidhean a' Chatha, 'the Fairy Knoll of the Battles' (NN358162). In *A Gaelic Topography of Balquhidder* Revd Alex MacGregor explains that this is a very exposed stormy place at the head of the pass, and the 'battles' of the name refer to the great winds.

Paul McGinlay's *Tales of the Trossachs* gives the origin legend of Loch Tinker, which lies below Beinn Chochan at NN445067. A tinker kidnapped a little boy from a nearby cottage; when they reached the loch he lifted the lad onto his shoulders and started to wade across. A huge, ferocious water bull, the loch's resident monster, rose from the depths and ate both man and boy.

7

STRATHYRE, BALQUHIDDER AND LOCH EARN

LOCH LUBNAIG

Robert Forsyth's five-volume *The Beauties of Scotland* (1805–1808) has a very Romantic description:

> About the middle of this lake there is a tremendous rock called Craig-na-coheilg, The Rock of the Joint Hunting, which is the boundary between two estates… Upon hunting days the two chieftains met there with their hounds and followers, hunted about the rock in common, and afterwards separated, each turning away to his own property.

Craig-na-coheilg is probably Creag-na-Comh-sheilg, on the west side of the loch (NN581125). There is a submerged crannog in the southern end of the loch, at NN58471112. High up on Tom na Moine, on the east ridge above the loch, are two adjacent cup-marked boulders, one with nine cups, some 4in (11cm) across, and the other with at least one (NN579149).

St Bride's Chapel – the site of the wedding in *The Lady of the Lake* – is now just a nondescript disused walled burial ground on the west side of the A84 (NN58500981). Two fragments of very weathered cross-incised stones are built into the north and south walls.

STRATHYRE

At the bottom of the Forestry Commission car park is a reconstruction of part of the wall of an Iron-Age broch. The project was undertaken by the Dry Stone Walling Association in 2004 (with further work completed in 2006). No modern tools were used as it was an experiment to try and determine the amount of effort required to build a prehistoric broch – based on the DWSA's experience it was estimated a real broch would have needed twenty people working for a year and using 2,500 tons of stone. The arc of wall includes part of the stairway and the entrance complete with triangular lintel.

In the village, Airlie House B&B has an arrangement of Edwardian standing stones in its garden, and another garden hosts the statue of a heron awarded to John Sutherland, station-master 1878–1919, for Best Kept Station (the line closed in 1965). Kilkerran, at the north end of the village, has a carved bearded head above the door, and the doorstep of the village shop is inscribed with the Latin motto *Nihil satis nisi optimum*, 'Nothing enough if not best'. The tourist information panel in the adjacent car park notes:

> Celtic folklore is rich in stories of fairies, who were known as the people of the hollow hills. Unlike the tiny fairies of modern fiction, Celtic fairies looked much like us but lived in a mysterious underground world. Even in recent centuries rural folk believed in fairies and you can find fairy hills all around the National Park.

An Sidhean, the Fairy Mountain, taken from Cnoc an t-Sithean, the Fairy Hill in Strathyre.

To visit Cnoc an t-Sithean, the local fairy hill, walk through the Munro Inn car park and take the gate marked Strathyre Recreation Group. Straight ahead you will see the war memorial on a knoll. From there the prominent fairy hill can be seen to the east, reachable by negotiating an area of bog and burns and vague paths. Cnoc an t-Sithean itself is covered in bracken. It provides good views of An Sidhean and Beinn an t-Sidhein, the fairy mountains, on the opposite side of the strath. Also across the river is a place called Sidheag, the name meaning a little fairy knoll. The minor back road to Balquhidder passes through an area called Bruach-an-Tannaisg, which translates as 'the bank haunted by the ghost' (NN559177). By coincidence, the avenue of beech trees here – which is certainly much younger than the name – has produced many specimens of simulacra, with the boles and twisted branches forming an entire gallery of faces.

Twisted face simulacrum at Bruach-an-Tannaisg, 'the ghost-haunted bank,' near Strathyre.

BALQUHIDDER

The Kingshouse Hotel, the local community and commercial focus at the junction of the A84 and the minor road to Balquhidder, is said to be haunted, although I have no details. The road to Balquhidder passes through the hamlet of Auchtubh, on the south side of which is the gloomy Macgregor Murray Mausoleum, built in 1830 and still in good condition (NN55532062). The gates are locked but the building can be easily viewed from the end of the drive. Further on, a whitewashed cottage on the north side of the road boasts a wrought-iron gate decorated with numerous sets of numbers and initials, flowers, a swift, a crab and a pair of handcuffs, along with more obscure, abstract patterns.

Handcuffs on a gate near
Auchtubh, Balquhidder.

Across the road from the house signposted as Beannach Aonghais is a smaller building, the
eastern gable of which holds a heavily eroded stone (NN54982071). It is no longer possible to
tell what the carving was, but it was clearly revered, because it was once known as the Stone
of Blessing. The old folk at this point would doff their bonnets and offer a prayer: *Beannachd
Aonghais ann san Aoraidh*, 'Bless Angus in the worship place (or chapel).' The tradition is that
this is where St Angus (of whom more soon) sat to rest when he first ventured into the glen.
(Another version of the blessing was *Beannach Aonghais san Aithroenis*, 'Bless Angus at the Point',
the Point being where the two waters of Balvaig and Kirkton met.)

Some 400yds (266m) east of Auchleskine Farm, a field gate on the north side of the road
gives access to rough pasture. Diagonally to the right is a massive boulder with seven obvious
cup marks (NN54582087). Auchleskine was once home to Clach-nan-Sul, the Stone of the
Eyes, a large boulder with a natural cavity. Water from the hole was used to bathe sore eyes,
money being left behind. It was broken up for road metal in 1878. (Apropos of eye cures,
in 1901 Revd George Williams showed a chain at a meeting of the Stirling Natural History
and Archaeological Society. It had been presented to a 'Miss D.' some sixty or seventy years
previously by a Balquhidder woman, as a cure for her weak eyes.)

Another lost stone is Basan An Sagairt, the Priest's Basin, described as being five-sided with
a hollow 18ins (45cm) across and 6ins (15cm) deep, on the side of the road at NN54192089.
Despite extensive searching I failed to locate it. A community woodland signposted gate just
east of Broomfield cottage leads south to Puidreag, a standing stone of considerable interest
(NN54062079) In 1887 James Mackintosh Gow reported the stone's history in the *Proceedings
of the Society of Antiquaries of Scotland*. The wedge-shaped stone is about 4½ feet (1.37m) high and
has an unusually flat top. The local men would compete in a trial of strength, trying to lift a large,

The old and new churches, Balquhidder. Site of Rob Roy's grave and much more.

round, water-worn boulder, weighing between 224–336lbs (102–152kg) and placing it on top of Puidreag. There was once a ledge on the east side used as a resting-place in the lift but it was broken off about 1857. The minister stopped the contest on health and safety grounds and had the lifting-stone either thrown into the river or built into the manse dyke. Elizabeth Beauchamp, in her recommended 1981 book *The Braes O' Balquhidder*, has more details. Mrs Peter McDiarmid told Beauchamp that when she first came to live in the glen her elderly neighbours told her it was unlucky to harm Puidreag. Apparently someone did try to move it and duly received a broken leg for his pains. Beachamp also thought the stone was aligned on Ben Vorlich to the east, a supposition I am happy to endorse – the wedge lines up directly on the peak, which just peeps over the shoulder of the intervening hill. Where you rejoin the road next to Broomfield the slight knoll was Tom Na Croich, the Gallows Hill, NN54062089, where the condemned were both executed and buried. The next field to the west, entered via a field gate then down a very boggy slope to the flat waterlogged ground, brings you to the 'is-it-or-isn't-it?' stone circle called Clachan-Aoraidh, the Stones of Worship (NN53892076). Gow identified these as a seven-stone circle in 1887, but recent investigators are dubious. At best the northernmost upright stone and its fallen neighbour may be considered candidates for some sort of stone setting, but the other three (there are only five stones in total now) are some distance away and appear to be just random boulders.

Entering Balquhidder village, the big house known as The Keep has three crowned heads on the exterior.

When discussing the Europe-wide agricultural fertility rituals of the Corn Mother and the Corn Maiden in *The Golden Bough*, his monumental 1922 study of ritual and magic, Sir James George Frazer mentioned a ceremony he had witnessed in Balquhidder in September 1888. The last handful of corn was cut by the youngest girl on the field, and was fashioned into an approximate of a female doll, called the Maiden. It was clothed with a paper dress and ribbons, and kept in the farmhouse, above the chimney, for several months, sometimes till the Maiden of the following year was brought in.

Balquhidder parish church and the ruined old parish church (NN53572091) are on a rise in the centre of the village. If you come here only to see Rob Roy's grave (which is just east of the gable of the ruined church), then you're missing out much more, as this is one of the most interesting sites in the entire area, a focus of beliefs and folklore for centuries, if not millennia.

The story starts, more or less, with fire. Behind the parish church (take the left path) and butting against the newer part of the burial ground is an overgrown knoll called variously Tom nan Ainneal, Aingeal, Ainil, Aingeil and Angeae – the Hill of Fire. Twice a year, at the Celtic festivals of Beltane (1 May) and Samhain (1 November), all fires were extinguished, and then relit using the sacred fire on this spot. The practice was still going in the nineteenth century and was said to date from time immemorial – which of course makes it impossible to know exactly how far back it went. There was, however, certainly a suggestion among those who recorded it that the ritual was pre-Christian. Drawing on the presence of the Hill of Fire and the various prehistoric stone monuments, James Stewart in *Settlements of Western Perthshire* notes: 'There is a strong concentration of ritual sites at this focal spot and the implications are that this already venerated sanctuary was adopted by the first Christian missionary for his centre.' This missionary was St Aonghus or Angus, whose high degree of fame in the parish is inversely proportional to what we know about him, as even by the standards of the Dark Ages, this is one obscure saint. He may have come from Ireland, or Iona, or Dunblane, in the sixth, or the seventh, or the eighth century. G.A.F. Knight in *Archaeological Light on the Early Christianisation of Scotland* suggests Angus was Aonghais Mac Cridhe Mochta Lughmhaigh (Angus Dear Son of Mochta of Louth), recorded in the *Martyrology of Donegal* as having died in 535. Angus's feast day was 11 August, and Feill Aonghais, St Angus' Fair, was indeed held in Balquhidder on or near that date. But most writers see Angus as later. Or perhaps he is an amalgam of several saints. Traditionally Angus built a cell or oratory somewhere in the general area, possibly below the present kirk, or under the ruins of the old church, or in the field across the road, the later being the favoured spot. Elizabeth Beauchamp writes poignantly that for years the Kirkton farmers, with reverence and not a little inconvenience, ploughed round the stones, but finally agricultural pressure meant that in 1860 Duncan Campbell the schoolmaster witnessed the removal of the last of them. Angus preached from a spot further east, opposite the former Manse (now called Creag an Tuirc House), his congregation occupying the rising ground in front of him. This practice has been recently revived on the same site, where services partly held in Gaelic have taken place on St Angus' Day in August.

When he died Angus was buried where the ruined old church now stands. At some point the grave was covered with a slab carved with the figure of a cleric. And in about 1250, Abbot Labhran of Auchtubh built a small stone church over this grave, which later generations called Eaglais Beag, the small church, the first of three churches on the site. Bar a few foundations to the east of the gable of the ruined old church, nothing now remains of this medieval structure, and we know little about it – apart from its role in a gruesome 'ethnic swearing' ceremony by the MacGregors.

In 1589 some MacGregors from Rannoch, caught poaching deer in the Royal Forest of Glenartney, were sent home minus their ears. Other members of the clan returned to avenge the insult. They killed the man responsible, John Drummond-Ernoch, forester to Lord Drummond of Perth, cut off his head, wrapped it in a plaid and made their way to Ardvorlich House on Loch Earn side, where the forester's sister was married to the Stewart laird. They asked for hospitality and were duly given bread and cheese. Mrs Stewart left the room to obtain more substantial fare, and when she returned she found her brother's bloodsoaked head in the centre of the table with the bread and cheese stuffed into his mouth. Despite being several months pregnant the poor woman fled to the hills, temporarily losing her mind. After wandering for several days she was eventually persuaded to return by her husband. Dire predictions were cast for the effect the trauma had on pregnancy, and in the course of time the child became Major James Stewart, a man so violent and cruel that when he died his friends were forced to obscure his place of burial to prevent his enemies from desecrating the corpse. Drummond-Ernoch's murderers, instead of returning to Rannoch, went down to Balquhidder where the Chief's brother had a stronghold at the foot of Loch Voil. Word was sent to the Chief himself, Alasdair MacGregor, who arrived a few days later. The severed head was placed on the altar of Eaglais Beag and the Chief walked up it, placed his right hand on the trophy and vowed to protect the murderers. His followers all followed suit. The clan suffered terribly from the reaction to this outrage.

In 1631 Eaglais Beag was replaced by a new church (the current ruin). This now forms the focus for the older part of the graveyard, which has a rich crop of carved gravestones. The centrepiece is the triple grave of Rob Roy, his wife, and two of their four sons, Robin and Coll. Rob Roy died in 1734; his graveslab, with carvings of a sword, a primitive human figure, animals and interlace, is clearly a re-used stone from an earlier period. The slab next to it has a smaller sword. The A.K. Bell Library in Perth holds a series of press cuttings collected by the nineteenth-century historian Robert Scott Fittis. One cutting from an unidentified newspaper has the following letter, entitled 'Opening of Rob Roy's Grave':

> Rob Roy's grave has within the last few weeks been re-opened, his dust has been disturbed, and that of a female – and she not a Macgregor, but a McLaren – has been deposited in his grave. This merely caused a low murmur of local disapprobation, by which it would appear the spirit of kinship is defunct, when in the very country of the MacGregors such an event could have taken place without even a remonstrance.

The letter is signed 'Not a McGregor', Balquhidder February 1862. I have no further information on this incident.

From Rob Roy's grave, which is east of the ruined gable, and moving south then west through the graveyard keeping the ruined church to the right, you can find the following medieval carved stones: a Greek (equal-armed) cross; a Latin cross (where the shaft is longer than the arms and headpiece) and shears; a large sword (partly under moss); a Latin cross with a spike at the bottom of the shaft; a small sword, cross and two circles; and another two Latin crosses, one with an expanded foot and spike. This is one of the most important collections of medieval graveslabs in mainland Scotland. The graveyard also has many eighteenth- and nineteenth-century carved stones, including a winged soul, a pair of shears, an animal (lion?) crest, coats of arms, the blade, sock and coulter of a plough, and a pelican piercing its breast.

The south-west corner has the gravestone of Robert Kirk's first wife Isabel, who died in 1685 aged twenty-five (see the parish church, below), but the inscription, said to have been carved by his own hand, is now illegible. Further east from Rob Roy's grave is a memorial plaque to Alasdair Alpin MacGregor (1889–1970), a particular hero of mine as he recorded great swathes of Scottish folklore and ghost stories in such books as *The Ghost Book* and *Phantom Footsteps*. His ashes were scattered in his beloved Hebrides. One stone I have not been able to find is an unlikely one described in an undated item (probably 1862) in Fittis' press cuttings, taken from 'Willis's Current Notes':

> …an oddly shaped stone, resembling in form and size a horse's collar. Traditionally it is said to have been an instrument of punishment in the days of superstitious requirements, and that it was formerly placed on the shoulders of the delinquent, whose head protruded through it.

The sill of the first window from the east gable of the ruined kirk is incised with a small cross. The Angus Stone was once the centrepiece of this church and the MacLaren Chiefs not only had the right of burial in the church but in front of the altar, under the Angus Stone, the most prestigious and holy crypt in the place. Beauchamp relates an episode from 1966. The MacLaren chief, Donald, died in London and the family claimed the ancient right of church burial in Balquhidder. The negotiations took so long – church burial no longer being, strictly, allowed – that the body had to be embalmed. Eventually it was decided only his ashes could be interred, beneath one of the windows of the ruined church. Later it was noticed a beautiful silver crucifix had been fixed to the holly tree growing beside the windows in the ruin. A few months later the crucifix was stolen.

Flat on the ground is a memorial plaque to David Stewart, last of the Stewarts of Glen Buckie lairds. He led the Balquhidder Stewarts to join Bonnie Prince Charlie in 1745 but did not get far, being soon found in bed at Leny House, Callander, shot through the head, with a discharged pistol in his hand. Suspicion fell on Leny's owner, Buchanan of Leny, who was not 'out' with the Jacobites. Buchanan was executed at Carlisle for the crime, although he claimed to the end that he was innocent. To this day it is not clear whether it was murder or suicide. David Stewart was buried at Balquhidder; about 1855, during the construction of burial vaults, a skull was dug up with a pistol ball still rattling inside. Both skull and ball were re-buried. The more recent part of the graveyard is behind the new church. In the far north-west corner, on the slope of Tom nan Ainneal, look out for the amazing headstone of Christina McNaughton, intricately carved with vegetation, two owls, and a portrait of Christina based on a photograph. Beautiful and moving.

The current Victorian parish church is filled with items of exceptional interest, pride of place among which is Clach Aonghais or Leac Aonghuis, the St Angus Stone, a large slab fixed to the north wall. It is carved with a figure of a cleric holding a chalice. Both feet are turned to the left, and there is possibly a galley on the lower part of the figure. The origin and history of the stone is obscure. It may be from Ireland or the West of Scotland, and may be of medieval or even Dark Ages date – it is quite a primitive carving. Certainly at one point it lay over the traditional site of Angus's grave in the 1250 church. It remained *in situ* in the 1631 church, where parishioners insisted on standing or kneeling on it to solemnise weddings and christenings. In 1722 Revd Duncan Stewart, a man of strong views on 'superstitious' practices, cast the stone out of the church. It languished in the graveyard for about a century before returning to the old church, but it did not transfer across when the new church was built. Finally in 1917 the Angus Stone was welcomed back into the fold and placed in its current location at a ceremony attended by a substantial congregation and conducted by the Moderator of the General Assembly of the Church of Scotland.

The same ceremony saw the installation of the enormous rough stone font which currently stands near the door. It was found in the mid-nineteenth century among the walls of the 1631 church, where it had been used just as building rubble. This may suggest it dates from the 1250 church, but it is otherwise undateable.

The church also holds a number of mementos of Revd Robert Kirk (or Kirke, the spelling varies), minister of Balquhidder from 1669, when he was just twenty years old, to 1685. Kirk's main claim to fame is his authorship of a description of Fairyland, *The Secret Commonwealth of Elves, Fauns, and Fairies*. Although the work was completed after he left Balquhidder, he probably started it here and many of its descriptions of fairies and second sight may well have come from his Balquhidder parishioners. For the full story of the fairy minister see ABERFOYLE. Kirk also donated a bell to the church, inscribed BALQUHIDDER CHURCH M ROBERT KIRKE MINISTER LOVE AND LIFE ANNO 1684. I like that 'Love and Life'; it's much more human that some of the portentous inscriptions you get on bells. The bell was in use until 1896, when it cracked, and was kept in the new church until being stolen in 1973. By chance it was spotted in a scrap merchant's yard in Airdrie, and returned. It now hangs above the entrance to the Friendship Room, which has a small but informative exhibition.

A path running left from the church provides a circular walk to Creag an Tuirc, the Rock of the Boar, with a monument to Clan MacLaren on top. It was at the foot of the cliff that the clan rallied in the old days in response to the call of the Fiery Cross. Revd Alex MacGregor, in *A Gaelic Topography of Balquhidder,* says that Creag an Tuirc was the old name – in the late nineteenth century it was apparently Creag-an-Bhuic, the Rock of the Buck. MacGregor relates the origin: about 1592 the Tullibardine family came to own the district. The tenants were said to be late paying their rents, and a demand came to send the money 'by a swift messenger'. So the locals caught a roebuck, tied a small bag with a few coins about its neck, and let it loose. Later it was found dead under the rock.

A stiff hill route runs up Kirkton Glen, over the summit and down into Glen Dochart to the north. On the way it passes a huge boulder called Rob Roy's Putting Stone, and the steep crags of Leum an Eireannaich, the Irishman's Leap (NN518245). It is up here, at the 2,000ft (600m) level, that strange things have been encountered. The tale is told in Rennie McOwan's *Magic Mountains*, a treasury of ghostly and legendary mountain lore. In 1990 two naturalists, one a friend of McOwan, were doing a bird count on top of Creag ab Eireannaich, the crag at the crest, when they both saw a man in old-fashioned clothing carrying an ancient musket or fowling gun and accompanied by two deerhounds. They thought he might have been poaching, so they each took different routes off the crag to intercept him. But he had vanished, an impossible act in the limited confines of the open mountain area. They made enquiries locally, but no one had noticed the striking figure and his dogs. McOwan publicised the story in several outdoor magazines, which prompted a letter from Donald Ferguson of Dundas, New South Wales, Australia: 'It brings to mind a story I was told in 1927, when I was six years of age, by my grandfather, Donald Ferguson, born in 1852. His father, Donald, owned a farm at Kirkton in the early 1800s and I was told that my great-grandfather had seen "phantom hunters and their deerhounds passing through a local forest".' Then Douglas N. Lowe, of Balerno, Midlothian, a tax inspector and director of the Scottish Rights of Way Society, wrote to McOwan on 30 September 1990. In June 1979 he had been walking from Balquhidder to Ledcharrie in Glen Dochart, and stopped for a bite to eat on the lower slopes of the top of the pass. The wind was cold so he took shelter in a crater-like hollow that was about shoulder deep. Bizarrely, it was even colder in the hollow, and his dog Briagha, normally all too keen to share a sandwich, refused to come in, just stood at the edge of the hollow with its hackles raised, giving a whining growl, and showing signs of wanting to leave. Lowe finally moved on when he saw the dog staring past him as if at something invisible to himself. He packed up and left, to the dog's great relief, but saw and felt nothing himself. The intense cold in the hollow did not affect the tea he had just poured, which was still piping hot when he returned it to flask.

A Gaelic Topography of Balquhidder mentions Carn Chailean, Colin's cairn, on the height of the Kirkton Glen pass, where 'Green Colin', so named from his green tartans, the son of Sir Duncan Campbell of Glenorchy, was killed by the Buchanans *c.*1514. I can find no trace of this cairn.

Back at Balquhidder, the road splits east of the church. The left-hand fork heads towards the Stronvar Bridge, Glen Buckie, and the back road to Strathyre, but not before passing, on the west, a small wooden totem pole marked 'HALF WAY.' The reason is explained in the May 2007 edition of *The Villagers,* the local monthly newspaper. The road is notoriously narrow, and the spot marks the halfway point between two passing places. Local sculptor Edward Chadfield put up the totem after he had a 'who's going to give way and reverse?' encounter with neighbour Vera Stewart. The happy owl is the nearer vehicle and the sad owl the reversing middle; if you've passed the totem you have the right to proceed and the other vehicle has to reverse. The road also gives a good view of the small artificial island at the east end of Loch Voil (NN53272062). In contrast to most such structures, which are ancient crannogs, this is a more recent addition, designed to encourage the nesting of waterfowl.

The back road towards Strathyre passes through an area with conflicting traditions of a clan battle. William Marshall, in *Historic Scenes in Perthshire*, gives the basic story. At the fair of St Kessaig in Kilmahog, a Buchanan of Leny (Callander) struck a MacLaren of Balquhidder on the cheek with a salmon and knocked off his bonnet (one is reminded of the Monty Python 'fish slapping' sketch). The MacLaren said he would not dare to repeat the insult at the next St George's fair at Balquhidder, and then, being apparently a simple-minded soul, promptly forgot he had issued a challenge to a rival clan. On the appointed day the Buchanans turned up in force, much to the consternation of the MacLarens, who were not expecting any conflict. Eventually the salmon slappee remembered the insult. The MacLarens eventually won the day, driving the Buchanans over a small cascade on the Balvaig stream, Linan-an-Seicachan, 'the Cascade of the Dead Bodies'. Only two of the clan escaped the field, the one was killed at Gartnafuaran, and the other at Sron Lainie (Stroneslaney).

The running nature of clan battles, and the vague nature of the supposed date (the battle is said to have taken place either between 1106–1286, or in the sixteenth century) means that it is virtually impossible to say where the fighting actually took place. The best guess (or the favourite tradition) is that it started in the market-stance, in the haugh below the current

The HALF WAY
totem pole near
Balquhidder.

manse, with the later action spreading across and south of the River Balvag. A new signposted footpath runs from beside Gartnafuaran Cottage (NN538203) north to the part of the river known as the Manse Pool, which is said to be where the bodies were thrown in. A human skull was discovered in the gravel river bed at this point some years ago. Even if you don't find any relics of an ancient clan battle, it's still a lovely spot, with good views of Creag an Tuirc.

The cairn of one of the Buchanan victims can be found east of Gartnafuaran Farm at NN54392008. Take the swing gate east of the stand of conifers and head diagonally left up the boggy slope to a wooden gate. Follow the track east and the cairn soon appears. What looks to be the original grassy stone mound has been surmounted by a modern cairn of white stones. There is a massive boulder near the house east of Gartnafuaran Farm, at NN54202026, decorated with five distinct cup marks.

GLEN BUCKIE

In 1925 William Thomson reported to the Society of Antiquaries of Scotland on Leac nan Saighead, 'the Flat Rock of the Arrows', a stone, possibly a millstone reject, carved with deep arcs of two almost concentric circles and a cup mark. In tradition, the man who carved them was killed here by an arrow fired from Bealach a' Chonnaidh, the heights to the south-west. The location is given as NN52041742, west of Ballimore. I failed to find it.

A Gaelic Topography of Balquhidder identifies several fairy placenames such as Glen Shoinnie, 'the Glen of Fairy Knolls' (NN513160), Sron Shoinnie (Sron a Chonnaidh), 'the Promonotory of the Fairies' (NN513168), and Sidhean Dubh, 'the Black Fairy Knoll' (NN539159). Some nearby flat ground was known as Lon an t-Sithein, 'the Meadow of the Fairy Knoll', and on the other side of the glen was Sithean Riabhach, 'the Brindled Fairy Mound'.

LOCH VOIL

This section follows, first, the minor road along the north side of the loch from east to west, and then the south lochside in the same direction. A signpost just west of Tulloch reads 'Rob Roy's Cave'. The very steep, not to say precipitous, waymarked path comes to the cave after about 700yds (640m). The cave is beside the curiously named crags known as Creag An Taxman, behind a small waterfall on the Tulloch Burn (NN51612130). Not surprisingly, it is dark and damp. The association with Rob Roy is through persistent tradition only, but there are no details. The house Dhanakosa (NN507203) has wooden carvings at its gate (a hand holding a flower and a meditating monk or Buddha) appropriate to its role as a Buddhist retreat, while Rhuveag has a pair of carved pelicans on its gate.

Further along, Uamh An Righ, 'Bruce's Cave' (NN49012019) is very difficult to find – you basically have to strike north through the steep forestry then scramble endlessly among the crags until you stumble across it. Alex MacGregor gives the tradition: in 1306 Robert the Bruce took shelter here with a few followers after being defeated by the Lord of Lorn at the Battle of Dalrigh in STRATHFILLAN. These 'few followers' must have been very close friends because this is just a small unimpressive rock shelter. The Bruce Stone in the shallows of the loch – a large boulder with a fir growing on the top – may have a dubious association with Robert the Bruce, but at least it is easy to find (NN48381972). It is the emblem of the Balquhidder Rural Women's Institute.

On the crags above is Creag nan Seichean, 'the Rock of the Fairies' (NN483201). The ruinous burial ground at Imirriabhach, at the west end of Loch Doine (NN46041911) has only one remaining graveslab, now illegible. Following the track west from the end of the road brings you to Carn Mhicgriogair, MacGregor's Cairn (NN42551745). Again, Alex MacGregor has the story: around the year 1780 two neighbours were cutting hay together. Some angry words were exchanged and one killed the other with his scythe.

Unauthorised vehicles are not allowed on the rough road on the south side of the loch, so unless you are staying at one of the places here access is by foot or mountain bike. Muirlaggan (NN514199) has self-catering cottages (see www.lochsidecottages.co.uk). Above the door of the old house is a primitive carving of a human figure, known as Am Bodach, the Old Man. It was brought from Glen Beich on north Loch Earnside in 1750 when members of the Clan Ferguson moved here. Other than this its provenance is unknown, although it probably originated from a medieval religious site. Am Bodach has suffered in his time, his nose being damaged by a drunken delivery van driver who didn't stop in time.

Catriona Oldham is the seventh generation of Fergusons to occupy the site, and she and her husband Lawrie kindly shared several stories from the area, such as a stand of alders north of the track on the way to Tuarach, where the former shepherd always felt the hairs standing up on his neck, and through which he didn't care to take the sheep, and the rock west of Muirlaggan on which one of Catriona's ancestors would stand and declaim his forthcoming Sunday sermon to the loch and the birds.

Another 2 miles (3km) further on the track reaches Monachyle Tuarach, home to the creative hotspot that is West Highland Animation, established in 1988. Over the years producer/director Leslie Mackenzie has created animations in Gaelic and English covering the gamut of Highland folklore and supernaturalism, from the Brahan Seer and the Lady of Lawers to Fingal, Vikings, shapeshifters, clan warfare, witchcraft and Nessie. Sample titles include *The Treasure Cave, Fighting Fairies, Warring Witches, Warrior in the Mist, The Black Toad of Clanranald*

Am Bodach, Muirlaggan, Loch Voil.

and *The Minister who saw the Fairies* (which deals with Robert Kirk – see ABERFOYLE). For more on the company's output, including work on Hindu and Siberian folktales, see www.westhighlandanimation.co.uk. Note that the studio is not open to casual visitors.

At the entrance to Tuarach is a fine modern stone circle (NN47901912). It was built in 1984 under the direction of Leslie and her husband, both stone circle enthusiasts, and was constructed by the digger driver one very wet day after he had completed the road to the site. The substantial stones are glacial moraines, taken from the rise on which the circle sits. Inevitably the circle has become a focus for the odd bit of oddness. When an engineer visited to track television signals – a process which involved wandering round with a backpack from which, surreally, sprouted a huge television aerial – the best signal was found to be received in the very centre of the circle. At one point Darrell Jonsson, a friend from Iceland, was staying at Tuarach. The Landrover wasn't working so, as you do, he decided to exorcise it. The vehicle was pushed into the centre of the circle and Darrell poured kerosene around the perimeter of the stones. As the evening darkened the kerosene was lit and within the ring of flames Darrell proceeded to 'sacrifice' beer cans and oranges with an axe. The entire episode provided great enjoyment, both dramatic and convivial, for all concerned, and clearly it was performed with a puckish humour. And of course after the exorcism the Landrover was as right as rain.

EDINCHIP

A long-distance walking path and cycletrack runs from the Kingshouse Hotel to Lochearnhead, thus avoiding the busy A84. Edinchip Chambered Cairn lies some way off the main route but is worth visiting (NN57502185). From a field gate at NN574212 follow the track (marked 'Old Military Road' on the OS map). Once you have passed three ruined houses the cairn is on the left. Three chambers are visible along its 61yds (56m) length, one of which has a large capstone still *in situ*. Just to the east a set of modern, metal animal feeders have been set up on the hardstanding of the disused Callander & Oban railway; their architecture is such that they mimic an old rural railway station, forever waiting forlornly for a train that will never come.

Stone circle on south side of Loch Voil. Built 1984.

In his 1887 report to the Society of Antiquaries of Scotland Mackintosh Gow described Fuaran n'druibh chasad, the whooping cough well, beside the Alt cean dhroma burn in the grounds of Edinchip House. It was a water-worn pothole 10–12in (25–30cm) in diameter and 6in (15cm) deep. As soon as it was emptied it immediately refilled itself. Children were still being brought 'in recent years' to drink the water in a spoon made from the horn of a living cow. Non-ambulants received it in bottles taken back to their homes. C. Randall's 1812 book *The History of Stirling* claims that in the glen behind Edinchip House there is a cave which sheltered Robert the Bruce after the Battle of Methven, and was capable of holding fifty men in full armour. Randall's book, clearly an attempt to cash in on the success of *The Lady of the Lake*, is full of errors – which may have something to do with the fact that he published, printed and sold the book himself – and here I believe he is thinking about other 'Bruce' caves elsewhere.

SOUTH LOCH EARNSIDE

Little remains of the shore-side St Blane's Chapel (NN59742304) other than some unimpressive rectangular foundations which appear to line up on the crannog in the nearby shallows (NN59852306). A report from 1927 mentioned a small boulder incised with two small Latin crosses in the chapel ruins, but these cannot be found now. Traditionally this is the burial place of the saint, who before his death predicted the possessors of the land where he was buried would forever be neither rich nor lasting. This is a pleasant enough wooded lochside site but there is no obvious access.

Edinample Castle (NN60172266, private) was extensively restored by architect Nicholas Groves Raines in the latter part of the twentieth century. There is a good view from the road above it, and it can also be seen from across the other side of the loch. In his book *Supernatural Scotland* Roddy Martine relates how Glasgow journalist Fidelma Cook and photographer Dave

Edinchip Chambered Cairn, with animal feeders in the background.

McNeil were doing a piece on Edinample's new interior decoration. On a personal tour of the castle Fidelma felt a push from an invisible source. In the room designated to become a child's bedroom the tense atmosphere increased to the point where she panicked. Over lunch, Nick and his wife Limma, when asked, told her the story of Black Duncan of the Cowl. Duncan Campbell was a bad egg, an avaricious thug who schemed to have the MacGregors proscribed in order to get his hands on their lands and property. He built the original sixteenth century fortalice. When inspecting the final results he tripped and fell on the wallhead walkway and so pushed the Master Mason off the roof to his death. When Dave's photographs were processed the next morning in Glasgow a sinister cloud-shaped shadow was seen in the background. As is traditional with spooky images, the negatives and all copies of these photos have mysteriously disappeared. For more on Fidelma Cook see ABERFOYLE. The road crosses the Falls of Edinample, where standing dramatically next to the cataracts is the splendidly gloomy late-nineteenth-century mausoleum of the Campbells of Menzie (NN60172245, locked). Adjacent are the castle gates, sporting statues of a unicorn and lion.

LOCHEARNHEAD

About 1840 a Lochearnhead man was returning from his work in Glasgow to the village. It was a dark midnight when, just south of the village, he saw a host of men, women and children he thought to be a benighted wedding party heading to a spot by the roadside. But a year or two later he saw in daylight the same company at the same place – it was the Balquhidder Free Church congregation, assembling to worship in their church, which had just been erected. The precognitive vision was described by Revd George Williams to the Stirling Natural History and Archaeological Society in 1901. Just north of the bridge over the Kendrum Burn a field gate leads into a field on the west, in which is a rocky mound hosting three cup-marked boulders, one of which has at least fifty cup marks (NN58752307).

Edinample Castle, home of the pushy ghost of Black Duncan of the Cowl.

Paul McGinlay's *Tales of the Trossachs* (2004) tells the extraordinary story of an unnamed fifty-year-old Lochearnhead man who encountered a 'Mothman' entity during a ritual at a Bronze-Age burial site on the south coast of England about 1989. The creature had two blood-red eyes and large wings. The man, a member of the Institute of Shamanic Studies, struck out with a knife, feeling a powerful electric shock at the impact. The Mothman vanished with a trail of red smoke, but its malign influence on the individual has remained, leading to loss of partner, friends and job, and near misses from falling rocks and tree branches.

NORTH LOCH EARNSIDE

Past the eastern edge of Lochearnhead is Leckine, the private burial ground of the McLarens of Ardveich (NN60192402). Access is up the private road to Earnknowe Holiday Cottages, past the bungalow and on the right. Ask permission at Earnknowe farmhouse. Within the small, walled cemetery there are thirteen standing gravestones, two of which have eighteenth-century carvings of winged souls. The entrance posts are crowned with white quartz. Further east, Glenbeich Lodge has a stone with a carved cross incorporated into the rockery beside the drive (NN615249), and there are several cup-marked rocks north-east of Ardveich farmhouse (NN61862482, NN61782486 and NN62132487).

8

BREADALBANE: FROM KILLIN TO TYNDRUM

Many of the magical and ritual elements in this Highland area (Breadalbane translates as 'the heights of Albane') are associated with St Fillan, so a little introduction is necessary. Like so many saints from the Dark Ages, Fillan's origins, activities and achievements are circumscribed by limited documentation, later speculative writings and quasi-history. We know he existed, and was venerated, but other than that much of his story is legendary. He has the compulsory miraculous birth-story, being thrown into a pool by his father because he was born with a stone in his mouth; rescued by angels, the infant Fillan was later baptised by St Ibar. At a best guess, Fillan lived in the early part of the eighth century and came as a missionary from Ireland with his mother St Kentigerna (see LOCH LOMOND) and uncle St Comgan. He was active in Pittenweem (Fife) – where he lived in a cave, his light for writing being supplied by his luminous arm – and possibly other parts of Scotland before settling in what became known as STRATHFILLAN, the valley from Crianlarich to Tyndrum. By tradition he set up a monastery in the strath. While building the church – or, depending on the version, ploughing a field – Fillan's ox was killed by a wolf. An interspecies negotiation followed, after which the predator saw the error of its ways and took up the burden of the ox. The name Fillan probably means 'little wolf'.

There was another St Fillan, who is associated with the area around Loch Earn and St Fillans in Perthshire; the two are easily confused, and details of their activities have certainly migrated from one to the other. The feast day of the eastern Fillan was 20 June, that of the one we are concerned with here is 20 January (9 January Old Style).

Fillan is associated with healing, but we have no details of his work in this area. After his death various relics of the saint circulated, but the monastery in Strathfillan, if it existed, may have decayed or been taken over; the site only comes into historical focus again in about 1317, when Robert the Bruce founded, or refounded, a religious establishment on the site. Bruce's act was one of pious gratitude: it was his belief the arm-bone of the saint had miraculously intervened at the BATTLE OF BANNOCKBURN. Other relics of St Fillan were, unusually, kept in Breadalbane by hereditary lay custodians known as Dewars. As part of the arrangement, each Dewar received a grant of land rent-free, known as Dewars' Crofts. Several attempts were made by senior ecclesiastical figures to claim the relics for the Church, but their protestations were always rebuffed by the courts, and the Dewars' rights even confirmed by the Crown. The relics were:

The Quigrich or crozier, now in the National Museum of Scotland, Edinburgh.

The Bell, also known as the Bernan or Bernane. In 1488 it formed part of the procession of coronation of James IV at Scone. It is also housed in the National Museum of Scotland.

The Farig, or Fergy, the wooden mallet used in the making of pot barley in the knocking stone or mortar. The ruinous burial ground at AUCHLYNE was called Chapeil na Farig; it was somehow connected to this relic, which is now lost.

The Mayne, usually thought to be the famous Bannockburn-winning enshrined left (luminous-in-life) arm of the saint, held in a silver casket. However, Ronald Black, in his notes for J.G. Campbell's *The Gaelic Otherworld*, translates the word as mionn, meaning a diadem. Whatever it was, like the Farig, it vanished at the Reformation.

The Meser, probably an illustrated Psalter. Black translates it as measair, 'dish'. It too is now lost.

Given the antipathy of the Reformers for 'Popish superstitions' it is remarkable that even two of the five relics have survived. The story of the Bell is told in the STRATHFILLAN section. The Quigrich was regarded as a sacred guarantor of oaths and was held by a succession of eldest sons, usually at Ewich near Crianlarich. A legal document of 1428 confirmed the ownership of Finlay Dewar, whose family had long held the relic. Further, if anyone had suffered theft of cattle or goods, they could charge the Dewar to take the Quigrich and seek out the property wherever it might be; the Dewar's fee for this was to be fourpence or a pair of shoes. In 1487 James III ordered that no one impede, deceive or assault the Dewar when he was carrying the Quigrich in the execution of his duty. The Quigrich was an item of power and awe; no cattle-rustler, however bold and law-despising, would dare to molest the holder of the sacred totem, or swear his innocence when touching it – to do so, which involved swearing an oath of purgation, would be to see his soul damned.

By 1782 the Quigrich, along with a certified copy of the charter of James III, was in the possession of Malice Dewar, a day-labourer living in reduced circumstances in Killin. Malice earned a small income showing the relic to interested visitors; it was also used to cure mad cattle – water was passed through the relic and given to the cattle; if the cure failed, the water boilded on the ground. The anonymous guidebook *Strathfillan and Glen Dochart in Bygone Days* quotes a French officer who had paid Malice to see it: '*J'ai été charmé de trouver une relique parmi les Presbytériens*' ('I was delighted to find a relic among the Presbyterians'). Malice later took the Quigrich with him when he emigrated to America. In 1876 his descendant, Alexander Dewar of Plympton, Canada, sold it for £100 and it was returned to Scotland. An examination by the National Museum of Scotland has found that the crosier head is a fourteenth- or fifteenth-century silver gilt reliquary which contains within it an earlier, eleventh-century bronze crook; nothing of the original wooden staff has survived. The exterior has a crucifixion, a head (probably Fillan), a piece of rock crystal (a charm stone for healing), and a vexillum, the word signifying a Roman military standard; here, its purpose is to guard the bearer and ensure victory in battle.

KILLIN

'The peculiarity of Killin is in its assemblage of such a variety of picturesque objects in so small a space.' (Lord Cockburn, *Journal*)

The Breadalbane Folklore Centre (which doubles as the Tourist Office) is located in a former mill beside the extended rapids of the attractive Falls of Dochart. It has a small exhibition, with artifacts and displays, on the clans of the area, including the MacGregors, as well as a sculpture of a young urisk (illustrating a well-known story of the creature being outwitted by a housewife), while there are also stop-motion animations on folkloric stories by West Highland Animation from LOCH VOIL, and a video presented by St Fillan. Pride of place, though, must go to St Fillan's Healing Stones. These are kept locked in a tray, but can be viewed on request. They are one of the few relics with a long-term magical tradition that can be seen and handled by anyone, and as such the stones are an incomparable treasure.

There is no verifiable origin for the stones; by tradition they were collected by St Fillan and associated with healing thereafter. Since 'time immemorial' they have been kept in a niche in the mill on the site, which was built in 1840, replacing earlier mills; whenever a new mill was built it always incorporated a new niche, and an iron grille constructed to protect the stones. There are eight stones; each is supposed to be effective in healing specific parts of the body. Of the two with socket-holes (which were possibly created through the workings of something such as mill-wheel machinery), the larger, face-like stone works on the head, while the other is applied to the chest and front. Of the others, the largest waterworn stone is designated the stone for the back, while the five small waterworn pebbles of various colours and shapes are for the upper and lower limbs. In 1836 John Shearer (*The Antiquities of Perthshire*) described the ceremony as practiced by the custodian: 'The old woman rubs the head three times one way, then reverse three times, then three times round the head; she at the same time pronounces a Gaelic benediction. They are then cured.' A similar process was undertaken for all the others. The stone for the back was said to have a resemblance of all the joints of the spine; one of the smaller stones had lines in the shape of the ribs, while one of the side stones had been taken away but had come back through its own accord. Shearer concluded: 'The matron is not allowed to charge any pence, but looks as a present as a recompense for curing the invalids of their pain. Her ancestors and herself pay no rent.' And, bizarrely, 'The miller is obliged to keep a number of geese, and a white cock, as an injunction left by the saint.'

These days, anyone who wishes to can apply the stones; there are no recent anecdotes of miraculous healing, but according to the staff a number of people have contacted them to say the stones had a beneficial effect, and Reiki healers have reported the stones emanate energy. One woman told the staff the stones had cured her son's persistent hand warts. Hugh MacMillan in *The Highland Tay* (1883) says that until recently the stones were also used for healing cattle, which would drink water in which the stones had been immersed.

Numerous travellers in the eighteenth and nineteenth century mention the stones, and also record a set of traditions which are still maintained to this day. The straw and reeds on which the stones lay is changed on Christmas Day, and is taken from the riverside. And on St Fillan's Day, 20 January (9 January, Old Style, before the calendar change of 1752), no work was done in the mill; these days, no one is allowed in the building on that day. Shearer records a miller who kept the mill going on the sacred day: the machinery broke into pieces and killed the sinner. 'The present miller would not set it going on that day, although he was to be made the laird of the glen.' The Centre staff told me that during the conversion of the mill into its present use a plumber disdained the tradition as mere superstition and set off to work on 20 January 1994; a snowstorm prevented him reaching the mill.

Perhaps inevitably, variants in the traditions are recorded by various writers. The most common dissonance is the exact number of stones. The *New Statistical Account*, 1845, says there were 'seven small round stones… Five of them are still preserved at the mill.' A report to the Society of Antiquaries of Scotland in 1880 mentions 'seven or eight.' Charles Stewart, in *The Gaelic Kingdom in Scotland* (1880) definitely says eight. Hugh MacMillan, in *The Highland Tay* (1901), writes:

> There were at one time five stones in the mill, but two of them were unaccountably lost. I found the missing ones, bleached to their original purity by long exposure to sun and shower, on a tombstone in a lonely burying-ground of the McDiarmids, called Cladh Dabhi, on the shore of Loch Tay, below Morenish.

MacMillan does not explain how he identified the stones. Cladh Dabhi is at NN59823465. When C.G. Cash visited in 1911 the number was eight again. So we have seven stones reduced to five; seven or eight; five reduced to three; and eight. Is it possible some of the current stones are not 'originals'? Cash's report to the Society of Antiquaries of Scotland also noted other variations:

> The tradition still remains in the district that these stones were used in cases of illness, though such use seems not to have been made of them for a very long time. The 'socket stones' were placed over the nipples of women's breasts, and the smaller stones were rubbed on affected parts… So far from having a bed of fresh straw, we found them lying in a thick bed of soot, for the recess communicates by crevices in the wall with the flue of the kiln, and recess and stones were alike thickly coated with dirt, and considerable cleansing was necessary before the stones could be examined with any comfort.

The Healing Stones of St Fillan, kept in the Breadalbane Folklore Centre, Killin.

The later twentieth century seems to have seen a revival: a report in *The Scotsman* for 19 December 1959 notes that Graham Wilson, whose family owned the mill – then operated as a weaving manufactory – conscientiously guarded the eight stones, and ensured their bed was changed on Christmas Eve.

The Folklore Centre staff very much regard themselves as the current guardians of the stones, part of a long line stretching back uninterrupted through Graham Wilson, and then beyond both living memory and written records. At a time when most of Scotland's various healing stones are either lost or largely forgotten, the survival of this set and of the continuing observance of their associated ceremonies is truly remarkable.

Other Fillan items have not fared as well. No local person would have touched a branch of St Fillan's Ash Tree, even leaving its fallen boughs to rot; to sacrilegiously use the wood was to invite supernatural retribution in the form of a house fire. The tree was blown down by a gale in 1893 but in 1912 the dead stump still stood against the south post of the mill gate. The saint's rock-cut seat, next to the tree, was swept away by a flood in 1856 (or, according to another report, thrown into the river). Just west of Killin are places called Tigh a' Mheanaich, 'the House of the Monk', and, above, Craig Neavie, 'the Rock of Heaven', but their traditions are in desuetude.

J.G. Campbell's folkloric masterpiece *The Gaelic Otherworld* tells of a man who saw a woman was making porridge in a fairy knowe near Killin. A spark flew and struck him in the eye, after which he could see the fairies with that eye. At the Féill Fhaolain, 'St Fillan's Market', he saw many of them riding about the market on white horses. Meeting one he recognised he said, 'What a number of you are here today!' The fairy immediately blinded the man in the revealing eye. The market or fair survived on the third Tuesday of January until at least 1912.

The Folklore Centre will also give out, on request, the key for the locked gate that leads from the bridge over the falls down to Innes Bhuidhe, the burial ground of the Macnabs

The entrance to the MacNab burial ground, Inchbuie, Killin.

(NN57303263). You first pass through an eighteenth-century screen wall with three arches and two large pillars topped with ball finials (allegedly each surmounted at one time by a huge dragon), then cross the low banks of two Iron-Age forts which defended this peninsula, before reaching the locked walled enclosure, its walls topped by a pair of curious carved heads. A plaque notes that within lie 'fifteen high-ranking members of the clan including nine chiefs,' and in 1883 Hugh MacMillan reported a huge slab with a kilted warrior, supposedly brought down from the shoulder of Ben Lawers to cover the remains of one of the earliest chiefs several hundred years earlier, and in a corner a flat slab with a round hole cut into the lower part of it, 'so the spirit could leave and return'. None of these things are discernable today, the gravestones being mossed over or damaged. Other members of the clan are buried outside the walls; one of the stones has a winged soul, coffin and crossed spades.

MacMillan was deeply affected by the atmosphere of this unusual site, comparing it to Philae, the Egyptian temple in a similar situation amidst the cataracts of the Nile, and writing:

> The effect of this ancient fold of the dead, appearing at the end of the long vista of the trees, is exceedingly striking. Situated in the densest part of the wood on the island, the shadows cast by the foliage create a perpetual twilight there. A rank smell of decay, almost autumnal, haunts the place, no matter what the season may be. Hardly any wild flower pushes from its snowy breast in growing the dead leaves of the past year that rustle beneath your tread. An air of utter neglect rests on the whole enclosure… An immemorial calm seems to brood over the spot. The world of the dead past folds you about.

An old postcard in Kay Riddel's collection *Killin in Old Photographs* is marked with a handwritten description: 'Relics MacNab's Island, Killin.' It shows a platform containing a grated hearth over which is placed a large cooking vessel, while a smaller pot hangs next to it, then a flagon with a small handle, a portable fire grate, and a square wooden building with a corrugated iron roof

Guardian statue on
the MacNab burial
ground.

which looks like a privy or shelter. I have no idea what this collection of domestic paraphernalia
has to do with the burial ground; was there once an on-site custodian?

A sideroad running north-east from the south end of the bridge leads to Killin stone
circle, one of the few stone circles in Stirling District, and the best (NN5770 3280). The six
stones, 'standing bleaching in the sun, like the unburied bones of a long-extinct faith,' (Hugh
MacMillan, *The Highland Tay*) range from 4ft (1.2m) to 6ft 6ins (2m) high and the northernmost
stone has three cup marks on the top. The circle is in good condition, probably because of
its proximity to Kinnell House. There is the possibility it may have been 'improved' in the
late eighteenth or nineteenth century, when antiquities in the parkland of great house were
fashionable. Note the gates at the start of the sideroad say 'Kinnell Estate Private' – you are
allowed to walk as far as the circle, but do not enter the field in which it stands. A good view
can be obtained from the two inner gateposts topped with snarling lions.

Back in the village, signposts point to Fingal's Stone (NN5712 3301), one of the mythical
Celtic hero's numerous graves around Scotland – one of the derivations of the Killin placename
is 'Cill Fhinn', the burial place of Fingal. About 1830 the stone is said to have been higher
up the hill, and was brought down because visitors to it damaged the surrounding crop. The
standing stone was re-erected in 1889 after having lain recumbent for many years, with part of
a smaller stone fixed on the top. Kay Riddel's *Killin in Old Photographs* has a photograph of the
re-erection ceremony, in which respectable hats and Victorian beards are much in evidence. By
tradition, the first church in Killin was said to be built somewhere near the stone. Many human
bones were apparently found up the slope in the nineteenth century, and transferred to the

Stone circle, Killin – the only remaining prehistoric circle in Stirling District.

old graveyard, within which was an early fourteenth-century church (now vanished, replaced by the 1744 church on the main road). The graveyard itself (NN 57113300), behind the Killin Hotel, has a very good selection of carved gravestones, including wonderful trumpeting Angels of the Resurrection, winged souls, clan crests, skulls and crossed bones, hourglasses, crossed ploughshares and coulters, mason's tools and a splendid panel with crossed spades, coffin and an arrow pointing at a heart. An unusual seven-sided font was found half-buried on the site; it is now in the parish church.

Both Pier Road, north of the village (signposted 'Killin Cemetery') and the walk along the disused viaduct and dismantled railway lead to the mound upon which sits the gaunt ruins of seventeenth-century Finlarig Castle and its adjacent mausoleum (NN 57503383). The castle was built on a site of earlier strongholds by Sir Duncan Campbell, better known as Black Duncan of the Cowl, one of the more ruthless of the lairds of the powerful and land-hungry Clan Campbell (for more on Duncan's misdeeds, see EDINAMPLE CASTLE). Evidence of a capacity for summary violence can be found in the castle's unique feature, the beheading pit, a well-constructed stone-lined rectangular pit 4ft (1.2m) deep on the north side of the castle. Two links of an iron chain are still embedded in a corner of the west side. Execution by beheading was only for those of noble birth; commoners were hanged, a process both less ceremonial and, given the imprecise nature of the art, more likely to result in a slow, lingering death. One of the two mounds to the immediate north of the castle is claimed to be the gallows hill.

The grounds were clearly landscaped at one point, and are scattered with sizeable, presumably ornamental, boulders. A path through the undergrowth between the mounds reveals itself to be the former avenue from the north gates. On either side of the gateposts curious stone shapes rise from the walls; they have no obvious purpose, but they must have been built for some reason. In *Folklore of Scottish Lochs and Springs* (1893) James MacKinlay makes the intriguing statement that some of the trees were 'believed to be linked with the lives of certain individuals, connected by family ties with the ruined fortress,' but gives no further details. On the east side of the castle is the brick-built bulk of the ruined Tudor-style Breadalbane Mausoleum, built in 1829 on the site of a chapel and burial ground erected in 1523 by Sir Colin Campbell, ancestor of the earls of Breadalbane (in 1688 Sir John Campbell of Glenorchy wrote to Alexander Campbell of Barcaldine, complaining that the garrison of Finlarig had taken up the gravestones and floored their stable with them).

Over the centuries the Campbells of Breadalbane acquired more and more land through aggression, strategic marriages and dubious legal moves. By the end of the nineteenth century – by which time fourteen chiefs of the clan had been interred in the vaults of the mausoleum – they

Finlarig
Castle,
with the
beheading
pit in the
foreground.

The chain links in the beheading pit.

The ruined Breadalbane Mausoleum, Finlarig.

owned everything from Kenmore to Oban, an area over 100 miles (160km) long and covering almost 440,000 acres (178,000 hectares). By the First World War the third Marquis of Breadalbane was the largest landowner in Britain, but taxation, mounting expenses, a depressed economy and death duties all took their toll and the estate was broken up and sold off. The last of the great Breadalbane family were Sir Gavin Campbell, the 3rd Marquis (d.1922) and his wife Lady Alma St Fillan (d.1932). At their own request, they were buried, not in the by-then decaying mausoleum, but in the two modern graves marked with Celtic crosses just to the north. The Breadalbane estate had taken 500 years to reach its apogee, and only twenty-eight to be dispersed for ever. 'Look upon my works, ye Mighty, and despair!' (Shelley, *Ozymandias*).

On the night of 5 September 2004 the Spectre Paranormal Investigation And Research Group (www.freewebs.com/ukspectre) set up their equipment at the castle. The beheading pit, allegedly a source of energy which could be detected by dowsing rods, registered not a thing on the electro-magnetic frequency meter. Before any serious investigation could commence, however, the group's activities were compromised by the local youths having a laugh, and so the group withdrew.

An old woman who died in 1900 told Revd George Williams (recorded in 'Local Superstitions') that when she was young they had a custom of climbing a hill near Killin at dawn on Easter day to see the sun mount the sky with a tripping motion 'in sympathy with the work of Him who redeemed mankind.'

GLEN LOCHAY

This attractive glen is notable for rock carvings. About 100yds (91m) of Murlaganmore farm, on a ridge of rock, is a 6in (15cm) deep shape which resembles a footprint, and which may well be artificial (NN54323483). There are no other carvings near it but 200yds (183m) south of the farm are two cup-marked rocks (NN54023455 and NN53953455). Ask at the farmhouse for permission. A stone by the fence beside the river at NN53453568 has its carvings obscured by a metal post and grass. The best rock art is on a prominent ridge south of the road, at NN53223582 eight separate slabs in a row are decorated with cups and rings, with the second and penultimate slabs (counting from the east) being particularly impressive. Ask permission at the house opposite. There are five more cup marks on a boulder above Duncroisk at NN53113640; above the second dyke, on the east side of the burn, there is supposed to be a rock face incised with three crosses within circles (NN53253641). I scoured every sloping rock in this area looking for these unusual carvings and failed to find them; perhaps they have been covered in moss. The other (west) side of Allt Dhuin Croisg has a good cup-and-ringed marked boulder (NN52813635) and further up the slope in the deserted buildings of Tirai is a single standing stone with a blasting hole (NN53083670); it might possibly be a survivor of a stone circle or cairn – the nearby gatepost and the walls of the buildings apparently re-use other megaliths. South of the river (ask permission at Corrycharmaig) a ridge has three areas of extensive cup marks (NN52783549).

In 1904 James Macdiarmid of Morenish near Killin gave an address on Breadalbane folklore to the Gaelic Society of Inverness, in which he related the tale of Duncan Campbell of Glen Lochay, a famous swordsman and a fearless prosecutor of ghosts. A terrible wraith haunted Lochan-nan-damh in the hills above Corrycharmaig (NN523336), waylaying travellers both by day and by night. Duncan successfully expelled the spirit, and this and other triumphs over the denizens of the supernatural, ensured his reputation spread far beyond his native glen. In old age he set out to lay a ghost which haunted a murder site at a place called Tibbert, somewhere between Callander and Gartmore. His concerned wife arranged for one of Duncan's friends to 'accidentally' meet him on the road and enquire where he was going. When Duncan explained the nature of his mission, the friend noted that, given the location, the ghost would only speak English. Duncan considered this for a moment, then returned home, never again to trouble the world of non-Gaelic ghosts.

Macdiarmid also told the tale of John Brown of Duncroisk, who buried a stolen ploughshare – a crime worse than hiding gold or weapons – and then died without revealing the location. His ghost could not rest and haunted the top of the bank above the ford on Eas Choimhlig, which may be one of the streams that flow into the Lochay east of Allt Dhun Croisg. The spirit appeared as a big black dog, a roebuck, a horse and a man, and no one had the courage to speak to it. Eventually a weaver named MacPherson addressed the dreaded entity, which revealed the future of the weaver's family and that his betrothed daughter would never marry. The weaver took to his bed and never rose. Mairi B. Copland, writing in *The Celtic Annual* of 1915, has the ghost's name as Peter Brown – who in this version did not steal the ploughshare, just bought a new one and buried it, feeling that the old one was good enough for the communal ploughshare – and the weaver as Alasdair Mor. The event was meant to have taken place in the early nineteenth century.

Local resident Ella Walker (1905–1996) wrote *A Village History – Killin* which was published online at www.killin.co.uk/news. She describes a woodland clearing in Glen Lochay about 3 miles (4.8km) from Killin. Here lived a weaver who one Hogmanay met the Devil. Satan aimed a blow at him, but missed, leaving a handprint in a treetrunk which for many a night thereafter shone in the dark. Nearby a woman killed the 'last bear in Scotland' by throwing a pot-full of boiling porridge in its face, upon which the blinded animal plunged over the cliff and drowned in the deep, dark river below. This is a variant on a widespread tale, the dispatching of the 'last wolf in Scotland' by a woman wielding some type of domestic item – a story told throughout the Highlands. Walker also mentions the Clach-an-Sgadain, the Herring Stone, a large flat-topped stone by the road high up the glen, where the people of Lochaber would exchange fish for the raw flax, butter and cheese of Killin.

SOUTH LOCH TAYSIDE

A cup-marked stone with an unusual basin 8in (20cm) across and 5½in (14cm) deep lies in the forestry south of the road near Allt An Airgid (NN57853179). The large hole may be a mortar or knocking stone. Somewhere north of the road is (or was – I failed to find it) Fuaran na Druidh Chasad, 'the Well of the Whooping-Cough', actually a large boulder with a natural cavity in its side which could hold a considerable quantity of rainwater. It had never been known to run dry. Hugh MacMillan, in a report from 1884, noted that the practice of visiting the well had died out because the proprietor of Auchmore had closed off the access; it had last been used about 1860. The landlady of the house at Killin where he stayed remembered distinctly having been brought to the stone to be cured of the whooping-cough; there were steps for children, and before drinking the patient had to go round the stone three times in a right-hand direction. In 'Local Superstitions,' a 1901 paper for the Stirling Natural History and Archaeological Society, Revd George Williams noted it was thought kink-hoast (whooping-cough) could be cured by the sufferer receiving a piece of bread and cheese from a woman or, if both man and wife had the same surname, from her husband. Williams was told by Donald McLaren of Killin that a cure could always be got by asking any passing stranger. The Macnab of Macnab was once riding past a house where a child was ill. The mother called out, 'I say, you riding the piebald, what cures kink-hoast?' 'Warm milk and oatmeal, wiffie,' said he, and the child recovered. The image of a Highland woman calling out 'I say!' like an English toff will stay with me to my grave.

In Ardeonaig, the path signposted Glen Lednock leads up to the steep slope to the graveyard of Cill Mo Chormaig (NN67143554). The ruined pre-Reformation church was dedicated to one of several saints called Cormac. The old stone font has been erected on a pillar. The last burial is dated 1988; taking the coffin up here must be quite a task.

A man who dwelt on the north side of Loch Tay went to visit a dangerously ill kinswoman who lived in Cloichran. He took the ferry to Ardeonaig and in the gloaming was walking over a bridge at Coille-Chromadain (c. NN652343) when he was asked where he was bound by a little woman wearing a green cap. On explaining his mission of mercy, she told him that his relative had already been cured – in Ardnamurchan, on the far west coast. And then disappeared in blue flames. The man found the woman better, as had been predicted. (Source: James Macdiarmid, 'More Fragments Of Breadalbane Folklore,' 1904.)

Cloichran is now a mournful collection of ruins and a boulder-lined road at NN579343, the tenants having been cleared in the nineteenth century. Several of the buildings incorporate enormous boulders. To visit, take the track south uphill from the road. Peter Fisher, who in his youth had been a herd boy on the farm of Briantrian, Ardeonaig (NN662344), told Macdiarmid of his experiences. One night in the barn the bedclothes were almost pulled off the bed, and he heard someone/something trying to untie the laces of his boots, and dragging the sheaves of barley across the floor. The next day he learned a woman in the adjacent house had died during the night. And when walking on the road west of Ardeonaig in the dark, something hard hit him on one leg. A week later, deliberately taking a different route, his other leg was attacked. His brother died the day after the first assault; and his widow passed on following the second incident.

William Gillies' invaluable book *In Famed Breadalbane* mentions that the disease-curing charm stone of the Campbells of Ardeonaig was transferred to Boreland, Fearnan, on the north shore of the Loch, but I do not know what has happened since to this pale red granite stone. Gillies also tells of a woman baking in one of the houses in Bealach, Ardeonaig. A young urisk nonchalantly strolled in, sat by the fire, and snaffled several oatcakes as they were made. The annoyed housewife swept a hot bannock from the brander direct onto the urisk-urchin's bare knees. The burned creature ran off to the waterfall to get its parent, so the woman barred the door; after threatening and grumbling, the old urisk slouched off, revenge unfulfilled.

GLEN DOCHART

A standing stone sits on the south verge of the A827 at NN56143160, a short distance out of Killin. It may have been moved slightly when the road was re-done. The nearby Acharn Lodges have, at the rear of the property, a small modern stone circle of four stones. A plentifully

Modern stone circle, Acharn Lodges, Glen Dochart.

carved cup-and-ring-marked boulder sits in the forest at Mid Lix (NN55253030). Walk south for 400yds (366m) along the A85 from the road junction at Lix Toll, and look for the low stile; the stone is 50yds (46m) into the trees. Its setting – a clearing within the gloomy forest – makes it more impressive. Several fallacious stories based on Roman numerals have been concocted to try and explain the unusual placename Lix, from the mundane – this was the fifty-ninth toll on the road – to the ludicrous, the still-repeated legend that it was here that the 59th Roman Legion were annihilated. No they weren't.

James Macdiarmid describes a death premonition. James MacIntyre of Innisewan and a neighbour were walking to Killin to tell a man called MacEwen that his brother had died suddenly at Ardchyle, when they met MacEwen coming towards them. To their surprise, his first words were 'when did my brother die?' 'How do you know that your brother is dead?' they asked. 'I was in the closet, and saw my brother's gealbhan at the window, and was sure he was dead.' 'Gealbhan' means glow or little fire.

Two impressive red metal dinosaur/dragons stand on the north side of the road near Ardchyle. Sith-a-bhruaich, a fairy hill, is just to the east of Bovain on the minor road north of the river (NN541306), while Sithean Dubh is half a mile (800m) west. William Gillies tells of an Auchlyne man who, with a neighbour, had walked to Killin for whisky to celebrate the birth of a son. On the way back they were lured into the Sithean Dubh by fairy music. After listening to the music for a time the neighbour went home, but the other man refused to leave, and it was a year and a day before his friend could rescue him. The fairies had a secret treasure but no mortal could find it:

> There is a treasure in Sith-a-Bruaich,
> Whichever time it comes out.
> It will never be found:
> It is in the place of the trout.

'The Spectre's Cradle-song,' a part of James Hogg's epic *The Queen's Wake* (an 1813 work filled with supernatural elements) has the following introduction:

Pair of metal dinosaur/dragons, Glen Dochart.

As I was once travelling up Glen-Dochart, attended by Donald Fisher, a shepherd of that country, he pointed out to me some curious green dens, by the side of the large rivulet which descends from the back of Ben-More… A native of that country, who is still living, happening to be benighted there one summer evening, without knowing that the place was haunted, wrapped himself in his plaid, and lay down to sleep till the morning. About midnight he was awaked by the most enchanting music; and on listening, he heard a woman singing to her child. She sung the verses twice over, so that next morning he had several of them by heart… she (the singer) had brought her babe from the regions below to be cooled by the breeze of the world, and they would soon be obliged to part, for the child was going to heaven, and she was to remain for a season in purgatory. I had not before heard anything so truly romantic.

The mother is introduced thus:

Came first a slender female form,
Pale as the moon in winter storm;
A babe of sweet simplicity
Clung to her breast as pale as she,
And aye she sung its lullaby.
That cradle-song of the phantom's child.

After singing her lullaby and commending her child to heaven, the woman wanders into the wilderness, sadly saying to the baby:

The time will come, I shall follow thee;
But long, long hence that time shall be.

The burial enclosure of Caibeal Na Fairge opposite Auchlyne (NN51322933) has a few niches but there are no gravestones and the site is in a very poor condition. In the seventeenth and eighteenth centuries it was a Campbell burial place, but has an earlier association with the FERGY, one of the relics of St Fillan. Back on the A85, the burial ground of the Macnabs of Inishewan, at Suie, near Luib, on a low knoll north of the road, is a more worthwhile visit (N49012799). There are two excellent carved gravestones, and in the rubble of the south-east corner, a faint early medieval cross. Coirechaorach, marked on the map as 'Rob Roy's House,' (NN45772756) is just the gable of a house allegedly occupied by Rob Roy, visible to the south of the road. For Rob Roy completists only. The Robster is erroneously attached to the nearby Loch Dochart Castle (NN40612573) – Victorian photographers and guidebook writers, noting the unimpressive remains of Coirechaorach, decided this island castle was a residence more befitting the great man. The castle was also supposedly where Robert the Bruce licked his wounds after the Battle of Dalrigh in STRATHFILLAN, an impressive claim given that it wasn't built until several centuries later, by Duncan Campbell, Black Duncan of the Cowl (see FINLARIG CASTLE). The castle was captured in 1646 by Marquis of Montrose, and then burned down by the Campbells after recapture. Hugh MacMillan, in *The Highland Tay*, has a story, presumably from an earlier period, that when the loch was frozen the MacGregors crossed it and sheltered from the defenders' arrows by making large fascines of straw and boughs of trees, and advanced behind these until they were close enough to attack and take the castle.

The castle was an overgrown ruin until 1890, when a group of young people picnicked on it. Among them was a woman later called Mrs Place, whose family owned the estate, including the island. After lunch she expressed a desire: 'Oh, I *do* wish we could clear all these stones away, and see what the castle was really like, and put it right and take an interest in it.' Half the party poo-poohed the idea, and went fishing; when they returned the other half had something to show them; 'A dungeon 8ft deep, quite cleared out!' Over the next few years Mrs Place and her volunteers cut down the choking vegetation and consolidated the ruins, finding a hoard of eighty-seven small copper coins of Charles II, and a great deal of domestic items. The entire charming story is told in Mrs Place's 1906 paper to the Society of Antiquaries of Scotland. The castle is not accessible but can be easily viewed from a path leading to the lochside from the layby on the A85.

Robert Forsyth (*The Beauties of Scotland*) describes a floating island on the loch. It was 51ft (15m) long, 29ft (9m) broad and 25in (64cm) deep, and was composed of roots and stems of water plants. It could be propelled about the loch by poles, and cattle feeding unsuspectingly upon it were liable to be carried a voyage of discovery.

STRATHFILLAN

Saint Fillan's blessed well,
Whose spring can frenzied dreams dispel,
And the crazed brain restore.
(Walter Scott, *Marmion: A Tale of Flodden Field*)

An extract from *A Journal of a Tour in Scotland*, author unknown:

Aug. 9, 1798.—Arrived at Tyndrum by 4 o'clock. Rode, after dinner, with a guide to the Holy Pool of Strathfillan. Here, again, is abundant cause for talking of the superstition of the Highlanders. The tradition avers that St Fillan… consecrated this pool, and endued it with a power of healing all kinds of diseases, but more especially madness. This virtue it has retained ever since, and is resorted to by crowds of the neighbouring peasantry, who either expect to be cured of real diseases, or suppose

St Fillan's Holy Pool.

themselves cured of imaginary ones. This healing virtue is supposed to be more powerful towards the end of the first quarter of the moon; and I was told that if I had come there to-morrow night and the night after I should have seen hundreds of both sexes bathing in the pool. I met five or six who were just coming away from taking their dip, and amongst them an unfortunate girl out of her mind, who came from thirty miles' distance to receive the benefits of the waters… but had never derived the smallest advantage… A rocky point projects into the pool… on one side of which, the men bathe, and on the other the women. Each person gathers up nine stones in the pool, and after bathing, walks to a hill near the water, where there are three cairns, round each of which he performs three turns, at each turn depositing a stone; and if it is for any bodily pain, fractured limb, or sore that they are bathing, they throw upon one of these cairns that part of their clothing which covered the part affected; also if they have at home any beast that is diseased, they have only to bring some of the meal which it feeds upon, and make it into paste with these waters, and afterwards give it to him to eat, which will prove an infallible cure; but they must likewise throw upon the cairn the rope or halter with which he was led. Consequently the cairns are covered with old halters, gloves, shoes, bonnets, nightcaps, rags of all sorts, kilts, petticoats, garters, and smocks. Sometimes they go as far as to throw away their halfpence… When mad people are to be bathed they throw them in with a rope tied about the middle, after which they are taken to St Fillan's church.

The Holy Pool (NN35032880) is signposted from the track from the A82 to Auchtertyre Wigwams and Farm, where there is ample parking. Lacking any kind of structure or archaeology, it is one of those places – just a slightly wider part of the river, with two slight shallow bays divided by a steep rocky outcrop – that you would normally pass without giving it a second glance, were it not for its extensively documented history of healing through sympathetic magic, just one example from many of which is given above. The comparatively late survival of the practice – the last mentally ill person was treated in the pool in 1850, and apparently made a full recovery, although by the 1840s the practice was already slipping out of use – allowed

The font in which the head of the patient was placed, St Fillan's Priory.

many writers, both local and visitors, to record the rituals, something which elsewhere had to be reconstructed from historical documents. Sometimes the mentally ill were described as needing to pick up nine stones from the bottom of the pool, as above, and sometimes just three. In each case they had to be deposited on the cairns. Sometimes quartz pebbles are said to be required, elsewhere they are just whatever stones come to hand. Other variants are noted, as in R. Heron's *Observations made in a journey through the western counties of Scotland* of 1793:

> About 200 persons, afflicted in this way, are annually brought to try the benefits of its salutary influence. These patients are first conducted by their friends; who first perform the ceremony of passing with them, thrice round a neighbouring cairn, they then deposit a simple offering of clothes, or perhaps of a small bunch of heather... the patient is then thrice immersed in the sacred pool.

But although minor details may vary, the essence of the ritual always remains the same – immersion, circling the cairns sunwise, the number three or multiples of it, and deposition of a votive offering – and all incorporating a brand of sympathetic magic which derives its alleged efficacy from the power of objects and places associated with a great saint, Fillan.

The origin legends are obscure. Fillan was said to either have thrown a miraculous stone into the pool to prevent its acquisition by bandits, or broken his staff and thrown it into the water, or simply had his monastic cell on the site and blessed the water. The antiquity of the rituals is unclear, but Fillan's Bell (see the priory, below) is on record from the fifteenth century and the rituals surely must date back to long before the Reformation, possibly even early medieval times. In which case the pool gives an insight into how Highlanders had been thinking about and dealing with both physical and mental illness for perhaps a millennium.

The cairns on which the offerings were deposited are long gone. They appear to have been on the central ridge; quarrying operations uncovered many old coins, the organic items presumably have long decayed away. In *The Highland Tay* Hugh MacMillan states that on one particular flat

Carving of the saint's quigrich
on the interpretation panel at
St Fillan's Priory.

The saint's bell on the
interpretation panel.

part of the rock, the cakes of meal for diseased cattle were made, and where also 'holy bread made of the first corn of the harvest every year, mixed with the water of the pool, spread out on the rock and baked by the heat of the sun, was offered in homage to the fertile powers of nature.' Mackinlay's *Folklore of Scottish Lochs and Springs* records that the pool lost its power when a farmer drove a mad bull into the sacred waters. The anonymous tourist guide *Strathfillan and Glen Dochart in Bygone Days* (1900) claims that the pool was also used for testing witches, who were thrown in it bound, a story which appears in no other work, and is unlikely in the extreme.

If you came to the pool with a physical ailment, you went home after the ceremony. But for the mentally ill the cold-water immersion was just the start:

> In some parts of this island it hath been a common practice in the *mania*... to reinforce the power of the cold bath by shutting up the patient alone, and properly secured, in a solitary church, where his fancy might be haunted all night long. (Tobias Smollett, *Essay on the external use of water* 1752)

Patients were taken to St Fillan's church (also known as St Fillan's Priory or Strathfillan Priory), two-thirds of a mile (1km) downstream ((NN35922841), bound hand and foot, covered in straw, had St Fillan's Bell placed on their head, and left overnight. If in the morning – having absorbed the benefits of what MacMillan calls 'a whole galvanic battery of relics' – the bonds had been loosened, the prognosis was favourable; if they were still taut, the insanity would continue. We have very few records of specific patients. Moray MacKay's *Doune: Historical Notes* mentions a seventeenth-century kirk session record from Bridge of Teith, in which a young man drowned in the pool and the member who had taken him there was reprimanded severely. In 1733 John McLauchlane of Auchintroig, near Drymen, was washed, 'dooked' and tied up all night long, during all of which he was calm, in contrast to his previous extreme behaviour. The pool was clearly the first resort; not until a month later was a Glasgow doctor was called in to treat John.

Descriptions of just how and where the patients were bound vary with the writer. Several mentions are made of ropes, but the SMITH MUSEUM in Stirling has links of an iron chain said to have been used. The anonymous author of *A Journal of a Tour in Scotland* says patients were placed in 'a large stone with a nick carved in it just large enough to receive them... [and] fastened down to a wooden frame-work.' Others describe the head lying in a stone trough; both are probably the same as the damaged old baptismal font (which is still there). And J.G. Campbell (*The Gaelic Otherworld*) says the stone bowl was filled with water to be consecrated – were there priests, and later ministers, present? – and poured on the patient's head; and the patient was stretched between two sticks laced up with simple rope, which were arranged for easy escape. Campbell also quotes a former assistant at the pool who remembered as many as twelve 'lunatics' being left tied there at a time, which would have made access to the font difficult, not to mention St Fillan's Bell, although to be fair A.D. Lacaille ('Antiquities in Strathfillan') says that the Bell was only placed on the head of the patient for a few moments.

The Bell, one of Fillan's five great relics of power, usually lay on a gravestone in the churchyard, and was described by the author of *A Journal of a Tour in Scotland*, who also, through personal intervention, noted its fate:

> St Fillan caused it to fly to this church; and a soldier seeing it in the air, fired at it, which brought it down, and occasioned a great crack in it, which is still to be seen. I was told that wherever this bell was removed to it always returned to a particular place in the churchyard next morning... In order to ascertain the truth or falsehood of the ridiculous story of St Fillan's bell, I carried it off with me, and mean to convey it, if possible, to England. An old woman, who observed what I was about, asked me what I wanted with the bell, and I told her that I had an unfortunate relation at home out of his mind, and that I wanted to have him cured. 'Oh, but,' says she, 'you must bring him here to be cured, or it will be of no use.' Upon which I told her he was too ill to be moved, and off I galloped with the bell, back to Tyndrum Inn.

The gentleman concerned then departed for England with the Bell in his bag. On 24 October 1869 A.P. Forbes, the Bishop of Brechin, reported to the Society of Antiquaries of Scotland that he had met someone who had a relative in Hertfordshire; that relative was the son of the Bell-thief; and that he no longer wished to retain the Bell. As a result the relic was returned to Scotland, where it now resides in the National Museum in Edinburgh, next to the saint's Quigrich. The quotes from *A Journal of a Tour in Scotland* are in Forbes' paper.

The Priory of Augustinian Canons was founded in 1317 or 18 by Robert the Bruce, one of several such chapels he set up in gratitude for the saint's posthumous intervention at the BATTLE OF BANNOCKBURN. There may possibly have been an earlier structure on the site but the records are unclear. The traditional site of Fillan's cell was nearer the Pool; using 'time-based dowsing,' J.C. Orkney (*St Fillan of Glen Dochart*) claims to have identified the imprint of two rectangular Dark-Age buildings under the Victorian church on the west side of the road (NN34952865, now a private house), but of course this can only be confirmed by excavation.

The priory was dissolved in 1607, since then the structure has crumbled rather badly. It is now an undistinguished ruin next to Kirkton Farm, reachable by a well-made track (part of the West Highland Way) south from Auchtertyre. Within it can be found the font, plus a quernstone and a fragment of a cross. The supports of the modern interpretation board are carved with the saint's bell and crozier. Immediately east is the old graveyard (NN35952841), an attractive mound with many lichened stones, including two recumbent slabs carved with medieval crosses. Slightly further north, on the east bank of the burn, a piece of dilapidated circular ironwork covers the site of what was once called the Priest's Well (NN36022845). In 1924 a rectangular enclosure named the Priest's Garden was identified further south-east at (NN36122818); there is nothing to see now.

In 1901 Hugh MacMillan had a surprise when he attempted to reconstruct a smashed gravestone which lay alone in a field somewhere nearby: 'When I put together the fragments, I was greatly startled to read my own name in the inscription, "Sacred to the memory of Hugh Macmillan" etc.' His namesake, suffering from depression, had committed suicide by drowning himself in the Holy Pool; he had therefore been consigned to be buried outside the consecrated ground of the graveyard.

Donald MacGillivray, the minister of Strathfillan in 1813–16 and 1819–20, was once afflicted by a wasting disease, suffering burning pains all over his body. Early one morning a parishioner from the opposite side of the river, on her way to meet MacGillivray, saw another woman who had the reputation of being a witch. Suspicious of the woman's behaviour, she watched her bury something in a hollow and then leave. A little later the first woman arrived at the manse, and found the witch present; she produced what she had just dug up – a piece of wood stuck all over with pins. The witch was shocked and embarrassed, the pins were withdrawn and the minister's pains stopped. The episode is in John Gregerson Campbell's *The Gaelic Otherworld,* which also has the curious tale of a Strathfillan man who wished to slaughter a goat for food. In the evening a stranger dressed in green came to the door. He said he could not enter as he was in a hurry to go to Dunbuck (a famous fairy place near Dumbarton), but that 'many a day that goat had kept him in milk.' And then disappeared. Clearly Breadalbane fairies had a fondness for goats' milk.

The field below Dalrigh, to the north-west of the pool and priory (NN342289) is by tradition the site of a 1306 battle between Robert the Bruce and the MacDougalls of Lorne, with the latter the victors. As Bruce's men fled eastwards they are supposed to have thrown their weapons into Lochan-an-arm, Loch of the weapons (NN339287). A MacDougall is said to have caught Bruce by his cloak; Bruce shucked off the garment along with a grand brooch, which is a prized relic of the MacDougalls to this day. None of the early writers on Bruce mention the episode, however. After the defeat Bruce is supposed to have taken refuge on the island in LOCH DOCHART, in Rob Roy's Cave on LOCH LOMOND, in another cave in Craig Royston, or in Bruce's Cave above LOCH VOIL.

All that remains of the Priest's Well near the priory.

TYNDRUM

Beinn Dorain to the north was haunted by a urisk. In winter it came down to the Tyndrum area, where it lurked around a waterfall near Clifton which was later known as Eas na h-ùruisg, 'the Urisk's Cascade'. St Fillan banished the creature to Rome. For some reason. In the nineteenth century some boys saw a urisk: 'In the hill, when the sun was setting, something like a human being was seen sitting on the top of a large boulder-stone and growing bigger and bigger till they fled.' Shortly after sheep and grain were stolen. A man from Killin was passing the fairy mound at Lawers on Loch Tay one night when he heard fairy music. He joined the fairy group, who welcomed him and gave him a white horse on which to ride home. It flew through the air at great speed, overshooting his destination. When he finally shouted 'Woah' the horse threw him off its back, right down a chimney of a house in Tyndrum. His sudden appearance in the hearth startled a wedding party, but he stayed there the night and made his way back to Killin, where he was still telling the story in the 1880s. (Sources: J.G. Campbell, *The Gaelic Otherworld* and William Gillies, *In Famed Breadalbane*.)

GLEN FALLOCH

Clach Na Briton (NN33712161), also known as Clach Nam Breatann, the Stone of the Britons, is one of those monuments rich in suggestion and speculation and poor in certainty. Alistair Moffat in *Arthur and the Lost Kingdoms* calls it 'one of the hinge-points of dark ages Scotland.' It is an impressive site, a circular mound some 60ft (18m) in diameter and about 26ft (8m) high, ringed with large boulders and with one large jagged boulder protruding from the top in the manner of the capstone of a chambered cairn. Despite being marked as 'cairn' on the OS map, it does not have any of the features of a burial site. It is probably a natural feature whose striking size and appearance has been partially improved. W.F. Skene (*Celtic Scotland*, 1880) identifies it

Two-headed lamb, the Drovers Inn, Inverarnan.

with a stone called Minvircc, where a battle where fought between the Britons of Strathclyde and the Scots of Dal Riata in 717. A more secure suggestion is that it was, in Moffat's words, 'a geographical, linguistic and political boundary' of the Dark Ages, marking the upper limit of the kingdom of Strathclyde, the eastern boundary of the Dal Riata Scots of the West, and possibly the south-west edge of Pictland. The 'landmark' nature of the site means it is easy to imagine messengers and ambassadors meeting here. The RCAHMS 'Canmore' website notes that similar boundary markers between the kingdoms of the Britons and Scots are found 6 miles (10km) to the south above Lochgoilhead (where the placename is Clach nam Breatunnaich) and 15 miles (24km) to the west in Morvern. Clach Na Briton was still being recorded as a bound-mark in sixteenth and seventeenth century references. Getting to the stone, you have to take account of the railway line. 1 mile (1.6km) north-west of the Falls of Falloch car park, just after the bridge crossing the Eas Eonan, a track runs to the north. From here can be seen a footbridge over the railway. Clach na Briton is to the west across the moorland and over seven burns.

INVERARNAN

The Drovers Inn markets itself as 'Scottish Pub of the Year... 1705', and certainly entering the atmospheric main bar you do appear to be stepping back in time – not in a 'theme pub' way, but because the establishment has genuinely been serving travellers for over 300 years. Two enormous fireplaces flank the dark, convivial space, which is ornamented with weapons, plaids, mounted animal heads, old paintings and a large gong. Elsewhere the building is stuffed with animal specimens, including a wolf, lynx, wildcat, bear – and a shark. The must-see specimen, however, is the two-headed lamb.

9

THE ROAD WEST TO ABERFOYLE AND AREA

THORNHILL

The burial ground (NN670000) next to the church is in excellent condition and has a very good collection of carved stones. Alongside the usual symbols of mortality (skulls, crossed bones, hourglasses, winged souls) and of occupations (mason's tools, several ploughshares and coulters, often crossed) there is a large panel, possibly unique in Scotland. It shows a haloed St Martin, depicted as a Roman centurion, sitting on a horse and cutting his cloak with his sword to give to a beggar. The main road junction is enlivened by the towering Masonic Lodge.

'Local Superstitions,' a paper given to the Stirling Natural History and Archaeological Society by Revd George Williams in 1901, has a number of stories from the Thornhill area. John Miller from Ruskie suffered loss of cattle: 'They were witched, but I did for the blasted witch in the long run.' He cut the heart out of a dead cow and stuck it full of nails, pins, and needles and put it in his peat stack. The heart disappeared after a time and he was not bothered again. The edge of the field belonging to Hillhead Farm (NN676003) was called The Guidanes, derived from the Goodman's Field – a common practice in which one small part of a farm was dedicated to the Goodman (the Devil) so he would leave the rest unmolested. Nellies Glen, between the village and the Skeoch to the north, was either named after a serving girl from the Commercial Hotel (now the Lion and Unicorn) who fell out of an upper window while watching a shooting party in the glen, or, the more usual story, from Nellie Christie, an old woman with a reputation as a witch who lived in the park by the hotel. An outgoing Thornhill tenant said in 1897, 'I am too fond o' J. N. and her bodies to leave a clean house for them to come into.' (It was thought unlucky to move into a clean house.) A man was bitten by an adder in the Moss of Boquhapple. John Marshall, who told Williams the tale, was instantly sent to get a live pigeon. It was torn to pieces and the warm remains applied to the wound to remove the venom, the flesh of the gentle dove being thought the opposite of the poisonous viper. The man recovered.

Stuart McCulloch, in *Thornhill and its Environs*, has more. Road-widening east of the Lion and Unicorn revealed many skeletons, possibly a plague pit dug on the boundary of the settlement. On 5 September 1857 lightning struck three men in a field west of Thornhill. One was stunned, another recovered from a death-like unconsciousness, but James McQuarry was rendered a charred corpse. On 26 June 1913 another lightning strike killed four cows under a tree on Easter Torr farm. One day, shortly after the regular mail coach to Aberfoyle passed through, the horses appeared back in Thornhill with broken harnesses. The coach was found overturned at the side of the road a short way along the Aberfoyle road, with the mail stolen and the driver murdered. The perpetrators escaped. The spirit of a coachman in period dress has been sighted in the area. A friendly spook inhabits 15 Main Street, another resides at Hillview, and 'the Spectre' demonises a house in Low Town. McCulloch quotes an unnamed source from 1886: 'the de'il himself in the guise of a big black dog, jumped out of one of the high windows of Ballinton following an interview with the Napier laird who had vigorously refused the terms of the contract proposed by his satanic majesty.'

St Martin as Roman centurion, Thornhill graveyard.

FLANDERS MOSS

> The damp green heart of the Carse of Forth, 3–4 miles wide by about 14 miles long – say, 50 square
> miles of level marshland through which the Forth and its tributaries, great and small, coil and
> meander… (Nigel Tranter, *The Queen's Scotland: The Heartland*)

The Moss, now much reduced, occupied the flood-plain of the upper Forth, and once stretched almost from the fringes of Stirling to the next boundary of high ground, the hills at Aberfoyle. It was formed when the sea slowly retreated between around 9000 BC and perhaps 2000 BC. A treeless mixture of wetlands, peatlands, bogs and watercourses, the difficulty it presented to north-south travel made Stirling and Stirling Bridge the geographical bottleneck. The twelfth-century map of Matthew Paris (a copy of which is in the STIRLING SMITH MUSEUM) shows the mistaken but potent medieval conception of Scotland as being divided in two with seas coming in from east and west to meet at Stirling. Tranter describes the area as 'the moat of half of Scotland… The Flanders Moss and the Firth of Forth between them cut Scotland in two,' and 'an almost impassable barrier – save for the utterly desperate, the notably light-of-foot and the MacGregors, who knew the secrets of its hidden tracks, reaches and islands' Rob Roy's success as a cattle drover/thief is partly attributed to his clan knowledge of the area. In 1715 he offered to guide the Jacobite Army across the Moss, which would have outflanked the Government forces at Stirling, but the offer was declined and the Jacobites were forced to fight at SHERIFFMUIR.

A more successful manoeuvre was conducted in 1745 when Bonnie Prince Charlie's Jacobites, on the advice of Gregor MacGregor of Glengyle, Rob Roy's nephew, crossed the Moss on their southwards march, thus avoiding Stirling, where the bridge had been rendered impassable. The key crossing point was the old Fords of Frew, 2½ miles (4km) south of Thornhill, where the Forth could be forded. The route, however, was always risky, and in wet weather impassable;

a guide was essential. The main ford was east of the present Bridge of Frew (NS667960) and just west of Fordhead Farm.

As a slight correlative to this dramatic picture, a 2003 report for Scottish Natural Heritage by J.G. Harrison, *A historical background of Flanders Moss*, challenges the widespread view of the 'great morass' as a myth, citing documentary and environmental evidence to show that while there were a number of different mosses, which were indeed difficult to cross, they were discrete from each other, and there were small settlements on the fringes between the rivers and the mosses by at least the fifteenth century. Harrison also notes that the area was often referred to as 'Moss Flanders' prior to the nineteenth century. This may point to a Gaelic name-origin – in Gaelic origin the adjective comes after the noun – but there are no records of what the original name may have been. As Harrison notes, 'Any connection with Flanders is purely fanciful.'

Fancy, of course, is what drives part of folklore. Sir Michael Scot of Balwearie, Kirkcaldy, was probably the most learned man of his time, which inevitably meant he gained a reputation as a great wizard, even getting a mention in Dante's *Inferno*: 'Michael Scott, practised in every slight of magic wile.' He constructed a man of brass and instructed the brazen golem to perform various tasks, such as bringing Flanders Moss from, yes, Flanders on the Continent. The supports broke west of Stirling, hence the reason for the current location of the Moss. Dun, in *Summer at the Lake of Monteith*, cites the peculiar tradition that Scotland had to pay taxes to Denmark for the use of the Moss, and the preacher George Buchanan threatened the Danish Government that if the tax was not cancelled the Moss would be returned. I'm not clear how that would have been achieved.

Another long-running legend is that the Romans cut down all the trees in the area to deny the shelter of the *horrida sylva Caledoniae* to the local insurgents, and the absence of tree cover caused the carse to flood.

Systematic clearance of the Moss was underway even in the eighteenth century, and gathered pace thereafter, creating rich agricultural land. Today the Moss is about a third of its former size, and is a valued and managed natural environment. The clearance revealed several archaeological finds: huge animal horns, immense bones (possibly whale), the skeleton of a horse, an untanned cowhide, a native tent or camp, an iron hammer, a canoe, and a timber track 12ft (3.6m) long. Many of the items were kept in the various big houses but were stolen by soldiers, burnt, or otherwise lost.

INCHMAHOME PRIORY

> From the old decaying trees on Inchmahome the mottled leaves of sycamore and ash flutter down
> gently, looking like giant ghosts of moths in the still misty air. (R.B. Cunninghame Graham, *Notes*
> *on the District of Menteith*)

Historic Scotland. Open 1 April–30 September, 9.30–16.30 (last outward sailing), and in October, Saturday–Wednesday only, 9.30–15.15 (last outward sailing). Admission fee.

The priory (NN57440055) is one of the most delightful historic sites in Scotland, being set on an attractively wooded island in the middle of an equally scenic loch (much is made of this being the only 'lake' in Scotland, but this is just due to an early transcription error). A small boat takes you across.

The choir has a number of graves, including that of R.B. Cunninghame Graham (see GARTMORE) who is buried alongside his wife Gabriella; he dug her grave with his own hands. An older gravestone has an incised skull and crossbones. A thick-lipped face peers down from between the two left lancets in the east window of the choir. The chapter house now houses a collection of medieval sculpture. Attached to the wall, the gravestone of Sir John Drummond features the armoured knight flanked by St Michael the Archangel, with wings issuing from his head, and a figure in bishop's robes with staff and hand raised in benediction. Both are standing on dragons; Michael's is accurately described in John Stewart's *Inchmahome and the Lake of Menteith* as resembling 'a reptilian chicken.' Below Sir John's feet are two cats, possibly lions or wildcats. Another, very faded, slab has a knight drawing his sword – the fact that his legs are crossed does *not* mean he was a Crusader, this being a Victorian-era myth. The charming double effigy of Earl Walter Stewart and Countess Mary shows, unusually, the couple affectionately facing each other and embracing; below their feet are a lion and a dog. Alongside lies the legless effigy of a Stewart knight, and there is also a graveslab carved with an interlaced crosshead and a sword, a badly eroded effigy of an ecclesiastic with an eroded figure at its right shoulder, a human head from a corbel, and a five-hollow cresset stone in which lighted wicks were floated in oil.

At some point the warming house and latrine south of the chapter house gained the name 'the Nunnery,' even though there were never nuns on the island. 'The Nuns' Walk' runs alongside the wall leading south-east to the slight eminence known as 'the Nun's Hill'. William Marshall, in *Historic Scenes in Perthshire* has the legend. A nun fell in love with the son of the Earl of Menteith. She arranged to leave the convent at Cambuskenneth (where there was in reality an abbey but no nunnery), walk from Stirling and row a boat across to the island. But the young man died in a clan battle, in his last moments confessing the assignation to a monk. Enraged by the insult to the church, the monk disguised himself in warrior's clothes, met the nun when she rowed across, and drowned her. Next day her body was taken from the water and buried in an upright posture on the knoll, where a large stone on the top was erected to mark the site. A dark figure is supposed to have been seen on the hill at a certain hour of evening, although this could just as easily be the wraith of Duncan II, who Marshall says was murdered here on the orders of his brother Edmund. There is no stone on the hill.

The future Mary Queen of Scots was sequestered on the island for three weeks for safekeeping following the Battle of Pinkie in 1547. The walled Queen Mary's Garden contains a bower of box trees which, with a teethgrinding degree of inevitability, are supposed to have been planted by the young princess. Who was just four-years-old at the time. The short walk around the island takes you past the ancient, gnarled sweet chestnuts, named as some of Scotland's Heritage Trees. *Buchanan's Popular Guide* of 1902 advises, 'the visitor, matrimonially inclined, should not omit trying to throw a particular stone over the certain branch of a given tree. If this feat be successfully performed, a happy marriage is assured within the year.' It does however omit to mention which stone, which branch and which tree.

INCHTALLA

The west shore of Inchmahome gives a view of the smaller island of Inchtalla, on which can just be glimpsed the ruins of seventeenth-century Talla Castle, occupied by the earls of Menteith. Further west again is the miniscule Dog Isle, supposed to have been where the earl's hounds were kept. It is a crannog, an artificial island, one of several in the loch, although the others are not usually visible above water. Nimmo, in his *The History of Stirlingshire* (1880) relates an episode connected with a town-clerk called Mr Finlayson, who had been visiting the last earl on Inchtalla:

On taking leave, [he] was asked by the earl whether he had seen the sailing cherry tree.

'No,' said Finlayson, 'what sort of a thing is it?'

'It is,' replied the earl, 'a tree that has grown out at a goose's mouth from a stone the bird had swallowed, and which she bears with her in her voyages around the loch. It is now in full fruit of the most exquisite flavour. But Finlayson,' he added, 'can you, with all your powers of memory and fancy, match my story of the cherry tree?'

'Perhaps I can,' said Finlayson, clearing his throat, and adding: 'When Oliver Cromwell was at Airth, one of his cannon sent a ball to Stirling, which lodged in the mouth of a trumpet that one of the troops in the castle was in the act of sounding.'

'Was the trumpeter killed?' asked the Earl.

'No, my lord,' replied Finlayson; 'he blew the ball back, and killed the artilleryman who had fired it.'

MacGregor Stirling, in *Notes Historical and Descriptive on the Priory of Inchmahome*, has another wild goose case, where a sport of the earls was apparently to attach bait to a goose's leg, then paddle alongside the bird until a pike took the bait and a combat ensued, with the goose usually being the victor. Stirling finishes his anecdote with; 'This merry doing of the good old times has, alas! Gone out of fashion in this degenerate age.' *Notes Historical and Descriptive* also has a tradition related by Revd Duncan Macfarlan. The Earl of Menteith was entertaining guests, but, catastrophically, the wine ran out, so the butler was despatched to Stirling. The next morning the man was found asleep with a full barrel beside him. He said that at the shore he 'spied two honest women, mounted each on a bulrush, and saying one to the other, "Hae wi' you, Marion Bowie, Hae wi' you, Elspa Hardie' Hae wi' you, too, says I", mounting, like them, on a bulrush. Instantly we found ourselves in the King of France's palace.' As he was invisible he filled his cask from the store of wine in a sideboard, then popped a cup into his pocket and returned the same way as before. At dinner the guests were astonished at the quality of the wine. To confirm the story the cup was produced, with the *fleur-de-lys* of the House of Bourbon. In 1814 the loch froze, and the ice was as clear as glass, in many place invisible, with huge stones seen beneath. MacGregor felt 'stationed in mid air.' The ice cracked with hisses and explosions: 'another peal succeeds, and another, and another. The effect is terribly sublime.' The locals walked and drove loaded carts on the ice. To this day curling competitions take place when the ice is thick enough.

PORT OF MENTEITH AND LAKE OF MENTEITH

The graveyard of Port of Menteith parish church (NN58290116) has a unique table tomb; the flanks of the north support are carved with a smiling bewigged head with long tassels hanging from its ears, and a happy skeleton below a cheerful grotesque face, while the south support has a leering face sticking its tongue out, and a very strange mummiform figure in which the face is replaced by a rosette – it looks very much like some representations of extraterrestrials. The outer faces of the supports have a skull and crossbones, and a shield displaying a ploughshare, hammer, square and compass. It's probably all a cipher indicating the presence of smiling longhaired ancient Egyptian Masonic alien contactees. Other stones have the usual symbols of mortality. The church tower has a gargoyle on each face, but only one remains complete.

The Stewarts of Appin under Donald of the Hammers returned home from the Battle of Pinkie via the Port of Menteith, where they discovered a wedding feast all set out; chicken was a major factor on the menu, and the Stewarts dug in with relish. Enraged by the insult on a marriage day, the Earl of Menteith (of the Graham line) gave pursuit and attacked the marauders at Craigvad or the Wolf's Cliff. On the Stewart side only Donald and one other man survived, but as all Menteith's men were killed the Appin crew were technically the winners, and the losing side were thereafter known as Gramoch-an-Garrigh, 'Grahams of the Hens'. 'Local tradition heightens the flavour of the story with an additional and very wonderful circumstance, which the dignity of history has not deigned to notice.' A Graham and a MacGregor quarrelled on the hill of Coille-don on the north shore of the Lake. The latter was about to call out 'Hen Grahams!' when the other cut his head off, which then rolled to the foot of the hill, crying out 'Hen Grahams, Hen Grahams!' (Source: Marshall, *Historic Scenes in Perthshire*.)

A composite image of three of the carvings on a table tomb, Port of Menteith.

MacGregor Stirling includes a note from the Port of Menteith Kirk Session, 1 June 1704:

> The session, considering that there is a scandalous practice frequently used in this parioch at publick marriages, in the time, and immediately after the solemnization thereof, by the parties, there using of charms and inchantments, and that notwithstanding they have been sharply and openly rebuked for the same, by using circular motions &c.; wherefore the session, for preventing this abominable and heathenish practice in all time coming, do statute and ordain the guilty will have to appear publicly before the congregation and be rebuked.

A few decades earlier Andro McJohn of Port of Menteith had been hauled before the Presbytery of Dunblane for witchcraft, although the practices – easing a sore gut using water and butter, something obscure to do with broken bones – were clearly healing. Other than this single record, no more is heard about Andro.

Stirling also tells of the Red Book of the earls of Menteith. If it was opened, a supernatural event would always follow. One opening caused a group of fairies to appear. The little folk demanded to be given work, so the earl set them to make a road from the south shore to Inchmahome. They speedily built Arnmach (NN576003), the 500m-long peninsula on the south shore of the lake which points towards the isle. The earl, worried that either they would mutiny when the work ran out, or the security of the isle would be compromised, stopped the job and asked them to twist a rope of sand instead. Finding the task too hard the fairies departed in shame, so the earl granted them Coire na Uruisgean on the side of Ben Venue (see LOCH KATRINE). Stirling got this tale from a Mr Buchanan of Cambusmore, a noted local expert in folklore. Most later writers, seduced by the placename, set the episode on Cnoc-n'an-Bocan, Bogle Knowe, to the east (NN586997), but Stirling is quite clear. He mentions Bogle Knowe and calls it Hobgoblin Hill, but relates no traditions associated with it; the workaholic fairies are definitely said to have constructed Arnmach, which is described as west of Bogle Knowe. There is an actual *Red Book of Menteith*, but it is a massive two-volume work produced in 1880 by William Fraser, a history of the Earls of Menteith and their properties and descendants, with numerous family portraits and hand-coloured drawings of the various ruins. I have opened it several times and as yet nothing paranormal has resulted.

The Peace Stone lies about two-thirds of a mile (1km) south of Malling farmhouse at NS56419954. Its surface is entirely covered with cup-and-ring marks, with multiple circles, radial ducts, curves and straight channels. The stone is the subject of a prophecy apparently uttered by a Gaelic seer named Pharic McPharic, recorded in Dun's *Summer at the Lake of Monteith* (1867; Dun was station master at Port of Menteith). The stone would be buried underground by two brothers who would as a result die childless. The stone would then rise to the surface, and a fierce battle would be fought on Auchveity, Betty's Field (near Malling). Gramoch-Cam of Glenny, Graham of the One Eye, would sweep from the Bay-wood and decide the fight. After, a raven would alight on the stone and drink the blood of the fallen. About 1817 or so two brothers, tenants of the farm of Arnchly, found the stone agriculturally inconvenient and buried it in a trench. Both were married but died childless. With the work on the field over the years the stone has reappeared. When Dun was writing, a descendant of the Grahams of Glenny was alive and was blind in one eye. Dun concludes with: 'and the ravens are daily hovering over the devoted field. Tremble, ye natives!' Certainly the stone has been moved a few metres from its original position when it was first recorded in 1899 (in A.F. Hutchison's *The Lake of Menteith*).

For many years the Peace Stone was the only known prehistoric rock art in the area. By 1989 another twelve sites were known. During a three-day survey in October 1989 Maarten van Hoek and his wife located twenty-three new rock art sites. He found three more in 1990, and others have been found since (and some remain disputed). All of this makes the Lake of Menteith area one of the richest sites for rock art in this part of Scotland. The sheer volume of the new discoveries has meant a complete new naming system, so the Peace Stone is Menteith 1, and other stones are Menteith 2, 3 etc. Most of them are on the slopes above the farms of Ballochraggan, Arntamie and Nether Glenny. There are far too many sites to list in detail, so the main ones are given here (all numbers are Mentieth 10, 12 etc.)

10, a good grouping (NN56150176)

12, the best site in the whole area (NN56180175)

26, the largest group (NN56500211)

28, a very large outcrop (NN56230223)

32, another very extensive outcrop (NN56730246)

41, heart-shaped groove enclosing three cups, 42 is nearby (NN5610180 and NN56130183)

14, five cups and one cup with crook-like groove (NN56190189)

16, numerous cups, several rings (NN56240194)

17, large outcrop with numerous cups and rings (NN56240194)

9, the rings include a horseshoe maze design (NN56100171)

The best sites are Menteith 10, 12, 26 and 28. I direct the interested reader to the RCAHMS 'Canmore' website, and van Hoek's 1992 article in *The Forth Naturalist and Historian*.

Dun's book is a potpourri of facts and folklore; it is hard to distinguish which is which. The 'last wolf in Scotland' – one of several dozen 'last wolves' – was killed at the Claggans on the farm of Malling. The said wolf attacked a girl near Gartmore; she threw the beef and potatoes she was carrying down and made her escape while the wolf scoffed the lot. Somewhere east of Cardross House was a spring that cured gout. Dun was not sure if patients drank or bathed in the water. Cardross House itself (NS60469765) was bounded by a 'Roman pathway', and was home to a

74in (1.9m) long sword allegedly deposited there by Robert the Bruce. This may have been a confusion with Cardross near Dumbarton, where Bruce died.

ABERFOYLE

In Walter Scott's *Rob Roy* (1817), set in the early eighteenth century, Bailie Nicol Jarvie, Frank Osbaldistone the Englishman and his servant inadvisedly try to stay at the inn at 'Clachan at Aberfoyle'. There, they meet an unsavoury trio and get into a fight. Jarvie's sword is rusted through disuse so he wields the fire poker – actually a re-used coulter, the iron spike on a wooden plough that stuck down into the earth and divided it ahead of the plough proper. The red-hot poker burns a hole in the plaid of one of the Highlanders. The fight fizzles out with no one being hurt, and honour is satisfied, although the Highlander demands compensation for the damage. This mixture of high adventure and comedy was very popular, and soon hordes of Scott's readers came in search of the inn, or at least its site, and were delighted to find the genuine authentic coulter suspended from a tree on the village green. So delighted were they, in fact, that they stole it several times, and each time the village blacksmith forged another genuine authentic coulter. A fine example of the combined power of expectation, wish-fulfilment and commerce, building on a fiction to produce a legend which itself becomes the 'truth'.

ROBERT KIRK AND THE FAIRIES

> These Siths, or FAIRIES… are said to be of a midle Nature betuixt Man and Angel, as were Daemons thought to be of old; of intelligent studious Spirits, and light changable Bodies (lyke those called Astral), somewhat of the Nature of a condensed Cloud, and best seen in Twilight. (Robert Kirk, *The Secret Commonwealth*)

> Mr Kirk, the astral vicar of Aberfoyle. (R.B. Cunninghame Graham, Introduction to the 1933 edition of *The Secret Commonwealth*)

> We cannot help wondering whether Mr Kirk really believed that he had knowledge such as he professed, and if so, in what category his mental capacity would be reckoned to-day. (Alexander D. Cumming, 'Superstition and Folklore of Scotland')

Robert Kirk is easily one of the most important and influential people in the history of the Scottish magical tradition. His reputation rests on a truly extraordinary work, *The Secret Commonwealth of Elves, Fauns and Fairies*, written in 1691. 'The Secret Commonwealth' of the title is both the world (or Otherworld) and the culture of the supernatural beings, who Kirk calls the Lynchnobious People or Subterraneans. Deriving from and related to this place and way of life are many other elements such as second sight and ghosts; Kirk also discusses witchcraft and magic. He apparently acquired his information from his parishioners; it is possible he may have deliberately cultivated informants, such as seers or other tradition-bearers. The degree to which *The Secret Commonwealth* is a work of observation (recording the words of the locals), invention (did he make any of it up?) or even participative anthropology (did Kirk directly experience any of the things he describes?), is moot; we will never know for sure.

The Secret Commonwealth is a dense work, written in archaic prose and filled with now-obscure concepts. Briefly, its main points regarding fairies are:

Fairies are variable in physical nature, some astral, others more corporeal, but often invisible. Some eat the essence of food, others the food itself. They once existed and farmed above ground, but were displaced by humans, although much human labour is unknowingly carried

The 1893 and 1933 editions of *The Secret Commonwealth of Elves, Fawns and Fairies*.

out on the fairies' behalf. In terms of their origins, they may be the spirits of the dead or the ancestors, a vanished race, or beings neither angels nor demons, the undecided in the primeval War in Heaven. They dress and speak in the same manner as the humans in the country under which they live, and have a hierarchical social order which reflects human society. They have books – but not the Bible – weapons, spinning wheels, politics, marriages, births, combats and funerals. They live for a very long time but when they die they return to the great revolving circle of life. They move their lodgings at the beginning of each Quarter of the year, during which time those with second sight will commonly encounter them. They attend human funerals and eat the food supplied for the mourners, and at their own meals are served by 'pleasant children like enchanted puppets'. A man may have a great appetite but remain thin, the essence of his food being consumed by an invisible fairy called a 'joint-eater'. Fairies often steal nursing mothers for their own offspring, leaving behind an unpleasant substitute-woman, and blind or otherwise mutilate those who practise arts to penetrate the Fairy Mysteries.

In terms of second sight, seers can see 'double-men', apparitions co-existing with their human originals; these Co-walkers sometimes operate independently, or in advance, of their mortal counterparts. Other wraiths are perceived just before violent death. Seers can deliberately engage the services of the fairies, but accidental encounters are often terrifying. Visions could be painful and could involve combat with the fairies, during which times the seer would become temporarily invisible. Seership required an initiation ceremony involving a tether which had tied a corpse to a bier, and looking upside down between the legs at a funeral party as it crossed a boundary, a whole set of liminal elements. The same effect could be achieved by looking through a knot in a tree. The operation was perilous – 'But if the Wind change Points while the Hair Tedder is ty'd about him, he is in Peril of his Lyfe.' Second sight could be temporarily transferred if someone stood on a seer's foot and the seer put his hand on their head. In one of the few cases where Kirk names a person, a man called Stewart, one of Kirk's neighbours, scoffed at second sight; a seer caused 'many fearful wights' to appear before him, such that Stewart lost the power of speech, and collapsed.

Other elements can be found in the book. A death-messenger would appear in the form of a little rough dog. If the sign of the cross was made over it and an incantation or prayer said, it would be 'pacified by the Death of any other Creature instead of the sick Man'. Dying people exhale fumes which congeal into Astral Bodies; these can be agitated by the wind but are neither souls nor external spirits, but of the same nature as the apparitions of ships and armies sometimes seen in the sky. 'Skilful Women' can extract the essence of the milk from their neighbours' cattle by using a rope of hair or a spigot attached to a post. The cheese made from all that remains of the milk will swim in water like a cork (this may be a way of detecting milk-robbery caused by witchcraft). The theft can be reversed through counter-charms, although the theft can be prevented by placing a little of the cow's dung in the calf's mouth before it sucks. The astral bodies or supernatural forms of witches and were-wolves, if hurt, will replicate the wound in their true bodies which remain at home. There is much more in this truly fascinating work.

Perhaps the most surprising thing about *The Secret Commonwealth* is that it was written to prove the existence of God. At the end of the seventeenth century a wind of change was sweeping through the intellectual world: scepticism, rationalism and materialism were coming into vogue, based in part on the writings of Descartes, Hobbes and Spinoza. In this new mechanistic worldview, God was a clockmaker, matter and spirit were separate, and witchcraft, prophecy and fairies were mere superstitions. Kirk was one of many religious people who believed that scepticism towards the supernatural was a slippery slope. God made the fairies; to disbelieve in them was to perhaps doubt the very existence of God. The title page of *The Secret Commonwealth* makes his aim clear. It is 'an Essay to suppress the impudent and growing Atheisme of this Age,' a point underlined by one of the Biblical quotes that follows: 'This is a REBELLIOUS PEOPLE, which say to the Siers, sie not; and to the Prophets, prophesie not unto us right Things, bot speak unto us smoothe Things' (Isaiah, 30: 9–10). It is somewhat difficult to conceive of a modern Christian minister citing the existence of fairies as proof of the reality of God. So the times change.

Kirk was the seventh son – a notable factor – of Revd James Kirk, minister of Aberfoyle. Unlike his Anglophone Lowland parents, Robert grew up bilingual in English and Gaelic, which enabled him to go native and converse freely with his parishioners when he was appointed to the ministry in BALQUHIDDER, where he may well have collected material for *The Secret Commonwealth*. Certainly he was meditating on the supernatural. In 1921 David Baird Smith purchased a slim notebook at a sale in London of the estate of the Professor John Ferguson of Glasgow University, the title page of which reads: *First Manuscript | A | miscellany of occurring | thoughts on various | occasions | Ro: Kirk | Love and live | August i at Balquhidder | 1678*. Among the musings on clan feuds, misbehaviour, vice, the death of his first wife, religious disputes, farriery and his digestion, Kirk records a premonitory dream presaging the demise of his mother – an event he suggests may be due to a message delivered by a 'courteous angel' – and includes passages such as:

> The ancient tradition of evil spirits sucking of witches and dead carcasses (raising a storm while a magician's dead body is unburnt)… likewise the story of the human-shaped *incubi,* and stealing of children and nurses, give probable surmises that there are divers clans and kinds of spirits who make their vehicles seen to us when they please, though they are not so gross as terrestrial bodies, but most part aerial needing to be soakt and fed some way as ourselves. Such may be the fauns, fairies, satyrs and haunters of woods, hillocks, wells, etc.

In 1685 he was appointed to his father's old parish and served in Aberfoyle until his death in 1692. His masterwork on fairies notwithstanding, Kirk was a considerable scholar, with a clear sense of his own linguistic abilities. In 1659 the Synod of Argyll produced the first fifty psalms in Gaelic, and set about translating the rest (Highlanders could not read English). Driven by a powerful sense of competition, Kirk produced the first complete metrical Psalter in Gaelic (the Psalter is a copy of the Book of Psalms); his *Psalma Dhaibhidh an Meadrachd* came out in 1684, a full decade before the Synod published their version. D. MacLean (*The Life and Literary Labours of Rev. Robert Kirk, of Aberfoyle*, 1927) notes how Kirk worked through the night for months on the translation, putting a piece of lead in his mouth and a basin of water below him. If he fell asleep the splash woke him up. Between 1667 and 1688, Kirk was the well-regarded clerk to the Session of Dunblane; during his time there, in contrast to some of his predecessors, the minutes are recorded in beautiful, legible copperplate handwriting. In his introduction to the modern edition of J.G. Campbell's *The Gaelic Otherworld,* Ronald Black also suggests Kirk was the principal author of *A Collection of Highland Rites and Customes*, another superb early work of folklore. The manuscript is usually attributed to Revd James Kirkwood, but Black thinks this was because Kirkwood was better known than Kirk. Certainly many of the passages on second sight and fairies are very similar to those in Kirk's masterpiece. Kirk also compiled a Gaelic glossary, published posthumously in 1702.

In 1685 Bishop Bedell and William O'Donnell had produced a Bible for Gaelic speakers in Ireland, but it was written in Irish script, which Scottish Highlanders could not be read. Kirk set himself the task of transcribing Bedell's entire Bible from Irish characters into Roman ones, so Gaelic-speaking Highlanders could have a Bible in their own language. In 1689 Bedell sent Kirk to London to oversee the printing of the new edition, which came out the following year. In London, Kirk, in a remarkable example of religious toleration and enquiry, sampled three different sermons every Sunday, to see what he could learn from, and about, the various denominations, from Calvinists to Catholics. Kirk's religious moderation had already stood him in good stead. Throughout the seventeenth century Scottish Protestants of various sects, possibly having run out of Catholics to persecute, turned on each other in an unedifying display of internecine bloodletting. When Presbyterianism was re-established in 1688 Kirk, a lifelong Episcopalian, was the only one of his colleagues in the diocese who was not driven from his pulpit. Clearly his parishioners in Aberfoyle, especially the powerful and influential ones, thought highly of him. And while his colleagues of a previous generation had led the charge against witchcraft and fairy magic, Kirk – at a time when witchcraft and consulting witches was still a capital crime – assiduously explored the outer reaches of belief.

The Secret Commonwealth may have been actually written in London, when Kirk was participating in the intellectual ferment of the day on bulwarks against atheism. The costs of the printing of the Gaelic Bible were initially met by the deeply pious Robert Boyle, scientist, originator of Boyle's Law on the behaviour of gases, secret alchemist, seventh son, enquirer into the occult and contributor of papers on both natural and supernatural phenomena to the newly formed Royal Society. Boyle was the poster boy for the period's transitional nexus of religious, scientific and magical thinking. Kirk appended a letter to *The Secret Commonwealth*, a response from George MacKenzie, Lord Tarbat (1630–1714), to a query from Boyle on second sight (Boyle's original letter was suppressed by his biographer). Tarbat's letter later came to the attention of Samuel Pepys, who was interested in second sight because of the possibility it could provide naval intelligence – the 'remote viewing' psychic experiments of the Cold War were based in the same principle.

One of Boyle's confidantes was Edward Stillingfleet, eventually Bishop of Worcestor. Stillingfleet, a sceptic, invited Kirk to dinner and tackled him on the reality of fairies. Kirk's diary for 6 October 1689 records the exchange. Discussing a case of fairy abduction, Kirk told Stillingfleet it was,

Reported by many that knew the woman, which was taken out of her bed when lying of a child, and a lingering likeness of her decayed, died and was buried, and yet the same woman was said to return to her husband two years after, and he after a long whiles trial received her and had children by her.

The subject moved onto second sight, and a degree of verbal jousting ensued:

I urged to the doctor that as lynxes and cats see in the night beyond men, and as telescopes aid the natural sight by art, so may not some men have, or attain complexionally to such a habit or faculty.

Stillingfleet answered:

1. That by many subtle, unthought of insinuations the devil interposed in such cases, and sought no other invitation than the eager curiosity of the enquirer as of him that caught a fly and put it in the box, &c. 2. That it was not an art or faculty in use or of good fame among men, or recommended of God. 3. If it be diabolic, it was no reality, but apprehension.

Kirk riposted:

I opposed 2 Kings 6. 17: 'And Elisha prayed, and said, Lord, I pray thee, open his eyes, that he may see. And the Lord opened the eyes of the young man; and he saw: and behold, the mountain was full of horses and chariots of fire round about Elisha.'

Unable to counter this Biblical endorsement, Stillingfleet conceded defeat, and even gave Kirk ten Guineas for the printing of the Bible.

Kirk was a liberal intellectual of great energy and learning who habitually wrote after his name the words 'Love and Life'. 'If it be true that Mr Robert Kirk was chosen as her chaplain by the Fairy Queen, Her Majesty is to be congratulated on her good taste.' (David Baird Smith).

[Kirk]..became personally entwined with the very traditions that he dedicated the latter part of his life to studying, a paradoxical situation in which the historical figure was absorbed as part of the folk tradition.
(Lizanne Henderson and Edward J. Cowan, *Scottish Fairy Belief*)

The Secret Commonwealth was probably completed in 1691. On 14 May 1692 Robert Kirk went for a walk and dropped dead. A much-repeated legend says he was taken by the fairies as punishment for revealing their secrets. His spirit then appeared before a family member and urged him to tell a mutual relative to attend the christening of Kirk's child – his wife was pregnant at the time of his death – and, when Kirk himself appeared, to throw an iron knife over his head. Kirk kept the appointment, but the relative was so astonished at the apparition that he failed to throw the knife, and so Kirk remains trapped in Fairyland, specifically in the lone Scots Pine on Doon Hill.

The tale is much-loved by fairy-fanciers, new agers, casual visitors, children and the tourist industry, so I'll say this as gently as I can. It's a fib. A fiction. An invention. A madey-uppy story. A big fat fairy lie.

The origins of its creation lie, indirectly, with Walter Scott. Patrick Graham, minister of Aberfoyle, wrote *Sketches Descriptive of Picturesque Scenery of the Southern Confines of Perthshire* in 1806. It contains much lore about the fairies, called the Daoine-Shie or Men Of Peace – such as the fact that they 'sometimes held intercourse with mistresses of mortal race, and were inconsolable when their suits were rejected' – but there is nothing about Robert Kirk. The book was moderately successful. Then in 1810 Scott wrote *The Lady of the Lake,* a publishing sensation. The modest number of tourists to the area became a flood. In publishing, as elsewhere, everything counts in large amounts. Graham's book was hurriedly reprinted in 1810 with just

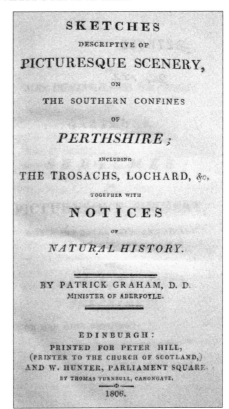

SKETCHES

DESCRIPTIVE OF

PICTURESQUE SCENERY,

ON

THE SOUTHERN CONFINES

OF

PERTHSHIRE ;

INCLUDING

THE TROSACHS, LOCHARD, &c,

TOGETHER WITH

NOTICES

OF

NATURAL HISTORY.

BY PATRICK GRAHAM, D. D.
MINISTER OF ABERFOYLE.

EDINBURGH:
PRINTED FOR PETER HILL,
(PRINTER TO THE CHURCH OF SCOTLAND,)
AND W. HUNTER, PARLIAMENT SQUARE.
BY THOMAS TURNBULL, CANONGATE,

1806.

The first edition of Patrick Graham's
Sketches, 1806.

the title-page changed to show that it included 'that district of country in which the scene of the 'Lady of the Lake' is laid.' Two years later a revised second edition came out as *Sketches of Perthshire*, complete with a detailed map of the locations in *The Lady of the Lake*, a stanza from the poem itself – and the complete story of Kirk's abduction. The Kirk insertion is noted as having a resemblance to the story of the captivity in Fairyland of Ethert Brand, in 'The Ballad of Alice Brand,' a part of *The Lady of the Lake*. Graham gives no source for the Kirk story, and Kirk's biographer MacLean notes that none of Kirk's friends such as Colin Campbell of Carwhin or Revd James Kirkwood mention it in their letters within a month of his death. MacLean was the first to suggest Graham had created the story as a compliment to Scott, who had freely acknowledged that he had gleaned a number of local superstitions used in *The Lady of the Lake* from Graham's 1806 work. Lizanne Henderson and Edward Cowan in *Scottish Fairy Belief* gently suggest: 'We may be forgiven the suspicion that the learned minister was inventing, rather than preserving tradition'. In my opinion, sometime between the 1810 publication of *The Lady of the Lake* and 1812, Graham's fertile imagination, possibly assisted by commercial pressures, made up the fairy abduction story. In 1830 Scott, the most popular author of his day, included the episode in *Letters on Demonology and Witchcraft,* thus ensuring the fictitious episode became widely known. Local historian Louis Stott's article 'The Legend of Robert Kirk Reconsidered' – which has been invaluable in compiling this section, along with his booklet *The Enchantment of the Trossachs* – makes the point: 'The legend of Kirk's death has taken on a life of its own… The legend is interesting because it is of comparatively recent origin, it is unusually complex, involving a number of folk elements, and it is *continuing to evolve.*' (My italics.)

By 1911, when W.Y. Evans Wentz (*The Fairy-faith in Celtic Countries*) visited Aberfoyle, most people he talked to knew the legend; some thought it was just Kirk's spirit that had been taken,

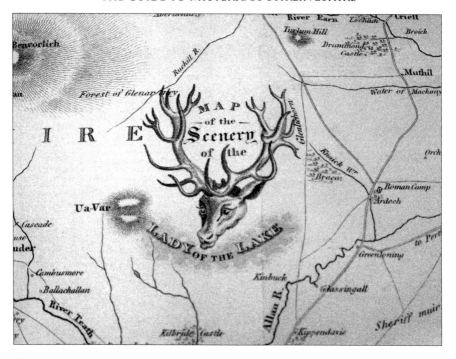

The fold-out 'Map of the Scenery of *The Lady of the Lake*' in Graham's 1812 edition.

but others believed his coffin was full of stones, and both body and soul were inside the Fairy Knoll. Evans Wentz interviewed the current minister, Revd William Taylor, who dismissed the story as mere fabrication – 'of course there is not the least doubt of his body being in the grave' – yet the story persists, possibly because, combined with the posthumous appearances of Kirk's spirit, it blends folk-tale with popular elements of the Resurrection.

In 1943 folklorist Katharine Briggs heard another story from a pregnant woman who had rented the Old Manse at Aberfoyle:

> If her baby was born in the Manse and christened there, Kirk could be freed from fairyland if a dirk was thrust into the seat of his chair. The chair was still there – or the chair supposed locally to be his – so that it would have been still possible to disenchant him.

Briggs thought 'this was only a whimsical belief on her part, but she had learnt it from the local people, for she was a stranger in the place.' Briggs wrote this to Stewart Sanderson on 10 March 1964; it is quoted in Sanderson's introduction to his version of *The Secret Commonwealth*. Louis Stott pours cold water on part of the episode: the manse was not let during the war, as it was occupied by the minister and his family; nor was there any chair supposed to be Kirk's. It seems likely the young woman concerned was the wife of an officer billeted in Manse Road. Her baby was born in Aberfoyle and named Robert.

Exactly *where* Kirk was taken, and resides to this day, is a subject for debate. The overwhelming consensus is that the spot is Doon Hill, east of Kirkton at NS525002. Mrs J. MacGregor, who kept the key to the old churchyard which contains Kirk's tomb, told Evans Wentz in 1911 that Kirk was 'taken into the Fairy Knoll, which she pointed to just across a little valley in front of us, and is there yet, for the hill is full of caverns, and in them the "good people" have their homes.' From the description this can only be Doon Hill. And the official Fairy Hill walk signposts this hill, complete with images of the *Amanita muscaria* fairy toadstool (follow the waymarked track

The Minister's Pine on Doon
Hill, Aberfoyle.

east from the car park at the end of the Kirkton road until you meet the Fairy Hill signpost, then ascend). The clearing on the summit provides a scene guaranteed to astonish: a single Scots pine decorated with hundreds of offerings and messages to the fairies, with countless others attached to the trees and bushes for a great distance around. Stones, crystals, ceramic fairies, beads, Tibetan prayer flags, clothes, crosses, messages on postcards, messages hidden in bags, messages on tourist flyers – the profusion is overwhelming. In *Scottish Fairy Belief* Henderson and Cowan say the practice was first noticed in 1996 following the DUNBLANE massacre – hundreds of ribbons or cloths offering prayers for the dead and injured were attached to the pine. Louis Stott (private communication 22 April 2008) notes that although the massacre undoubtedly prompted an upsurge, 'It was commonplace for local children to leave tokens (coins embedded in the Minister's Pine) long before Dunblane.' The practice is subject to fashions: when I first visited in 2002 the offerings had colonised the nearby vegetation, and many of the messages were addressed to 'Fairy Rose'. By 2008 Rose had disappeared, with the messages addressed only to 'the fairies'. Here we have a recently instigated, inchoate, evolving piece of modern folklore. It is a very powerful place. Of course, many of the messages are trivial in the extreme – wishes for lottery wins, promotion, even for the weather to improve. But others are deeply moving – photographs of relatives suffering from cancer; messages such as 'I wish to heal my relationship with my parents,' or a woman's wish for her terminally ill husband to have a good quality of life and not to suffer when the end comes.

There is indeed something striking about the focus of the shrine, the so-called 'Minister's Pine,' in which Kirk's spirit is sometimes said to be trapped. Seen from a distance, say the graveyard, outwith summer, it is a bright evergreen splash towering over the bare branches of the deciduous trees that surround it – it is very much an *omphalos* tree, a singular distinctive point on the summit. It seems to *mean something*; it's no surprise it has attracted attention.

In 1936 the literary weekly *John o'London's* published a series of letters from people who had seen fairies. In March that year Struan Robertson reported meeting a fairy on Doon Hill. It was

One of the many fairy figures
on Doon Hill.

very friendly and showed him 'a wonderful sight', although there are no more details. Robertson
also saw several fairies on the Isle of Arran (see my *The Guide to Mysterious Arran*). In the summer
of 1982 R.J. Stewart was meditating beside a rowan tree on the hill when he found himself
'communing with someone… a short man, fairly plump, who declared himself to be Robert
Kirk, fully alive in the faery realm.' He informed Stewart that many men from different time
periods had been physically translated into Fairyland, and together they formed a brotherhood
or order called the 'Justified Men'. He then invited Stewart to join them. Stewart felt as if a
doorway was being opened from one world to another, and was about to step through when
a car horn brought him to his senses. That night, Stewart experienced vivid dreams containing
teachings on the fairy mysteries, much of which appeared in his subsequent books (including an
edition of *The Secret Commonwealth*), and eventually enabled him to make mental, not physical,
journeys into the Otherworld. Stewart also mentions that 'other people have experienced similar
contact with him [Kirk] in the region.' So Doon Hill is the place to be.

And yet. And yet. Patrick Graham wrote that on the fateful day Kirk was walking 'upon a little
eminence to the west of the present manse.' Doon Hill is *east* of site of the former manse. The
only hill to the west is Kirkton Hill (NS511004), which has nothing of the fairy hill about it.
Perhaps Graham made a simple mistake – elsewhere, he gets Kirk's date of birth and age wrong.
But there is another, better candidate, south of Doon Hill and south-east of Kirkton – and it is
still called Fairy Knowe (NS527995). I am indebted to Louis Stott's articles for setting me on this
tack. Descend Doon Hill, turn left (south) and go straight ahead at the crossroads, ascending the
hill via the yellow waymarked trail. When the path turns east it passes three distinctive mounds –
the very essence of fairy hills. There are no offerings or messages at this atmospheric place. But I
suggest it is a possibility that if Robert Kirk is indeed in Fairyland, it is *here*.

Fairy Knowe from Doon Hill.

Kirk's legend continues to be embroidered. A quick check on the fount of all truth and knowledge, the internet, brings up sites claiming he ran seven times around the top of Doon Hill trying to summon the Devil and died on the seventh circuit, that his graveslab is deliberately aligned on Doon Hill, that his grave has been searched and found to be empty except for stones, and similar nonsense.

The Secret Commonwealth remained in manuscript form for well over a century. The first (very limited) edition was published in 1815, with another, only slightly less limited, edition coming out in 1893, accompanied by an erudite but not always helpful introduction by Andrew Lang. 1933 saw the first widely available version, garnished with a poetic introduction by Cunninghame Graham (quoted above). 1976 saw a revised edition with a very good academic commentary by folklorist Stewart Sanderson; R.J. Stewart's 'new age' version came out in 1990 (revised edition 2007). Probably the best version to get is the 2006 edition introduced by Marina Warner. For local insights and analysis, *the* source is the various works by Louis Stott.

Kirk's gravestone is in the east end of the old cemetery in Kirkton (NN 51840050), between Aberfoyle and the walk to Doon Hill. The inscription reads *Hic Sepultus Ille Evangelii Promulgator Accuratus Et Linguae Hiberniae Lumen M. Robertus Kirk Aberfoile Pastor Obiit 14 Maii 1692 Aetat.48* ('Here lies the body of a promoter of the true Gospel and light of the Irish language [i.e. Gaelic] Robert Kirk Pastor of Aberfoyle died 14 May 1692 aged 48') and is accompanied by a carving of a thistle and a crossed sword and pastoral staff. The inscription was renewed in the 1890s. On the day I visited the stone was home to a small ceramic fairy. The fact that the flat stone is aligned directly on Doon Hill is of no consequence — so are all the other table stones, it being conventional to have them face east. Outside the roofless church are a pair of large iron *morte gardes*, mortsafes used to protect recently buried corpses from bodysnatchers. A contribution by 'J.H.' to *Northern Notes and Queries* in 1889 describes their use. Two thick planks were placed in the bottom of the grave, and four strong iron bars screwed into the planks; the bars were hinged near the upper ends. The coffin was lowered into the gave, the mortsafe put over it, and the

Robert Kirk's gravestone, Aberfoyle.
Note tiny fairy figure.

hinged rods bent over, interlinked, and padlocked. The keys were given to the nearest relation. The grave was then filled up. When sufficient time had elapsed for the corpse to have decayed, the rods were unlocked and unscrewed, the mortsafe lifted, and the planks left *in situ*.

There are a few eighteenth-century gravestones carved with symbols of mortality but the best example is a shadow of its former self. In 1904 David Christison drew the extraordinary carvings on the gravestone of David Tod, died 1756. On the west face a skeleton Death, with spade in one hand, is impaling a man dressed in a short striped jacket and wide breeches. The point of the spear is sticking out of the man's back, but he still grasps the shaft as if to remove it, and brandishes a nondescript but feeble-looking weapon at the Grim Reaper. Beside him are two items, a glove and what appears to be a one-handled quaich turned upside down. The stone is now toppled and this face is no longer visible, and the east face is so mossed over it is difficult to make out the carvings Christison recorded – at the top, a winged soul hovering over a recumbent figure in a kind of dressing gown shroud, with a cloth covering the face, below which is a large half-human half-animal face with protruding tongue, and mason's tools in the side pilasters. The corners of the stone each have a sculptured man's head. The term 'the Cosmic Joker' is shorthand for the way the universe sometimes seems to toy with us when it comes to things like personal names: here the Joker works things so that just as 'Kirk' is a good surname for a minister, 'Tod' is German for 'death'.

AROUND ABERFOYLE

The B829 west of the village goes through the Pass of Aberfoyle, with the craggy height of Craigmore to the north. In *A Week At Bridge of Allan* Charles Roger claims that when huge rocks fall from the crag, it precedes a death or disaster in the ducal house of Montrose, while

Pair of anti-bodysnatching
iron mortsafes, Kirkton
graveyard, Aberfoyle.

Buchanan's Popular Guide dryly notes, 'Legend has it that when a rock falls a Macgregor dies, not
at all an unlikely story if the Macgregor were lodged underneath when the rock was dislodged.'
The foot of the loch just west of Milton (NN501015) is the site of a battle of the Civil Wars,
in 1653, when the Royalist John Graham of Duchray defeated a detachment of Cromwellian
soldiers under command of Colonel Kidd, governor of Stirling Castle. One of Kidd's officers
was shot by a private gentleman from the window of his house, and his body was interred in a
little knoll called Bard nan Sassenach, the Englishman's Thicket.

In *Notes on the District of Menteith* Cunninghame Graham notes a number of long cairns
above the slate quarry of Aberfoyle on CraigVadh (presumably Creag a' Mhadaidh, NN513037),
said to mark fallen Lochaber raiders overtaken by the pursuing men of Lennox and Menteith.

LOCH ARD

In another example of fiction becoming 'reality', coachmen and guides would point out a
gnarled oak on the north shore where Bailie Nicol Jarvie, having lost a contest, was suspended
by his clothes. An episode from Scott's *Rob Roy*. Which is a novel. Scott worked on the book at
Ledard, a MacGregor focus, and the nearby Helen's Pool and Waterfall (NN459028) is named
after Rob Roy's wife Helen Mary MacGregor, although this may be another one of Walter's
constructs. The path to Ben Venue passes the spot. Rob Roy's name is also attached to a cave
on the south shore (NN481015), although whether the connection is genuine is unknown.
Buchanan's Popular Guide notes that a gentleman in the district had a gamekeeper who was
black. When the gentleman took his friends to the cave, he would call out, 'Are you in, Rob?' –
at which point the gamekeeper, sequestered in advance, would pop out, 'greatly to the alarm
and discomfiture of the company.' Oh how we laughed.

LOCH CHON

Teapot Bridge, between Lochs Ard and Chon (NN440031) is named for a cottage where whisky was sold as tea. The name of the loch itself, meaning Loch of the Dog, apparently refers to the dog-headed monster that lurked within and would drag unsuspecting travellers into the depths. It could swallow a child whole. In *Sketches of Perthshire* (1812) Patrick Graham mentions a fairy cove, Coir-shi'an, somewhere above Loch Chon, and another round eminence near the head of the loch, 'by the skirts of which many are still afraid to pass after sunset.' If a person goes alone round this hill or one of its neighbours nine times on Hallow-eve, a door opens: but if venturing within, beware of the usual fairy traps designed to befuddle and imprison mortals.

GARTMORE

On the village green (NS522974) stands a memorial to R.B. Cunninghame Graham, aristocrat, Scottish nationalist, South American adventurer (the names of Uruguay and Argentina on the memorial attest to this), horse-lover (there is also a portrait of his favourite steed, Pampa) and all-round character. He was also an author of considerable note; he wrote the introduction for the 1933 edition of *The Secret Commonwealth*, and had an interest in folklore and the supernatural. His book *Notes on the District of Menteith* has the following chapter titles: 'Atavism,' 'Traditional,' 'Pantheistic' and 'Some Reflections on the Incontinence of Kings'. Chapter one includes '…a digression as to whether religious belief may not modify the human countenance.' Fairies, he mused, would soon adapt to the modern world, and 'dance as merrily upon the girders of a railway bridge as formerly upon the grass and tussocks.' My favourite passage from the book is very appropriate on an autumnal day in the area:

> Mist and more mist, mist which clings mysteriously about the hills, it makes one feel they hold some mystery, and that behind the vapoury canopy something is brewing fatal to mankind. Figures and faces seem to peep out from the folds of the intangible and awful covering, and contemplate a raid upon the world, and a sheep's bleat borne down the wind sounds just as if some spirit, prisoned in the mist, bewailed itself and asked for sympathy.

(For more on Cunninghame Graham, see INCHMAHOME PRIORY.)

The ruin of Gartartan Castle (NS53019780), almost invisible in vegetation on the estate of Gartmore House, is barely worth visiting. Dun, in *Summer at the Lake of Monteith* (1867) wrote that old people could remember the gibbet-pin and some other items required for neck twisting remaining on the old walls, and was sufficiently taken by the castle's then atmosphere to pen some lines:

> Gartartan, 'mid thy dungeons deep
> The spirits nightly revels keep;
> And ghosts of those that went the way
> When Gartmore barons held the sway,
> Wander among thy vaults at will,
> And haunt thy dismal chambers still.

The elaborate seventeenth-century sundial which once stood in front of Gartmore House is now in the Cayzer family burial enclosure behind the parish church on the main street. Known locally as the moon-dial, its obelisk form is a design unique to Scotland. The Flanders Moss once extended to the hills of Gartmore. A huge stone, known as the Clach nan Lung (the stone of the waves), set with an iron ring for the mooring of boats, once stood of Fir Hill (NS537969) but was broken up by a farmer.

In the late 1980s journalist Fidelma Cook moved with her family to Gartloaning, a seventeenth century farmhouse 'constructed on an ancient ley line' north-west of Gartmore. The stairs were originally in front of the door, but later they had been rotated and the front entrance repositioned. Fidelma's mother started seeing an elderly woman with full skirts and apron, and her hair in bun, who walked down the stairs that were no longer there and passed through the vanished door. Fidelma's four-year-old son Pierce spoke of 'My Lady' who tickled him in his bedroom at night. When Pierce's nanny was downstairs there would sometimes be a sudden rush of air and she would sense the swish of skirts going past. An octogenarian local man told Fidelia it was a well-known ghost named Old Mary. In 1991 Fidelma's mother had an aneurysm and died in hospital. The previous owner then revealed to Fidelma that her mother had told her she knew she would not be returning from the hospital, because just before she left for the last time she saw Old Mary who was this time sweeping and dusting. In the kitchen she suddenly turned to look straight at Fidelma's mother, who therefore knew her time was up. (Source: Roddy Martine, *Supernatural Scotland*.) For another Fidelma story, see EDINAMPLE CASTLE.

In the nineteenth century the Gartmore miller knew when he was grinding dead-bread (the meal to be made into funeral cakes) because the machinery made a distinctive sound (George Williams, 'Local Superstitions').

There is a small crop of rock art to the west and south-west of Gartmore. A slab in the farmyard of Blarnaboard (NS508977) has a cup mark with four rings, and slightly further north-east there are nine cup marks on a rock outcrop (NS50979795). The west end of a long rocky ridge at Spittal has a footprint which may be artificial, or may be just due to natural weathering (NS507972). Corrie has two sculptured boulders: 380yds (350m) south of the farm (NS49559504, seven cups and one ring, and at least eight cups) and 330yds (300m) south-west (NS491951, twenty-three cup marks). In 1969 the farmer was about to blow up the former boulder, and was dissuaded at the last minute.

The 'moon dial' sundial, Gartmore church.

10

THE SOUTH-WEST FROM TOUCH
TO STRATHBLANE

TOUCH

Somewhere on the summit of the Touch (pronounced 'Toosh') Hills was St Corbet's Well. Anyone who drank its waters before sunrise on the first Sunday in May (or on May Day) would be guaranteed health and life for another year. It seems to have remained popular until the early nineteenth century, but the crowds attracted hucksters and food vendors and eventually the sacred virtue withdrew in protest at the amount of whisky being consumed on site. The scenic waterfall of Gilmour's Linn has a deep cave behind it; unlike caves further to the west, this was said to have provided refuge not to Rob Roy or Robert the Bruce, but Bonnie Prince Charlie after fleeing the field of Culloden in 1746. There is a chance this might be true, because the 'Young Pretender' stayed at Touch House during his triumphant march south the previous year, so presumably he had sympathisers in the area. Take the minor road west out of Cambusbarron, park near the waterworks, follow the path north then west to Touch Glen.

In August 1897 a heavy, but not exceptional, shower of hail followed a thunderstorm. Shortly afterwards a shepherd walking on the hill about 5 p.m. saw what he supposed was a sheep on its back, possibly killed by lightning. He then realised it was not a member of his flock, but a block of ice the size of a sheep. It was lying in bracken on the west side of the road leading to farmhouse of Sheilbrae, about 400yds (365m) from the public road, which would put it about NS752904, off the minor road between the Carron Valley Reservoir and Cambusbarron. The ice block was seen the following morning by another shepherd, by which time hot and sultry weather had broken it into several pieces covering about a 1 square yard (0.84m²). David Morris got the news from the local vet, Mr Stewart, and then interviewed the second shepherd, before giving a report to the Stirling Natural History and Archaeological Society. There have been many reports of large hailstones from around the world (the technical term is megacryo-meteors); this is the first time I have heard of one the size of a sheep.

GARGUNNOCK

The 1774 church has three external stairways leading to separate galleries, presumably for lairds wishing not to meet. The cross and crescent on the finials are from the older church on the site – from some angles the crescent looks more like a pair of horns. The well-kept graveyard has stones with coats of arms, blacksmith's tools and one with the quill, ink-bottle and ruler of a schoolmaster.

A fallen standing stone lies on a ridge at Broompark (NS704943). The signposted Waterfall Walk passes Downie's Loup, named after a horseman who is reputed to have tried to leap the fall and may have been killed on the third attempt. Excavations at Leckie Broch (NS69269399) have shown that it was built and destroyed in the first century AD, to be shortly replaced by a promontory fort which again had a brief life in the first half of the second century. As these dates were concurrent with Roman occupations, the suggestion is that the broch succumbed to Roman catapults. The finds are in the Hunterian Museum, Glasgow. A large rock on the outer wall has at least eight cup marks.

The kirk session had several dealings with charming. In May 1626 Stein Maltman (see chapter two) was summoned in connection with the healing of a cow. Five years later a remarkable case was recorded involving sympathetic magic, liminality, the transfer of disease, and name taboos. Margey Ker confessed she consulted Rosie Graham about a sick cow. Rosie told her to go to some of her neighbours' houses and seek from them 'the thing that slew the mice' without speaking the proper name and not allowing anyone else to say it. The cat was to be handed three times round the cow and then thrown out of the door. Margey was also to repeat the process with her left shoe, and each time slap the cow with it. She was then to take some of the cow's milk and throw it out at a hole of the house where no light came in, and take it from the outside and mix it with the water of a march or boundary burn, and bring it home and put in three times in the cow's' ear. Within four days from the cure the cow was fine. Margey was ordered to make her public repentance in sackcloth. Source: Horton McNeill, 'Glimpses of Church Life in Old Days: From Records of Gargunnock Parish'.

Helen Mitchell was brought before the kirk session for witchcraft on 7 May 1650. The background was a series of neighbourhood disputes. She had complained to Robert McIlchrist that he did not look after her cow which pastured with his herd. He reproved her and so she cursed his cattle. Shortly after he found in his yard four or five 'sundry sorts of flesh as raters eirs puddings' (I have no idea what this is) and within a year fourteen of his cattle died and he became ill. He desired she come to him but she refused until compelled to do so by Johne Gilfillan, officer of Buchlyvie. She then drank to Robert, said she hoped he would be well, and left just as the cattle were coming in. She asked about the first cow and was told it was Robert's only newly calfed cow. On hearing this she said she was sorry it happened to be in front, and immediately the cow began to 'ramish' and died shortly after, while Robert got well at the same time – Helen had taken the illness off Robert but had to transfer it to the first living thing she saw. James Monteth of Wester Carden said there was strife between him and Helen and she had caused a calf to be born blind and a cow to sicken. Helen entered Walter Parland's house in Buchlyvie; when she heard James was there she hid beneath a bed. James poked her out with a sword and took her to his house, vowing that if she did not mend his cow she would pay for it. She acquiesced, went in alone to the cow several times, and the next morning the animal ate as normal. One night Johne Ure met Helen, who tried to hide. When asked where she was going, she replied 'to get a grey stone for heart fevers but it would not be for the better that she had met him.' Johne told others about the encounter and when she heard this Helen vowed revenge. Shortly after Johne visited Johne McLaughlan's house when Helen was there. He then seemed to lose his senses, went out of the house, wandered west to Caslie, fell over a crag, and lay comatose for eighteen hours, and when carried home was speechless for fifteen days. When Helen agreed to visit him his speech returned. James McIlchrist said that his son Robert Watsone found Helen and others helping a sick cow by holding an 'old hobbill of a shoe' and goose feathers to its nose. Helen tried to prevent Robert from seeing what they were doing. Robert went away but lost his mind, and wandered aimlessly through ponds and mires. His grandmother Jonet Galbraith went to Helen and after a conversation Robert was well. A request was made for Helen to be imprisoned, but there is no record of whether this took place, or what the outcome was. (Main source: Fergusson, *Scottish Social Sketches of the 17th Century*.)

Later generations had a different take on the gravity of tales of witchcraft and magic. When J.W. Campbell delivered a paper on relics of folklore in the area to the Stirling Natural History and Archaeological Society in 1927, he called it 'Humorous Reminiscences'. Campbell's first informant was his old gardener, John Beaton, who related that in his youth a local woman named Mrs Macfarlane had told him she knew a local family who consulted a warlock about the death of some of their cattle. He told them to take out the heart of the dead cow, to stick needles or pins in it, and boil it on the fire. No one was to come into the house while this was being carried out. A neighbour, suspected of witchcraft, came to the door and demanded admittance, but was refused. She said, 'Tak' aff that pat frae the fire and the spell will be ta'en aff y're beasts.' When a boy Beaton was asked by a neighbour to dig a grave for a dead cow. He started to dig a suitably sized pit when the man interrupted him, telling him to cut up the carcass and bury the parts in holes made just outside the byre door, so the cows might walk over them and receive the virtue. These episodes probably date from before 1850, as does the episode involving Macdonald, the local doctor, who demolished an old byre on his property and found a bottle above the door. Filled with quicksilver and twigs, it had been placed there many years previously, prescribed by a witch-doctor from Campsie to counter cattle loss. The messenger who received it had to return to Kippen by a different road from the one by which she came. Macdonald's by-then elderly daughter showed the bottle to Campbell in the 1890s. When the manse was being upgraded about 1887 the workmen came across a disused chimney in which was suspended a piece of rowan tree wood, to prevent evil spirits descending the lum.

The ruined old church on Station Road (NS65179485) has a small number of occupational carvings on the gravestones. William Chrystal (*The Kingdom of Kippen*) records that Revd Potter, minister of the parish in the early eighteenth century, allowed his pigs to roam free in the graveyard, despite many protests. The locals therefore smeared a black pig with tar, tied its tail to the bell rope, and set it on fire. The bell rang furiously and it appeared that the Devil himself was the bellman. The pigs were thereafter penned up. The fate of the barbecued animal is not recorded. Contrary to Presbyterian orthodoxy, burials continued within the church until 1777. The original pre-Reformation church may, or may not – neither the documentary evidence nor the archaeology is clear – have been on the knoll at Keir Hill of Dasher, just to the north-east of the village (NS65299511), although yet another suggestion is the earthwork to the north at (NS65349511). Barely 100yds (91m) west from the first alleged church site, behind Kirkhill Cottage, is St Mauvais' Well (NS65259504), now just some dull stonework and a pipe. Mauvais may be Mobhi, usually spelt Dabhi, who according to the *Annals of Ulster* died in 544. St Mauvie's Fair used to held in Kippen on 26 October. Outside the current church is the shaft of the old market cross.

Boquhan House, to the east of the village (NS67029473, private) has a grotto containing Prince's Well, dated 1790. By tradition, Bonnie Prince Charlie's Jacobite Army stopped here on 1 February 1746; they were retreating and would shortly be annihilated at Culloden. Beside the walled garden is Lady's Well, with a stone inscribed MARIE CAMPBELL IFC POSUIT 1792. Nearby is a roofless octagonal folly. South-west along the minor road to Craigend is Dougal's Tower, a natural sandstone feature near Muirend named after either an excise officer whose mutilated remains were found near here, or a Covenanter hiding from dragoons. Tradition avers a suicide was buried somewhere in or near Boquhan Glen, at a liminal place where the boundaries of the lands of three lairds met. The *New Statistical Account* of 1845 records that an old tenant of Ballochleam (NS653912), searching for limestone in a spot long thought to be the site of an undated battle between the Leckies and the Grahams, 'found some pieces of brass armour, with the points of spears, and a great quantity of different kinds of bones. He said he intended to go on, but a thought came that he might raise the plague.' Chrystal notes the tradition of a house in the centre of Loch Laggan (NS625925); next to the house was a spring covered with a huge stone which, being removed, flooded the house. There was indeed a crannog in the loch, approached by a causeway from the north shore, but all was submerged when the level of the loch was raised.

ARNPRIOR

The Kingdom of Kippen speaks of Tamas, a man of prodigious creativity in his tales told to a credulous group who gathered at Arnprior Smiddy. In one story he tried to fathom a supposedly bottomless pool and got stuck underwater for twenty minutes until 'the king of the otters', the size of young cow, mistook Tamas' legs for a pair of salmon and accidentally freed him. He also met a bogle after midnight on Clash-brae. The entity looked like a handcart on end, and kept pace with him until a cock crowed and the bogle shot through a malt barn in a burst of flame. The next morning Tamas heard that about the time he encountered the unearthly thing, Donald Stalker had died.

BUCHLYVIE

The abused old graveyard at the abandoned North Church (NS57349386) is depressing and neglected; a few symbols can just be made out on the mossed and damaged stones but most of the eighteenth-century carvings recorded by David Christison in 1905 are no longer visible. The 'Fairy Knowe' east of the village is also a disappointment (NS58569425). Excavation found it to be a stout-walled broch occupied in the first and second centuries AD by people who were remelting Roman metalwork to make their own tools and ornaments; a stone cist containing human bones was also dug up sometime before 1796. These days it is very obvious, next to the main road, but is difficult to access, covered with gorse and thorns, and featureless.

North of Buchlyvie are the farms of Nether and Over Easter Offerance, names which clearly appealed to novelist Iain Banks. Banks set his 1995 novel *Whit* in a place called High Easter Offerance, home to the vision-inspired Luskentyrian love-and-peace cult. The sect avoid modern technology and believe that you should avoid the main highways of life and stick to the back ways – both metaphorically and literally – so when the nineteen-year-old Whit has to journey to London she starts by travelling to Stirling on the River Forth using an inflated tyre. *Whit* is one of Banks' funnier satires (on both religion and modern life), and he clearly enjoys the sound of nearby placenames such as the Pendicles of Collymoon.

In *Summer at the Lake of Monteith* Dun describes 'a Buchlyvie Lyke-Wake of the olden time,' as related to him by an old friend. The episode probably took place at the start of the nineteenth century. In November both the aged taxman of Upper Kepdourie and his old horse died the same day. The guests attending the wake arrived and got stuck into the whisky, toasting the departed whose corpse lay at the other end of the room. Some wags fixed a rope around the neck of the old man, hiding it with the bedclothes, and drew it out the window. They dragged the dead mare to the front of the kitchen door onto its back, the four legs dangling in the air. In this position no one could leave without stumbling over it and falling into the manure-pile. Inside, the blacksmith was telling of a twilight encounter he had recently had with the ghost of Mungo. Mungo's Tree was on the roadside a little below Buchlyvie station; he planted it and hung himself on one of its branches. On this occasion Mungo was dressed in his old red nightcap, blue trousers, and looking up at the branch while sitting on the barrow that wheeled home his corpse. The smith was about to ask his former neighbour, 'Is that you Mungo?' when the spirit flew off. The atmosphere suitably lubricated by this authentic tale of the supernatural, the wakers clamoured for more whisky. The smith banged on the table, jumped up, and drank the health of the departed, as did the others. The wags then pulled on the rope, the corpse slammed upright, and fell down in the midst of the drunken company. Everyone fled out the door, tripped over the horse – which, in the darkness and panic they mistook for the Devil – and landed right into the dung pit. Take note, writers of funeral scenes for soap operas.

BALFRON

The Balfron name has unusual associations both old and new. In legend, the villagers were on the hill – either working, or, depending on the version, attending some kind of pre-Christian or at least quasi-pagan ceremony – when they heard screams from the settlement. Rushing down, they found all the children had been devoured by wolves. Thereafter the place was known as Bail'-a-Bhroin, 'the town of mourning'. And in March 2001 the village heritage group set up a promotional website to point out that; a) Balfron village was a lovely place to visit and b) it had no connection with the inhospitable and dangerous planet Balfron featured in the *Star Wars* movies, the obsessive interest of sci-fi fans notwithstanding.

The Clachan, now on the northern edge of the village, was the historic heart. Here stands the venerable Clachan Oak, a traditional shelterer of William Wallace and home of the punishment jougs. *Buchanan's Popular Guide* relates a tale from the end of the eighteenth century. A thief was attached to the jougs. Her vagrant husband got bored of sitting with her so he repaired to the Clachan House inn. She got irritated at his prolonged absence, kicked away the stones on which she stood, and was strangled in the jougs.

The adjacent churchyard (NS54808926) has a few carvings including a superb 1827 stone with a large winged soul above two large serpents coiled around what may be an apple.

Ballikinrain Castle (NS56298724, Church of Scotland Child Services Centre, no access) is a grandiose example of Victorian Baronial Gothic, with gargoyles on the gateways. The estate was broken up in 1912 and the furnishings sold. In June 1913 the entire castle, having lain empty for eighteen months, was gutted by fire. Suffragettes were suspected but an account from an unnamed newspaper in Comyn Webster's *The Parish of Killearn* suggests something stranger:

> Much stress is put on the appearance of two ladies, thickly veiled, in the district one Sabbath evening. They were seen between Killearn and Strathblane, along with two men, consulting what appeared to be a map. The ladies had bicycles but the men had none. Later in the evening they were seen by an estate hand in the hollow near Ballikinrain Smithy consulting a paper, which they rolled up on being observed. A farm servant saw them… and their manner aroused his curiosity. Their method of crossing a burn convinced him that they were not women, but men.

DRYMEN

The elaborate, gloriously eccentric mid-nineteenth-century Buchanan Castle (NS46198860) is a fenced-off dangerous ruin but it can still be viewed easily as it is boarded by modern housing and a golf course. During the Second World War it was used as a military hospital, its most famous patient being Hitler's deputy leader Rudolph Hess who was treated for injuries he sustained on his bizarre parachute jump into Scotland, apparently an attempt to persuade the British aristocracy to sue for peace with Germany. Given that Rudie died in Spandau Prison in Berlin it is unlikely that it is he who is responsible for the ghostly moaning or gasping said to have been heard between 11 p.m. and dawn in the summer months (the specificity of this timeframe suggests a seasonal natural explanation, such as birds).

A still extant holy well dedicated to St Maha or Machar can be found between Creityhall and Moorpark, on the hill above Milton, north-west of Drymen (NS45739180). The water issues from a turf-covered horseshoe-shaped mound, and was once a cloutie well, where people would drink and leave pieces of cloth behind on the adjacent tree; as the rag decayed, so would their ailment fade away.

CROFTAMIE

A stone on the north bank of Endrick Water at NS48478655 bears the simulacrum of a footprint, created by natural weathering. Close to the south bank of the Endrick, somewhere west of Finnich Blair and south of Dalnair was the site of the now-vanished St Vildrin's Well (given as NS49108568). It was apparently much-visited in pre-Reformation times and as late as 1851 the well still had a stone 2ft 6ins (76cm) high, incised with a figure said to be the patron saint. Within a few decades the carved stone had been broken up for building material. St Vildrin is an entirely obscure saint; this is possibly the only site dedicated to him (or her).

THE WHANGIE

A moderate walk from the Queen's View car park on the A809 gives access to the Whangie, a spectacular and twisty rock canyon some 50ft (15m) deep, 2–10ft (60cm-3m) wide and 300ft (91m) long. 'Whang' means a slice, or anything long and supple, like a whip or a bootlace. The creation story is that the Devil was flying back from a social with the Campsie witches when he flicked his tail, the pointed tip of which scored the Whangie in the rock. Further north-west across the moors is Stockie Muir Chambered Cairn (NS47908127). The chambers have collapsed and one of the two portal stones has fallen, but this is still a reasonable site. A broken rotary quern was found in the cairn (it is now in Kelvingrove Art Gallery and Museum, Glasgow); 'Canmore' suggests that this find indicates that the cairn 'may have provided both material and a site for an Iron Age dwelling.' Further north-west again a single slab of stone is all that remains of the large cairn at Cameron Muir (NS46908271) removed about 1825, at which date were found two cists containing bones. Catythirsty Well sits on the east of the main road (NS510813). Webster's *The Parish of Killearn* suggests it is named after a servant girl named Katie who was making her way home to Drymen from Glasgow with her wages when she was robbed and murdered at this spot; me, I'm betting it's really a corruption of a Gaelic word.

KILLEARN

The old church, dated 1734, with human faces carved on the keystones of the upper window, is now roofless (NS52298587). The large old graveyard has a couple of skulls and crossed bones. Between this and the Victorian parish church is the towering 103ft (31m) high obelisk of the Buchanan Memorial, erected 1788. George Buchanan (1506–82) was a local boy who went on to become a great Latin scholar and poet and tutor to both Mary Queen of Scots and James VI. Buchanan's reputation was clearly the reason why he was thought the very person to threaten the Danish King with the magical return of FLANDERS MOSS.

Nicholas Buchanan – a woman – was accused of making wax and clay images of Lords Cochran and Hamilton, and putting them over a fire to kill them. She was first arraigned in Dunbarton on 5 September 1679 but the trial was deserted. Another trial was held in Stirling, where she was ordered to appear at Edinburgh, but the High Court there also abandoned the case on 5 January 1680. This case is so far from the usual run of Scottish witchtrials – image magic used to murder two high-ranking individuals – that it is doubly frustrating to have no further details.

John Napier, the inventor of logarithms, lived at the now-vanished Gartness Castle to the west (NS50258652). The 1845 *New Statistical Account*, referencing the cultural climate of the sixteenth century, notes:

> The seclusion of Gartness, an isolated corner, far from the haunts of men, was congenial to a mind devoted to the mysteries of theological and mathematical science. In that sequestered spot, living like a hermit, and engaged in studies, which few, if any, in these parts could comprehend, it is not to be wondered at, that he was looked upon by the common people as a wizard, and was consulted as one who had insight into futurity, and intercourse with invisible beings.

STRATHBLANE

Between the West Highland Way and the Blane Water is Dumgoyach, another of Stirling's stone rows (NS53288072). The five stones run in a south-west to north-east line, although one has no socket hole and has presumably been added via field clearance, making this a four-stone row, now ruined (only one stone remains standing). Excavation obtained a radiocarbon date of 2860+/-270BC, that is, Neolithic – Aubrey Burl in *From Carnac to Callanish* suggests this means it is not a stone row but the remains of the façade of a chambered cairn. Dumgoyach Farm itself (NS52818121) has a cross-marked medieval graveslab in the buildings, possibly re-used from a burial-ground elsewhere. The East Gates of mostly Victorian Duntreath Castle have swans' heads above the gatepiers (NS53648108). Somewhere to the east of the castle was Blane's Well, where St Blane or Blaan is said to have baptized the pagan locals.

In 1697 the Kirk Session of Killearn issued a warning against necromancy, and particularly the spells and charms of Donald Fergusson in Strathblane; we know nothing more about Donald. Inside the parish church of 1802 is a worn heraldic slab set into the floor; a brass plaque claims it marks the grave of Princess Mary, sister of James I, but this has not been verified. The old graveyard (NS56367939) contains the Edmonston Mausoleum and a prehistoric standing stone 3ft 9ins (1.1m) high. A second standing stone 4ft (1.2m) high is at Broadgate Farm just to the east (NS56927940). When it fell down an excavation took place, revealing a Bronze Age cinerary urn containing the cremated remains of a child, inserted next to the earlier Neolithic stone. The stone has now been re-erected. The *New Statistical Account* says in the seventeenth century Mr Stirling of Ballagan was murdered at this stone. In 1861 an 'immense deposit' of human and horse bones was dug up when cutting the railway embankment to the south (NS56617915). St Kessog's Holy Well once stood 200yds (183m) north of Glasgow Road at NS55717969; it is now covered by the houses of the Netherton area. In December 1793 a Strathblane couple were sawing up a block for firewood. It turned out to be hollow, containing a hoard of coins from various periods. They had been using the block as a seat; prior to that it had supported the roof of a house.

MUGDOCK

Mugdock Country Park provides easy access to both Mugdock Castle (NS54997716, fourteenth to nineteenth century) and Craigend Castle (1812); both are ruined but worth seeing. You can also explore the 'chapel' (sixteenth century, possibly never used as a religious building), the lookout/folly, the Moot Hill or justice mound, and Gallowhill where men were strangled on the gallows and women drowned in the pool at the foot of the gibbet. Pick up the history trail leaflet. The park is open all year round and is free. Mugdock Castle tower (small entry charge) is open every weekend between 26 May and 16 September, 14.00–17.00.

In 1875 writer and antiquarian John Guthrie Smith (1834–1894) built a grand mansion which was linked by a covered passageway to the first floor of the south-west tower of Mugdock Castle (the mansion was demolished in 1967). Smith was a noted antiquarian and his 1886 book *The Parish of Strathblane and its Inhabitants from Early Times* provides a wealth of information on archeological discoveries, many of which are now lost. In 1885 a skeleton with a fractured skull was found in a shallow grave on the edge of Mugdock Wood (NS546767). It was lying in the ruins of an old building, and was interpreted as someone killed in an encounter in 1818 between the operators of small illicit stills in Mugdock Wood and Revenue officers and soldiers. At NS561766 on the north side of the minor road east of the country park (the one south of the main entry to the park) there was once a row of standing stones, aligned north-west – south-east. The largest was called the 'Law Stone of Mugdock'. When the millennia-old monument was removed in the nineteenth century a number of stone-lined cists were uncovered. A few yards south, on the other side of the road at NS56347643 was the sacred well of St Patrick, still visited on 1 May up to the start of the nineteenth century by pilgrims who left coins, stones and rags. The well was still extant in 1951 but has now vanished.

FINTRY

Fifteenth century Culcreuch Castle (NS62028767) is now a fine hotel (open to non-residents) with original features such as a medieval bottle dungeon, an aumbry, paneling and carved fireplaces, as well as a large colony of bats. It is also celebrated for its ghosts. Martin Coventry in *Haunted Places of Scotland* lists three. The Phantom Harper is the ghost of a woman whose sad clarsach music is heard late at night in the Chinese Bird Room (the current hand-painted wallpaper dates from 1723), the adjoining room and the Laird's Hall. In 1582 the Harper's lover, a Buchanan, was mortally wounded by Robert, son of the sixteenth chief of the turbulent Galbraiths, and died in the Bird Room. The severed head of a boar on a silver platter flies around the battlements and plunges to the ground, but vanishes before impact. And, most unpleasantly, there is a cold grey mass of turbulence, about the shape of a man, seen in all the rooms. Perhaps as a way of deflecting attention from these nasties and reassuring prospective guests, the website states: 'We also have a ghost who wanders in and around the castle from time to time. We think she's a lady and we know she's friendly, though she only seems to appear to people who think no castle would be complete without a resident ghost!'

Knockraich standing stone (NS60898774) is a strange beast. 3ft 6ins (1m) high, it has a substantial artificial basin on the top, several other large cavities which may be natural or not, and the sides are heavily pockmarked. According to the 'Canmore' website a human figure is pocked into the north-west face, about 1ft (30cm) above ground level. I have to say I completely failed to find this carving. There are other standing stones in the area. On Balgair Muir, on the west side of the B822, north-west of a gate itself 340yds (310m) north of where the road crosses the Lernock Burn, is a single stone 3ft 3in (1m) high; it may well be a medieval boundary stone. The two large Machar Stones (NS65708393) can be found by taking the firebreak (tough, boggy going) in the forest leading east from the track going past Waterhead, off the Lennoxtown road. Of the pair, one is upright and 5ft (1.5m) high, while the other much larger stone is now virtually recumbent. The almost hidden face has seven cup marks.

Dunmore, west of Fintry, has a Covenanters' Hole or Meeting Place (NS60608665), where religious dissenters held illegal meetings. According to *Buchanan's Popular Guide* a cave leads from Dunmore to the hill of Dechrode, half a mile (1km) to the south, but it is 'difficult to find'.

John Monteath, in *Dunblane Traditions*, has much to say about Doctor Ure, a medicine man who lived somewhere nearby on the banks of the Endrick Water in the first half of the eighteenth century. 'He had nostrums for all diseases, and salves for all sores.' He could banish ghosts, prescribe love and fidelity charms, unwitch the enchanted and use the power of second sight – which involved 'revolving his eye-balls upwards in their sockets' – to discover the location of bodies, or predict an individual's future. Monteath regarded him as 'one of those sagacious mortals who profited by the foolish credulity of the vulgar of the times in which he lived.' To cure the cattle disease of black-leg, he had a young and uninfected heifer buried alive, then chanted his incantations around the pit. A shoemaker from Muirmill by the River Carron was haunted by an apparition which constantly mimicked his own actions, and which was undeterred by having various tools thrown at it, because they passed right through. Blue flame came out of its mouth, and red fires sparked in its eyes. The doctor applied an ointment when caused the tailor to sleep; when he woke up, the ghost, in the form of a set of bones rolled up in a brown cowhide, was physically present in the corner of the room. The man was instructed to return home, making sure to throw his trousers over his shoulder as he crossed the moor, and not to look behind him until he reached his house, and he would be bothered no more. And it was so. For more examples of the doctor's art, see KILBRYDE and CROMLIX.

SAUCHIEBURN

The Battle of Sauchieburn of 11 June 1488 is Stirling's forgotten battle. No visitors centre. No iconic statue or imagery. No movie. Perhaps this is not surprising: a conflict where the forces of a fifteen-year-old Scottish prince defeat and kill a Scottish King, who happens to be that prince's father, is hardly the kind of thing that makes patriotic hearts swell with pride, and it does little to bolster the myths of identity and history in which Scotland, like most countries, needs to wrap itself.

James III had numerical superiority, with perhaps 30,000 men from Huntly, Errol and Athol, and the Highlands, but the 18,000-strong forces of the rebellious nobles, which included spearmen from the Borders, won the day. This was the only time Highlanders and Borderers were opposed in battle. The conventional story told is that James fled the battle, his horse bolted, and he was thrown. Dazed or injured, he was taken to nearby Beaton's Mill at Milton, and was there basely murdered by an assassin disguised as a priest. None of the early chroniclers mention a single word of this story. The tale does not start to appear until the sixteenth century, with works by Edward Hall (1548) and Robert Lindsay of Pitscottie (*The Chronicles of Scotland 1436–1565*, written in the 1570s). Even the locations are dubious. John Shearer in *The Battlefields Around Stirling* identifies Nimmo's *History of Stirlingshire*, published in 1777, as the first work to place Sauchieburn as the site. Shearer is convinced it was nearer Bannockburn for both practical and symbolic reasons: not only was it close to where Robert the Bruce had defeated his enemies, but James carried Bruce's very sword into battle. Pitscottie places the mill as being at Bannockburn, and does not name it. Later, the Bannockburn mill was lost and forgotten, so the existing mill at Milton was pressed into service for the story. Almost certainly, then, everything about the conventional story is a fiction. James was probably either killed falling off his horse, or was finished off by enemy soldiers. His son, Prince James, became King James IV, and for the twenty-five years of his reign wore a heavy iron chain around his waist, next to the skin, as an act of contrition for his role in the death of his father.

Two splendid seventeenth-century sundials, rescued from Barnton House in Edinburgh, stand in the grounds of Sauchieburn House (NS77368926, private). Another sits outside Auchenbowie House to the south (NS79888739, private). James Stevens Curl, in *The Art and Architecture of Freemasonry*, suggests that Freemasonry is the mystery religion the Protestants never had. Denied the opportunity to build cathedrals, they 'endlessly redesigned Solomon's temple instead'. This explains all those tomb and temple follies in landscaped gardens, and why sundials were so popular in Scotland, a country where the climate doesn't often allow a sundial to function.

Ghost's Knowe, a low mound by the track to Craigengelt off the minor road to Carron Bridge (NS74768571), was once a spectacular site. The *New Statistical Account* describes it as 300ft (91m) in circumference and 'flanked around by 12 very large stones, placed at equal distances.' When it was removed a stone-lined cist was revealed which contained a skeleton wrapped in decayed material. Various prehistoric items were found, such as a stone axe and knife, as well as a golden horn or cup embossed with figures, and a gold ring. All this suggests the stone artefacts were the original deposit, and the skeleton and the gold items were a later, secondary deposit, probably Roman or medieval. All the finds are now lost. During the great Lisbon earthquake of 1735 Loch Coulter was seen to be much agitated and temporarily sank by about 12ft (3.6m).

11

LOCH LOMOND

The loch is the largest stretch of landlocked water in the country, covering 27 miles^2 (70km^2) and being up to 600ft (190m) deep in places. It has about thirty-eight islands (the number varies with the level of the loch), plus a number of crannogs. This chapter covers the east shore of Loch Lomond and the islands within the boundary of Stirling District. A narrow road runs along the shore from Balmaha to Rowardennan – after that access is by foot or boat, although there is a road-end at the ferry-point at Inversaid, which is only reached via Aberfoyle.

Loch Lomond has always attracted both legends and a sense of wonder. In *De Mirabilibus Britanniae* (attributed to the ninth-century monk Nennius, but author actually unknown) it is called the first Marvel of Britain. 'Nennius' was the first writer to mention Arthur, and lists the warlord's twelve great battles, none of which can be positively identified (which hasn't stopped generations of writers trying to do so). One battle is upon a river called Dubglass in the district of Linnuis. This could be north-east of Lincoln; or Lindinis, a Roman town in Somerset; or near Loch Lomond. Geoffrey of Monmouth's twelfth-century *History of the Kings of Britain*, a rich stew of propaganda, myth and pure invention, put the warrior Arthur centre stage. He is described as pursuing the Picts and Scots to Loch Lomond, where they take refuge on the islands, only to be starved into submission – 'Then the bishops and abbots of the realm, with divers monks and other orders, carrying in their hands bodies of the saints and many holy relics, came before the King beseeching him to show mercy on the Scots.' Protesting that they were good Christians who had been subject to the whims of the heathen Picts, the Scots pay homage to Arthur, who forgives them and releases all his captives. Arthur's companion Hoel is entranced by the size and beauty of the loch. Arthur then tells him of an even more marvellous sight nearby, a perfectly square pool, 20ft (6m) along each side and 5ft (1.5m) deep, with four kinds of fish. Despite sharing the same water, each species keeps to its own corner of the pool.

Hector Boece's fantasy-rich *History of the Scottish People* of 1527 described the loch as having fish without fins, waves without wind, and a floating island. P.J.G. Ransom, in *Loch Lomond and the Trossachs in History and Legend*, tried to map these wonders onto the real world. He found that in *Loch Lomond: A Study in Angling Conditions* (1931) the 'fish without fins' were identified as lampreys. The 'floating island' may be a relative of a clump of sedge and turf which broke loose in the eighteenth century and after an uneventful voyage joined the south-west corner of Inchconnachan. And the 'waves without wind' may be the phenomenon where wind on a previously calm day generates waves in advance of itself – it has to push the still air out of the way, a consequence of the loch being in a basin. Or it could be a seiche, an underwater wave.

In 1724 it was noted by Alexander Graham of Duchray that a water horse was sometimes seen where the Endrick Water flows into the loch, just south of Balmaha. The report is in 'Description of Kippen', quoted in Dalyell's *The Darker Superstitions of Scotland*. Walter Scott (*Letters on Demonology and Witchcraft*) tells of an encounter between a miller and an urisk in a mill near the foot of the loch (the miller came out on top). Tobias Smollett's 1771 novel *The Expedition of Humphry Clinker* is a satire on eighteenth-century life and manners, written in the form of letters penned by the book's six main characters. The most credulous is the maid Winifred Jenkins, who writes to her friend Molly about a holiday spent at a gentleman's house at 'Loff–Loming'.

The bell on the island with the churchyard – presumably Inchcailloch – always rings of itself before someone dies. Winifrid then gives a list of other strange phenomena in the area. A house was haunted by a ghost who would not let people lie in their beds. Fairies stole new mothers unless a horseshoe was nailed to the door. The wild men of the mountains lived in caves and ate young children. Winifrid met an ugly old witch, Elspath Ringavey, whom she paid to tell her fortune. The woman described the maid's beloved to a 'T', and advised her to bathe in the holy water of the loch to cure her fits. Winifrid and another maid consequently went skinny-dipping, and were observed by Sir George Coon, who declined to avert his eyes as the two naked women scrambled for their clothes. The cad. It is impossible to tell how much of this episode is based on Smollett's observations of the foibles of his contemporaries, and how much he simply invented.

INCHCAILLOCH

The island is owned by Scottish Natural Heritage and easily accessible by boat from Balmaha. The 2-mile (3km) nature trail passes the old graveyard (NS41109061), with gravestones carved with sheep, cattle and ploughs. When the enclosing wall was modified in 1966 several child burials were found beside the north wall of the church – a common burial place for unbaptized babies, who were interred secretly by the families as close to holy ground as possible. This was the site of the parish church from the thirteenth century until its abandonment in 1621 – the people had to row over each Sunday, until eventually a new church was built on the mainland. Only foundations of the church now remain, but burials continued until the mid-twentieth century.

P.J.G. Ransom describes the funeral of Archie Davie, who died in 1904. The service took place on Inchcruin, and then the coffin was placed on a cattle boat and towed here. Inchcailloch is one of those sites where placenames and tradition conflict with, or are unsupported by, archaeological and documentary evidence. The *Old Statistical Account* of 1791–99 states that Inchcailleach (the spelling then) means 'the island of the old women,' the women concerned being nuns. The island's small hill is Tom na nighean, 'Hill of the young women'. The church was dedicated to St Kentigerna, the Irish saint (and mother of St Fillan, see KILLIN) who died here about 733 AD, supposedly after founding a community of nuns. But Kentigerna was a recluse, and there is no evidence of a nunnery on the island.

CASHEL

An enigmatic structure sits on the low-lying promontory of Strathcashell Point (NS39329311). A low stone wall cuts off the point, and there are ruins of rectangular buildings inside and out, although these appear to be much more recent. Earlier interpretations were that this was a cashel, a monastic or religious site from the Dark Ages. It is now regarded as a small fort, albeit one that is poorly defended and undated. Just off the point is a crannog topped with a modern cairn. Alexander Graham, writing in the *Account of the Parish of Buchanan* in 1724, says the Cashel is the Giant's Castle, founded by Keich Mac-In-Doill, or Keith the son of Doillus, one of Fingal's fellow giants; Keith also built the crannog. Ronald McAllister in *The Lure of Loch Lomond* claims 'Giant's Castle' is a mistranslation of the old Gaelic name Rownafean as Point of the Fiann.

ROWARDENNAN

The road stops here. North of Ptarmigan Lodge, before Rowchoish headland, is 'Rob Roy's Prison,' a rock cell overhanging the loch, seen easily from a boat, but a climb down by the walker.

INVERSNAID

Half a mile (1km) north along the West Highland Way is a signpost to Rob Roy's Cave, also known as Bruce's Cave. Which is, frankly, a waste of time. After scrambling the last part you come across the painted word CAVE which leads you to… just a crack in the rock. The association with Rob Roy is, as with many caves, simply a conjectural equation: outlaw + cave = 'Rob Roy stayed here'. Supposedly, Robert the Bruce came here in 1306 with a few hundred followers. They settled down for the night in the cave – which could hardly hold a darts team, never mind an Army – and then in the darkness heard breathing and movement. Bandits? Enemies? The bringing of light revealed the culprits to be wild goats. For the rest of the cold night the animals helped keep the men warm, and later Bruce ordained goats could graze rent-free on royal manors, a fine example of the caprice of Kings.

The spectacular waterfall south of the car park inspired Scott, Wordsworth and Gerald Manley Hopkins, whose poem 'Inversnaid' expresses what many people feel about wild places:

> What would the world do, once bereft
> Of wet and wilderness? Let them be left,
> O let them be left, wildness and wet;
> Long live the weeds and the wilderness yet.

Long may it be so.

The end.

BIBLIOGRAPHY

Works that have been particularly useful are marked with an asterisk★.

ABBREVIATIONS:

FNH = The Forth Naturalist and Historian
PSAS = Proceedings of the Society of Antiquaries of Scotland
TSNHAS = Transactions of the Stirling Natural History and Archaeological Society

ARCHAEOLOGY AND HISTORY

Anon 'Riot in Stirling', broadside in National Library of Scotland, shelfmark Ry.III.a.2(35), (1823)
Anon *Strathfillan and Glen Dochart in Bygone Days* (Callander Advertiser; Stirling, c.1900)
Anon 'Visit to Sheriffmuir' in *The Scottish Journal of Topography, Antiquities, Traditions etc* Vol. II No. 40, (March to July 1848), John Menzies, Edinburgh
Armstrong, Pete and Angus McBride *Stirling Bridge & Falkirk 1297–98: William Wallace's Rebellion* (Osprey Publishing; Oxford, 2003)
Balfour James *The Historical Works of Sir James Balfour of Denmylne and Kinnaird* (including *The Annales of Scotland*) (Aitchison; Edinburgh, 1824)
Barty, Alexander B. *The History of Dunblane* (Eneas MacKay; Stirling, 1944)★
Beauchamp, Elizabeth *The Braes O' Balquhidder* (Heatherbank Press; Milngavie, 1981)
Begg, Tom *The Kingdom of Kippen* (John Donald; Edinburgh, 2000)
Beveridge, David *Between the Ochils and Forth* (Blackwood & Son; Edinburgh, 1888)
Boece, Hector *The History of Scotland* (Blackwood; Edinburgh, 1946)
British Association for the Advancement of Science *Excursion to Ardoch Camp, Doune Castle and Dunblane Cathedral* (The British Association for the Advancement of Science; Glasgow, 1901)
Buchanan, D.S. *Buchanan's Popular Guide to Strathendrick, Aberfoyle and District* (J. & C. Buchanan; Balfron, 1902)
Burl, Aubrey *From Carnac to Callanish: The Prehistoric Stone Rows and Avenues of Britain, Ireland and Brittany* (Yale University Press; New Haven and London, 1993)
Byrom, Bernard *Old Comrie, Upper Strathearn and Balquhidder* (Stenlake Publishing; Catrine, 2005)
————— *Old Crianlarich, Tyndrum and Bridge of Orchy* (Stenlake Publishing; Catrine, 2006)
————— *Old Dunblane* (Stenlake Publishing; Catrine, 2006)
Cant, Ronald G. and Ian G. Lindsay *Old Stirling* (Oliver and Boyd; Edinburgh, 1948)
Cash, C.G. 'Archaeological Gleanings From Killin' in *PSAS* Vol. 46 (1911–1912)
Chambers, Robert *Domestic Annals of Scotland* (W. & R. Chambers; Edinburgh and London, 1874)
Charles, George *History of the Transactions in the Years 1715-16, and 1745-46* (Stirling, 1817)
Christie, J.G. 'Notes on Dunblane' in *TSNHAS* (1897–98)
Christison, David 'The Carvings and Inscriptions on the Kirkyard Monuments of the Scottish Lowlands' in *PSAS* Vol. 36 (1901–02)
————— 'Additional Notes on the Kirkyard Monuments of the Scottish Lowlands' in *PSAS* Vol. 39 (1904–05)
Chrystal, William *The Kingdom of Kippen: Its History and Traditions* (Munro & Jamieson; Stirling, 1903)
Clark, David *Battlefield Walks: Scotland* (Sutton Publishing; Stroud, 1996)

Cockburn, J. Hutchison *A Guide To Dunblane Cathedral* (The Society of Friends of Dunblane Cathedral; Dunblane, 1982)

Cook, W.B. 'Notes for A New History of Stirling' in *TSNHAS* (1897–98)

——————— 'Plaster Cast of Inscription on "Mar's Work"' in *TSNHAS* (1906–1907)

Cowley, David C., John A. Guy and Diana M. Henderson 'The Sheriffmuir Atlantic Wall: an Archaeological Survey on part of the Whitestone Ridge' in *FNH* Vol. 22 (1999)

Crawford, John *Memorials of the Town and Parish of Alloa* (J. Lothian; Alloa, 1874)

Drysdale, William *Old Faces, Old Places and Old Stories of Stirling* (Eneas Mackay; Stirling, 1898)

Dun, P. *Summer at the Lake of Monteith* (Oliver and Boyd; Edinburgh, 1867)★

Dunn, Ken *Walks and Forts* (Ken Dunn, 2003)

——————— 'Focus on Callander and Its Environs: A Personal Overview of its History' in *FNH* Vol. 29 (2006)

Elsdon, Sheila M. *Christian Maclagan: Stirling's formidable lady antiquary* (The Pinkfoot Press; Balgavies, 2004)

Eyre-Todd, George *Early Scottish Poetry, Thomas the Rhymer, John Barbour, Androw of Wyntoun, Henry the Minstrel* (William Hodge; Edinburgh, 1891)

Fergusson, R. Menzies *Logie A Parish History* 2 Vols (Alexander Gardner; Paisley, 1905)

Fittis, Robert Scott (comp.) *Miscellanea Perthensis* (1853–1861), copy in A.K. Bell Library, Perth

——————— *Chronicles of Perthshire* (The Constitutional Office; Perth, 1877)

——————— *Sketches of the Olden Times in Perthshire* (The Constitutional Office; Perth, 1878)

——————— *A Book of Perthshire Memorabilia* (The Constitutional Office; Perth, 1879)

Fleming, J.S. *The Old Ludgings of Stirling* (Eneas Mackay; Stirling, 1897)

——————— 'Regent Mar's Ludging, Stirling' in *PSAS* Vol. 39 (1904–05)

Forsyth, Robert *The Beauties of Scotland* 5 Vols (Thomas Bonar & John Brown; Edinburgh, 1805–1808)

Fraser, William *The Red Book of Menteith* (Edinburgh University Press; Edinburgh, 1880)

Gifford, John and Frank Arneil Walker *The Buildings of Scotland: Stirling and Central Scotland* (Yale University Press; New Haven and London, 2002)★

Gillies, William A. *In Famed Breadalbane* (Clunie Press; Strathtay, 1980) (first published 1938)

Graham, R.B. Cunninghame *Notes on the District of Menteith* (Eneas Mackay; Stirling, 1907)

Graham, Patrick *Sketches of Perthshire* first edition 1806, reprint 1810 and second edition 1812, all James Ballantyne & Co, Edinburgh★

Harrison, John G. 'Some Early Gravestones in the Holy Rude Kirkyard, Stirling' in *FNH* Vol. 13 (1990)★

——————— *A historical background of Flanders Moss* Scottish Natural Heritage Commissioned Report No.002 (ROAME No. F02LG22), Edinburgh (2003)

Heron, R. *Observations made in a journey through the western counties of Scotland in the autumn of MCCCXCII* 2 vols (Perth, 1793)

Hunnewell, James F. *The Lands of Scott* (Adam and Charles Black; Edinburgh, 1871)

Inglis, Bill *The Battle of Sheriffmuir Based on Eye Witness Accounts* (Stirling Council Libraries; Stirling, 2005)★

King, Elspeth 'The Stirling Heads and the Stirling Smith' in *FNH* Vol. 30 (2007)

Knight, G.A.F. *Archaeological Light on the Early Christianisation of Scotland* (Jas. Clark & Co.; London, 1933)

Lacaille, A.D. 'Antiquities in Strathfillan' in *PSAS* Vol. 58 (1923–24)★

——————— 'Ardlui Megaliths and their Associations' in *PSAS* Vol. 63 (1928–29)

MacAlister, R.A.S. 'The Greenloaning Stone' in *TSNHAS* (1937–1938)

McCulloch, Stuart J. *Thornhill and Its Environs: A Social History* (Munro Trust; Perth, 1995)

McCutcheon, Bob *Stirling Observer: 150 Years On* (The John Jamieson Munro Trust and Stirling Observer; Stirling, 1986)

MacDonald, James *Character Sketches of Old Callander* (Jamieson & Munro; Callander, 1938) (first published 1910)

McGinlay, Paul *A History of Tigh Mor Trossachs (The Trossachs Hotel)* (Trossachs Publications; Callander, 2002)

——————— *History of Lanrick Castle* (Trossachs Publications; Callander, 2004)

MacGregor, Revd Alex *A Gaelic Topography of Balquhidder* (Edinburgh University Press; Edinburgh, 1886) (computer enhanced reprint 2000)

MacKay, Moray S. *Doune: Historical Notes (Notes on the Parish of Kilmadock and Borough of Doune)* (Forth Naturalist and Historian Editorial Board; Stirling, 1984) (first printed privately 1953)★

McKean, Charles *Stirling and the Trossachs* (The Royal Incorporation of Architects in Scotland and Scottish Academic Press; Edinburgh, 1985)★

McKerracher, Archie *Portrait of Dunblane 1875–1975* (Stirling District Libraries; Stirling, 1991)

——————— *The Street and Place Names of Dunblane and District* (Stirling District Libraries; Stirling, 1992)★

McLaren, Archibald *Callander in the 1890s* (privately published, 1957)

MacLean, Ella *Bridge of Allan: The Rise of a Village* (Alloa Printing and Publishing Co.; Alloa, 1970)

MacMillan, Hugh *The Highland Tay* (Virtue & Co.; London, 1901)★

Main, Lorna *First Generations: The Stirling Area from Mesolithic to Roman Times* (Stirling Council; Stirling, 2001)

———————— 'An Early Historic Fort on the Abbey Craig' in *FNH* Vol.29 (2006)

Mair, Craig *Stirling: The Royal Burgh* (John Donald Publishers; Edinburgh, 1990)★

———————— 'Allan Mair – The Last Person To Be Executed in Stirling' in *FNH* Vol. 16 (1993)★

Marshall, William *Historic Scenes in Perthshire* (William Oliphant & Co.; Edinburgh, 1879)

Monteath, John 'Statistics of the Parish of Dunblane' Pamphlets collection in Press 10-C-18, Leighton Library, Dunblane (1831)

Morris, David B. 'Whale Remains, Prehistoric Implements &c., found at Causewayhead' in *TSNHAS* (1897–98)

New Statistical Account, Vol VIII. Dunbarton-Stirling-Clackmannan (William Blackwood; Edinburgh and London, 1845)★

Northern Notes and Queries, or, The Scottish Antiquary Vol. 3 (1889)

Paterson, P.T. *Bygone Days in Cambusbarron* (Stirling District Libraries; Stirling, 1993)★

Pearce, Wayne 'The Stirling Presbytery, 1604–1612: and the re-imposition of an erastian episcopy' in *FNH* Vol. 19 (1996)

Pitbaldo, Laurence O. 'The Gowanhill Roman Stone and its Epoch' in *TSNHAS* (1934–1935)

Randall, C[harles] *The History of Stirling* (C. Randall; Stirling, 1812)

Ransom, P.J.G. *Loch Lomond and the Trossachs in History and Legend* (John Donald Publishers; Edinburgh, 2004)

Riddel, Kay *Killin in Old Photographs* (Stirling District Libraries; Stirling, 1993)

Roger, Charles *A Week At Bridge of Allan* (Adam & Charles Black; Edinburgh, 1853)

Ronald, James *Landmarks of Old Stirling* (Eneas Mackay; Stirling, 1899)

Scottish Women's Rural Institutes, Stirlingshire and West Perthshire Federation *The Rural Remembers 1925–1965* (Bell, Aird & Coghill; Glasgow, 1965)

Shearer, John *The Antiquities of Perthshire* (Perth, 1836)

Shearer, John E. *The Battlefields Around Stirling* (R.S. Shearer & Son; Stirling, 1913)

Skene, W.F. *Celtic Scotland* (David Douglas; Edinburgh, 1880)

Smith, David 'Church Life and Customs in Olden Times' in *TSNHAS* (1897–98)

Smith, J.G. *The Parish of Strathblane and its Inhabitants from Early Times* (James MacLehose & Sons; Glasgow, 1886)

Smollett, Tobias *Essay on the external use of water* (The John Hopkins Press; Baltimore, 1935) (first published 1752)

Stair-Kerr, Eric *Stirling Castle: Its Place in Scottish History* (Eneas Mackay; Stirling, 1928) (first published 1913)

Steuart, Katherine *By Allan Water: The True Story of an Old House* (Andrew Elliot; Edinburgh, 1901)

Stevenson, Jack *Glasgow, Clydeside and Stirling – Exploring Scotland's Heritage* (HMSO; Edinburgh, 1995)

Stewart, James *Settlements of Western Perthshire: Land and Society North of the Highland Line 1480–1851* (Pentland Press; Edinburgh, 1990)

Stewart, John 'The Half-way Totem' in *The Villagers* Balquhidder (May 2007)

Stewart, John A. *Inchmahome and the Lake of Menteith* (John A. Stewart and the Stewart Society, 1933)

Stirling Council Libraries *Stirling's Talking Stones* (Stirling Council Libraries, Stirling 2002)

Stirling Sentinel 'The Stirling Cross' 2 September 1890

Stirling, W. MacGregor *Notes Historical and Descriptive on the Priory of Inchmahome* (William Blackwood; Edinburgh, 1815)★

Stott, Louis *The Ring of Words: Literary Landmarks of Stirling & Clackmannan* (Creag Darach Publications; Milton of Aberfoyle, 1993)

———————— 'Further Notes on the District of Menteith. 1. The Cunninghame Graham Country' in *FNH* Vol. 18 (1995)

———————— 'Further Notes on the District of Menteith. 2. John Graham of Duchray 1600–1700' in *FNH* Vol. 19 (1996)

———————— 'Bridges of the Forth and its Tributaries' in *FNH* Vol. 22 (1999)

———————— 'Writers and Artists of Loch Lomond and the Trossachs: The Scenery of a Dream' in *FNH* Vol. 25 (2002)

Thomson, J.E.H. 'The Mammet King' in *TSNHAS* (1885–86)

Thomson, William 'Notes on a Cross-Slab at Clanmacrie and Diamaird's Pillar in Glen Lonain, Argyll, and on a Sculptured Stone in Glen Buckie, Perthshire' in *PSAS* Vol. 59 (1924–1925)

Tranter, Nigel *The Queen's Scotland: The Heartland – Clackmannanshire, Perthshire and Stirlingshire* (Hodder & Stoughton; London, 1971)★

Van Hoek, Maarten A.M. 'A Survey of the Prehistoric Rock Art of the Port of Menteith Parish, Central Scotland' in *FNH* Vol. 15 (1992)

Walcott, Mackenzie E.C. *Scoti-Monasticon: The Ancient Church of Scotland* (Virtue, Spalding and Daldy; London, 1874)

Walker, Ella *A Village History – Killin* online at www.killin.co.uk/news

Webster, Comyn (ed) *The Parish of Killearn* (Mrs Ewen Cameron, Blanefield and Mrs George Garland; Killearn, 1972)

Whitbread, Harold *The Guildry of Stirling: Being the story of the Gild Brether and Toun Counsellors of Stirline* (Stirling Guildry; Stirling, 1966)

Wilson, W *The Trossachs in Literature and Tradition* (R.S. Shearer & Son; Stirling, 1908)

Wright, Isabella Murray *Stirling Letters* (Stirling Smith Art Gallery and Museum; Stirling, 1998)

KING ARTHUR

Alcock, Leslie *Arthur's Britain: History and Archaeology AD 367–634* (Penguin; Harmondsworth, 1980)

Ashe, Geoffrey *A Guide to Arthurian Britain* (Longman; London, 1980)

———— *The Landscape of King Arthur* (Grange Books; London, 1992)

Cook, W.B. 'The King's Park of Stirling in History and Record, Part I' in *TSNHAS* (1906–1907)

Fairbairn, Neil *A Traveller's Guide to the Kingdoms of Arthur* (Evan Brothers; London, 1983)

Glennie, John S. Stuart *Arthurian Localities: With a Map of Arthurian Scotland* (Llanerch Press; Llanerch, 1990) (first published 1869)

Graham, Alexander 'References to the Word "Knot" as a Term in Gardening in *TSNHAS* (1912–1913)

McHardy, Stuart *The Quest for Arthur* (Luath Press; Edinburgh, 2001)

Moffat, Alistair *Arthur and the Lost Kingdoms* (Phoenix; London, 2004)

Wace and Lawman *The Life of King Arthur* (Everyman; London, 1997)

ROBERT KIRK

Campbell, John Gregerson (ed) *A Collection of Highland Rites and Customes, copied by Edward Lhuyd from the manuscript of the Rev James Kirkwood (1650–1709) and annotated by him with the aid of the Rev John Beaton,* (D.S. Brewer/The Folklore Society; Cambridge, 1975)

Evans Wentz, W.Y. *The Fairy-Faith in Celtic Countries* (Oxford University Press; Oxford, 1911)

Henderson, Lizanne and Edward J. Cowan *Scottish Fairy Belief* (Tuckwell Press; East Linton, 2001)★

Kirk, Robert *The Secret Commonwealth of Elves, Fauns and Fairies* (Comment by Andrew Lang, Introduction by R.B. Cunninghame Graham) (Eneas Mackay; Stirling, 1933)★ [see also editions of 1893 (Lang), 1976 (Sanderson), 1990/2007 (Stewart) and 2006 (Warner)]

MacLean, D. *The Life and Literary Labours of the Rev. Robert Kirk, of Aberfoyle* reprinted from the *Transactions of the Gaelic Society of Inverness* Vol. XXXI (1927)★

Purkiss, Diane *Troublesome Things: A History of Fairies and Fairy Stories* (Penguin; London, 2001)

Smith, David Baird 'Mr Robert Kirk's Note-book' in *The Scottish Historical Review* Vol. 18, No. 72, (July 1921)★

Stewart, R.J. *Earth Light* (Element Books; Shaftesbury, 1992)

———— *The Living World of Faery* (Mercury Publishing; Lake Toxaway, New Carolina, 1999)

Stott, Louis *The Enchantment of the Trossachs* (Creag Darach Publications, Milton-of-Aberfoyle, 1992)★

———— 'The Legend of Robert Kirk Reconsidered' in *FNH* Vol. 21 (1998)★

MYSTERIOUSNESS

Adams, Norman *Haunted Scotland* (Mainstream Publishing; Edinburgh, 1998)

Adams, W.H. Davenport *Witch, Warlock and Magician: Historical Sketches of Magic and Witchcraft in England and Scotland* (Chatto & Windus; London, 1889)

Banks, M. Macleod *British Calendar Customs: Scotland* 3 Vols (The Folk-Lore Society; London, 1937)

Barty, James Webster 'Kirk Session Records' in *Bulletin of The Society of Friends of Dunblane Cathedral* Vol. VI, Part IV (1953)

Black, George G. *A Calendar of Cases of Witchcraft in Scotland 1510–1727* (New York Public Library; New York, 1938)

Campbell, John Gregerson (ed. Ronald Black), *The Gaelic Otherworld: John Gregerson Campbell's Superstitions of the Highlands and Islands of Scotland* and *Witchcraft* and *Second Sight in the Highlands & Islands* (Birlinn; Edinburgh, new edition 2005)★

Campbell, J.W. 'Humorous Reminiscences' in *TSNHAS* (1927–1928)

Coventry, Martin *Haunted Places of Scotland* (Goblinshead; Musselburgh, 1999)

————— *Haunted Castles & Houses of Scotland* (Goblinshead; Musselburgh, 2004)

Cumming, Alexander D. 'Superstition and Folklore of Scotland' in *TSNHAS* (1910–1911)

Curl, James Stevens *The Art and Architecture of Freemasonry* (Overlook Press; Woodstock New York, 2002)

Dalyell, John Graham *The Darker Superstitions of Scotland* (Waugh and Innes; Edinburgh, 1834)

Dean, James M. *Poems of Political Prophecy* online at www.lib.rochester.edu/camelot/teams/polpint.htm originally published in *Medieval English Political Writings* (Medieval Institute Publications; Western Michigan University, 1996)

Dyer, T. F. Thiselton *Strange Pages from Family Papers* (Sampson Low, Marston & Co.; London, 1895)

Elders, E.A. '"Healing Stones" of St Fillan' in *The Scotsman* 19 December 1959

Fergusson, R. Menzies *Alexander Hume: An Early Poet-Pastor of Logie and his Intimates* (Alexander Gardner, Paisley & London, 1899)★

————— *Scottish Social Sketches of the 17th Century* (R.S. Shearer & Son; Stirling, 1907)★

————— *The Ochil Fairy Tales; Stories of the Wee Folk for Young and Old Folk* (David Nutt; London, 1911)

Fleming, Maurice *Not of This World: Creatures of the Supernatural in Scotland* (Mercat Press; Edinburgh, 2002)

Forbes, A.P. 'Notice of the Ancient Bell of St Fillan' in *PSAS* Vol. 8 (1868–70)★

Gaskell, Malcolm *Hellish Nell: Last of Britain's Witches* (Fourth Estate; London, 2001)

Gotfredsen, Lise *The Unicorn* (The Harvill Press; London, 1999)

Gow, James Mackintosh 'Notes on Balquhidder: Saint Angus, Curing Wells, Cup-Marked Stones &c.' in *PSAS* Vol. 21 (1886–87)★

Grant, James *The Mysteries of All Nations: Rise and Progress of Superstition, Laws Against and Trials of Witches, Ancient and Modern Delusions Together With Strange Customs, Fables, and Tales* (W. Paterson; Edinburgh, 1880)

Hall, Alaric 'Getting Shot of Elves: Healing, Witchcraft and Fairies in the Scottish Witchcraft Trials' in *Folklore* 116, (2005)

————— 'Folk-healing, fairies and witchcraft: the trial of Stein Maltman, Stirling 1628' in *Studia Celtica Fennica 3*, University of Glasgow (online at http://eprints.gla.ac.uk/3102)★

Harvey, William 'Rhymes, Proverbs, and Proverbial Expressions of Stirling & District' in *TSNHAS* (1899–1900)

————— 'Some Local Superstitions' in *TSNHAS* (1900–1901)

Holder, Geoff *The Guide to Mysterious Perthshire* (Tempus; Stroud, 2006)

Jones, Richard *Haunted Britain and Ireland* (New Holland; London, 2003)

Kirk, James (ed) *Stirling Presbytery Records 1581–1587* (Scottish History Society; Edinburgh, 1981)★

Lamont-Brown, Raymond *Scottish Folklore* (Birlinn; Edinburgh, 1996)

Larner, Christina *Enemies of God: The Witch-hunt in Scotland* (Basil Blackwell; Oxford, 1983)

Macdiarmid, James 'More Fragments of Breadalbane Folklore' in *Transactions of the Gaelic Society of Inverness* Vol. XXVI (1904–1907)

McGinlay, Paul *Tales from the Trossachs* (Trossachs Publications; Callander, 2004)

MacKinlay, James M. *Folklore of Scottish Lochs and Springs* (William Hodge; Glasgow, 1893)

MacMillan, Hugh 'Notice of Two Boulders having Rain-filled Cavities on the Shores of Loch Tay' in *PSAS* Vol. 18 (1883–84)

McNeill, F. Marion *The Silver Bough: Volume 4 – The Local Festivals of Scotland* (William MacLellan; Glasgow, 1968)

McNeill, J.H. Horton 'Glimpses of Church Life in Old Days: From Records of Gargunnock Parish' in *TSNHAS* (1929–1930)

McOwan, Rennie *The Green Hills: Stories of the Ochils* (Clackmannan District Libraries, 1989)

————— *Magic Mountains* (Mainsteam Publishing; Edinburgh and London, 1996)

Martine, Roddy *Supernatural Scotland* (Robert Hale; London, 2003)

Maxwell-Stuart, P.G. *Witch Hunters: Professional Prickers, Unwitchers & Witch Finders of the Renaissance* (Tempus; Stroud, 2003)

——————— *An Abundance of Witches: The Great Scottish Witch-Hunt* (Tempus; Stroud, 2005)★

Monteath, John *Dunblane Traditions* (John Miller; Glasgow, 1835)★

Morris, David B. 'Large Hailstone at Sheilbrae' in *TSNHAS* (1898–99)

——————— 'Charm Stone Found At St Ninians' in *TSNHAS* (1911–12)

Morris, Ruth and Frank Morris *Scottish Healing Wells* (The Alethea Press; Sandy, 1982)

Orkney, J.C. *St Fillan of Glen Dochart: a Dark Age Religious Settlement* (Dr J.C. Orkney; Stirling, 2003)

Pitcairn, Robert *Criminal Trials in Scotland From 1488 to 1624* 3 Vols (William Tait; Edinburgh, 1833)

Robertson, Revd James 'Letter on the Superstitions of the Highlands, addressed to the Right Honourable James Drummond, of Perth' in *Archaeologia Scotica: Transactions of the Society of Antiquaries of Scotland Volume 3* (1831)

Roger, Charles *A Week at Bridge of Allan* (Adam & Charles Black; Edinburgh, 1853)

Rogers, Charles *Social Life in Scotland From Early to Recent Times* 3 Vols (The Grampian Club; Edinburgh, 1886)★

Scott, Sir Walter *Letters On Demonology And Witchcraft* (Wordsworth Edition; Ware, 2001) (first published 1830)

Simpkins, John Ewart *County Folk-lore Vol. VII. Printed extracts nos. LX, X, XL. Examples of Printed Folk-lore concerning Fife with some Notes on Clackmannan and Kinross-shires* (Sidgwick & Jackson; London, 1914)

Simpson, Sir James 'Notes on some Scottish Magical Charm-Stones, or Curing Stones' in *PSAS* Vol. IV (1862)

Spence, Lewis *The Magic Arts in Celtic Britain* (Constable; London, 1995) (first published 1945)

Van Vechten, Carl *The Tiger in the House* (A.A. Knopf; New York, 1922)

Williams, George 'Local Superstitions' in *TSNHAS* (1900–1901)★

FICTION AND POETRY

Banks, Iain *Whit* (Little, Brown; London, 1995)

Crumley, Jim *The Mountain of Light* (Whittles Publishing; Latheronwheel, 2003)

Hogg, James *The Queen's Wake: A Legendary Tale* (Edinburgh University Press; Edinburgh, 2005) (first published 1813)

Scott, Sir Walter *The Minstrelsy of the Scottish Border* (Constable; Edinburgh, 1802)

——————— *The Lady of the Lake* (Signet Classics; Harmondsworth, 1962) (first published 1810)★

——————— *Rob Roy* (Signet Classics; Harmondsworth, 1995) (first published 1817)★

Smollett, Tobias *The Expedition of Humphry Clinker* (Oxford Paperbacks; Oxford, 1998) (first published 1771)

WEBSITES

The Modern Antiquarian: www.themodernantiquarian.com★

Royal Commission on the Ancient and Historical Monuments of Scotland, 'Canmore' database: www.rcahms.gov.uk★

Scottish Big Cats: www.bigcats.org

Stirling Sites and Monuments Record: www.stirling.gov.uk/archaeology★

Spectre Paranormal Investigation And Research group: www.freewebs.com/ukspectre

Survey of Scottish Witchcraft: www.shc.ed.ac.uk/Research/witches★

University of Stirling anniversary: www.anniversary.stir.ac.uk

University of Stirling, Department of English, M. Litt in The Gothic Imagination: www.gothic.stir.ac.uk.

West Highland Animation: www.westhighlandanimation.co.uk.

INDEX